The Progressive Housewife

Politics and Culture in Modern America

Series Editors: Michael Kazin, Glenda Gilmore, Thomas J. Sugrue

A complete list of books in the series is available from the publisher.

The Progressive Housewife

Community Activism in
Suburban Queens, 1945–1965

Sylvie Murray

PENN

University of Pennsylvania Press

Philadelphia

10   9   8   7   6   5   4   3   2   1

Published by
University of Pennsylvania Press
Philadelphia, Pennsylvania 19104-4011

Library of Congress Cataloging-in-Publication Data

Murray, Sylvie.
   The progressive housewife : community activism in suburban Queens, 1945–1965 /
Sylvie Murray.
      p.   cm.—(Politics and culture in modern America)
   Includes bibliographical references and index.
   ISBN 0-8122-3718-8 (cloth : alk. paper)
   1. Women in community organization—New York (State)—New York—History—
20th century. 2. Housewives—New York (State)—New York—Political activity—
History—20th century. 3. Middle class women—New York (State)—New York—Political
activity—History—20th century. 4. Social action—New York (State)—New York—
History—20th century. 5. Community life—New York (State)—New York—History—
20th century. 6. Neighborhood—New York (State)—New York—History—20th century.
7. Queens (New York, N.Y.)—Social conditions—20th century. I. Title: Community activism in suburban Queens, 1945–1965. II. Title. III. Series.

HQ1439.N6 M87 2003
305.42'09747'1—dc21

                                                                        2002041256

To Marie and Lawrence,
loving parents and engaged citizens

Contents

Introduction:
Citizenship and Middle-Class Politics
in the Postwar Era

They are strangers to politics. They are not radical, not liberal, not conservative, not reactionary; they are inactionary; they are out of it. If we accept the Greek's definition of the idiot as a privatized man, then we must conclude that the U.S. citizenry is now largely composed of idiots.

—C. Wright Mills, *White Collar* (1951)

Dear President Truman:

We, a group of Alley Pond citizens, gathered at a barbecue picnic celebrating our first anniversary of the founding of our community, are gravely concerned at the delays and this weekend's breakdown in the Korean War truce talks. We are a group of veteran families who know well the horror and futility of war. We urge you to use your presidential power to hasten the successful conclusion of the talks so that our next barbecue may be held in a world of peace and prosperity and world amity.

—Letter to the Editor, *Meadow Lark*, August 9, 1951

Ironically, Betty Friedan could have written both statements, albeit at different times of her life. The famous author who in 1963 described the female citizenry in terms similar to those used by Mills had lived in northeastern Queens in the early 1950s. Like her neighbors from Alley Pond, she was a politically active resident of suburbia, not a "privatized" woman. Indeed in 1952, at a time when she lived in a garden apartment in the area, Friedan led a collective protest to stop a steep rent increase which threatened to destroy her racially and culturally integrated community. Of course, the young and radical Friedan has been eclipsed by the feminist best-selling author of *The Feminine Mystique*. Similarly, and not coincidentally, the political history of her suburban neighbors has been ignored, in fact, denigrated to serve as a foil for a renewed feminist movement. This book is an attempt to recapture this lost past. Its goal is to present in a more accurate light the experience of a generation of American men and women.

This study stems from a set of questions about women's public activism in the 1950s, and a conviction that it coexisted with the postwar domestic ideology—just as the two had coexisted in earlier times.[1] It evolved into an analysis of community politics in the neighborhoods of northeastern Queens, New York City, a newly developing suburban area in the immediate postwar period. Full-time mothers and housewives were a driving force among community activists who sought to build residential neighborhoods of quality in which to raise their families. This book examines the area's political culture; the debates and issues that engaged and divided its residents; and the residents' political consciousness or, more specifically, their understanding of themselves as citizens. An examination of their political experience reveals new ways of thinking about suburbia, the middle class, and women's experience in the 1950s. It also sheds light on the definition of citizenship prevalent in middle-class suburban neighborhoods. Finally, it presents my understanding of the position that this particular brand of neighborhood-based politics occupied in the context of New Deal liberalism.

The political culture in suburban Queens was infused with a celebration of the virtues of active citizenship. Men and women alike were encouraged to get involved in the public life of their community, and many did. An extensive network of community activists worked tirelessly to promote the interests of their residential neighborhoods. They organized collectively and fought political battles to build a better life, one that they expected as members (or aspiring members) of an upwardly mobile postwar middle class. By doing so, they shaped their living and political environment, although within constraints, and they revealed their political consciousness.

The definition of postwar suburban citizenship that I analyze here was centered on the local residential community (albeit one that was never seen as divorced from the broader national and international debates of the day). Second, suburban residents had a clear perception that as middle-class citizens they were deserving of certain social and economic rights (namely, the right to a residential neighborhood of quality) and that their government had an obligation for their welfare and that of their community. Third, this sense of entitlement was paired with a clear understanding of their obligations as citizens to participate in the collective life of their communities. These three elements, which defined their relationship to their fellow citizens and to the state, deserve further elaboration.

The focus on the residential community is perhaps the element that most clearly identifies these citizens as "middle class." This elusive socioeconomic category has been defined, historically, according to a number of criteria, including income level, occupation, education, even character. But students of the twentieth century, especially of the postwar era, have highlighted the importance of one's place of residence as a defining characteristic of social status: the home (along with its material goods and surrounding neighborhood) has become a crucial marker of one's location in the socioeconomic structure. For middle-class suburbanites, the home or, more accurately, the residential neighborhood was the defining element of their civic and political lives.[2]

The second core characteristic of suburban citizenship—the belief that "the good life" was an entitlement—has to be understood in the context of the right to economic well-being and security that entered the vocabulary of Western political culture following the Great Depression and World War II. In T. H. Marshall's words, this refers to the right "to live the life of a civilised being according to the standards prevailing in the society."[3] What these standards were for postwar Americans who claimed, or aspired to, a middle-class status varied slightly. But they could be summarized as the right to a residence of quality in an environment congenial to family and community living: this included sufficient and quality schools, safe and pleasant neighborhoods, parks, libraries, and the like. Compared with other racial and socioeconomic groups, the residents of suburban Queens had achieved a relative access to such material comfort. Yet the reality of a fast-developing residential area posed problems of its own. Schools were generally of good quality in northeastern Queens, but they were overcrowded. The neighborhoods were greener and less dense than elsewhere, but increased traffic on high-speed highways made them unsafe for pedestrians. Public transportation and libraries were insufficient by the residents' standards. Securing what they considered the "basic needs" of their communities was an ongoing preoccupation.

Third, along with an assertion of their rights to "the good life," Queens citizens had a clear and explicitly articulated sense of their obligations as active, or "good," citizens. The term *good citizen*, according to political scientist Judith Shklar, describes "the people of a community who are consistently engaged in public affairs." They "are public meeting-goers and joiners of voluntary organizations who discuss and deliberate with others about the politics that will affect them all."[4] This applies to a large number of Queens suburbanites, as it does to the residents of many postwar suburban communities.[5] Queens citizens joined home owners', tenants', and parents' associations, political parties and clubs, veterans' and religious groups. The issues that they discussed ranged from local to national and international affairs. Most important, participation in community associations reflected more than a commitment to abstract civic duties (although this was certainly part of the local political rhetoric); it served the more direct purpose of shaping the "good life" that these families aspired to.

Indeed, in contrast with an ideal version of disinterested civic participation, suburbanites' sense of civic obligation was directly related to their concerns for the immediate needs of their residential communities. Participation in community associations was necessary to lobby city officials for the construction of public services, such as schools. Civic involvement was also a means by which older residents of Queens, nervous about the rapid pace of demographic growth, tried to block the transformation of their beloved semirural communities through zoning regulations or opposition to public housing. Far from being disinterested or "apolitical" (as community leaders often claimed), the purpose of their civic involvement was to influence policy and the distribution of limited resources to bring about their own version of "the good life."

As was the case for the American citizenry as a whole, Queens citizens were a diverse group and disagreed at times over what the well-being of their communities entailed. Some, for instance, strongly believed that it was inextricably tied to national issues of racial justice, and their struggle to preserve the multicultural and multiracial nature of their neighborhoods was cast in this light. Others, like the group of Alley Pond residents cited above, believed that their own suburban peace and security were ephemeral in a world at war. The commitment to racial justice or world peace expressed by some was by no means shared by the majority of their neighbors. Yet in spite of their differences and disagreements they were united in their determination to shape their living environment.

One last point brings us back to the centrality of the residential community in the political lives of suburban citizens. Not only was it the object of their political activism but it constituted the public forum from which they acted as well. The residents' homes and neighborhood streets, their schools and places of worship, their community organizations and newspapers were all sites where public discussions took place. Parents gathered in the school's auditorium to discuss the lack of school seats or an alleged communist infiltration of the local PTA; housewives met informally in front of the supermarket to discuss the need for recreational activities; neighbors discussed the pros and cons of public housing in community associations; supporters of cold war policies brought their petitions to the local department store while their opponents held meetings in the Jewish Center or in their own living rooms. It was thus in the heart of their residential communities and with their neighbors, with whom they alternately disagreed and devised concerted action, that middle-class men and women acted as "good" citizens.

The suburban citizenship that I describe here—based on the dual conviction that one is entitled to a certain level of material well-being and that one has a responsibility to organize collectively to secure this social right—stands in sharp contrast to other models of citizenship prevalent in the twentieth century. It represented a departure from the value of simple living and the criticism of materialism found in the producer ethic of the late nineteenth and early twentieth centuries. The rich collective life and sense of collective responsibility that suburban citizens displayed (as producers had before them) is also at odds with the middle-American individualism that many social scientists assume dominated modern society. Finally, their concern for the good life, coupled with their determination to be good citizens, makes them hard to fit in the consumerist ethic that scholars such as Lizabeth Cohen argue shaped the political experience of Americans in the second half of the twentieth century. Queens residents' concerns for schools and neighborhoods of quality cannot be narrowly construed as an attempt to fulfill their desires as consumers. Also, they did not conceive of the state as merely a provider of goods and services. Just as they saw themselves as citizens, deserving of social rights and bound by collective responsibilities, they expected the state to be socially responsible and to ensure the well-being of local communities.[6]

This book is to be read as part of the broader reexamination of the immediate post–World War II period currently under way in the historical profession and, one hopes, among a more general public. The image that long dominated the historiography of the 1950s was not far from that depicted by C. Wright Mills in his thorough critique of his fellow Americans. Influenced by mass society theorists associated with the Frankfurt School, he diagnosed the deterioration in advanced Western societies of meaningful experiences of political deliberation. Alienation and manipulation characterized the lives of ordinary people, not involvement in the critical, rational debates essential to democracy. Devoid of access to the means of power, and unable or unwilling to transcend their private experience to take part in the public life of their nation, ordinary people were little more than spectators of life.

Their lives, like that of the Greek idiot, had no meaning beyond the singularity of their own private and familial experiences. They had no political significance and thus were historically irrelevant.[7]

Mills was not alone in his scathing condemnation of postwar society. The growth of a complex, bureaucratic society, the expansion of mass consumption, the burgeoning of "mass-produced" suburbs, and the revival of the domestic ideal—these were all developments that led many intellectuals to similar conclusions in the 1950s. Conformity and "keeping up with the Joneses" became keywords for describing a stultifying suburban experience that was dominated by empty materialism, rampant consumerism, and aimless peer pressures.[8]

In 1963, Betty Friedan extended this criticism of suburban conformity to the particular situation of women.[9] Her description of the exclusively private nature of her generation's experience is now familiar: "[Women's] only dream was to be perfect wives and mothers; their highest ambition to have five children and a beautiful house, their only fight to get and keep their husbands," she wrote in her 1963 bestseller, *The Feminine Mystique*. "They had no thought for the unfeminine problems of the world outside the home; they wanted the men to make the major decisions." Family-centered, homebound, and apolitical, "most American women" had fallen victim to the postwar ideology of passive femininity. As she also recounted in 1974, not only was suburban domesticity a stultifying experience but it stood in sharp contrast to the intense political environment of the pre-baby boom generation. "Having babies, the Care and Feeding of Children according to Doctor Spock, began to structure our lives. It took the place of politics."[10]

This classic criticism of 1950s culture is currently being revisited. From the work published in Joanne Meyerowitz's anthology, *Not June Cleaver*, to Daniel Horowitz's biography of Betty Friedan and Rosalyn Baxandall and Elizabeth Ewen's fresh examination of suburbia, among others, we now know that a tremendous complexity lies behind familiar stereotypes of the postwar generation.[11] The letter to President Truman cited above also confirms the need to rethink the long-standing academic wisdom on the period. Here, a group of families of World War II veterans are seen acting in collective and political ways. Assembled to celebrate the recent founding of their new suburban residence, these men and women discuss world affairs. They both identify with their residential community—introducing themselves as Alley Pond citizens—and express a deep concern for events happening beyond their own backyard. The letter is the expression of a collective opinion, reached after exchange among neighbors. More than a private communication between them and their president to whom it is formally addressed, their appeal is published as a letter to the editor of their community newspaper and, as such, it is a public statement intended to be read, and discussed, beyond their immediate neighborhood. Reflecting their understanding of themselves as public and political actors— as citizens—it is an example of the kind of evidence that, when one looks closely at the lives of 1950s ordinary Americans, shatters conventional stereotypes.

Our examination of suburban citizenship will proceed in three stages. In Part I, I examine the broad contour of suburban Queens as it was shaped in the immediate postwar era.

In Chapter 1, I look at the physical and demographic transformation that northeastern Queens underwent in the late 1940s and early 1950s as it became one of the nation's most active centers of residential development. Queens was certainly not a suburb in the technical or commonly accepted sense of the word. Administratively, it was located within the limits of New York City, and its built environment, which included an increasing number of large-scale garden-apartment complexes and publicly subsidized cooperatives for families of moderate income, contrasted with the more familiar suburban setting dominated by detached, single-family dwellings.[12] Yet the still undeveloped outer sections of the Borough of Queens offered key "suburban" qualities prized by families with young children: a relatively pastoral environment located within easy commuting distance of the city center. Families of unionized blue-collar workers, low-echelon white-collar workers, and professionals, many of them Jewish and some of them African American, joined the older residents of northeastern Queens to create a set of diverse communities.

From this physical and demographic portrait, I turn to an examination of the economic and political forces that shaped suburban Queens and dictated the terms by which postwar Americans could gain access to a residence of quality. The struggle over publicly assisted housing has been examined elsewhere, but it deserves special attention here. Not only was it central to the development of northeastern Queens in the late 1940s and early 1950s, but it was also instrumental in limiting access to the postwar middle class. That many families of the white race and of moderate income found themselves frustrated in their quest for the "good life" (defined in this context as affordable housing in a family-centered environment) needs to be better appreciated. Hence, in Chapter 2, I examine the difficulties that they encountered in their attempt to avail themselves of one of the basic markers of postwar citizenship in a context where the interests of private industry predominated.

As the debates over publicly assisted housing show, the so-called liberal consensus that has long been perceived as characteristic of postwar society concealed many conflicts.[13] Chapter 3, which examines the progressive and left-leaning forces at work in northeastern Queens, illustrates the vitality of ideological debates in postwar society. Changing voting patterns in the area show the electoral pluralism that was introduced by the immediate postwar migration. Especially in neighborhoods where a substantial number of Jews or unionized blue-collar workers lived, a strong progressive voice was heard on issues related to economic and racial justice, pacifism, and civil liberties. (One of these suburban radicals included Betty Friedan, who lived in northeastern Queens in the early 1950s and was anything but the apolitical creature that she later presented as typical of her generation.) Although by no means representative of Queens citizens as a whole, this radical minority had a significant influence on their communities. Indeed, by raising contentious issues for public debates, and doing so in their community associations, they rendered their suburban environment an ideologically lively place to be. Examining these debates is crucial to appreciating the diverse and divided nature of postwar suburban communities, as well as the way in which political debates were carried out in the very heart of residential communities.

In Part II, I turn from this contextual analysis of postwar Queens to a more specific exploration of its political culture and of its residents' political consciousness.

Debates over issues of national and international significance were everywhere present in community institutions but, as important as they were, they were not the defining element of community politics. Indeed, transcending the ideological differences that pitted neighbors against neighbors were issues related to the immediate residential community. The residents' keen interest for securing public services considered essential to their quality of life represented the essence of middle-class politics in Queens.

Chapter 4 examines the political culture of these neighborhoods, which was based on a celebration of participatory democracy. In line with a tradition of civic republicanism that has a long-standing history in American political culture, the editors of community newspapers and leaders of local organizations encouraged their neighbors to be "responsible" citizens, that is, to take an active part in the public affairs of their community. An important function fulfilled by these active citizens, as members of "the public," was also to be attentive to, and critical of, the action of their governments.[14]

As has often been the case in American history and continues to be so, the glorification of community-centered civic involvement was accompanied by a populist disparagement of politics. In ways reminiscent of the populist tradition traced by historian Michael Kazin, Queens political rhetoric pitted "the community" and its defenders, well-intentioned and sincere civic workers, against a less noble breed, the inherently corrupt and selfish politicians. The latter were seen as distant from or disrespectful of their constituents and their needs. Far from being simply a negative criticism of politics, however, this populist rhetoric served to strengthen the civic ethos described above. Indeed, the very corrupt nature of politicians demanded that citizens themselves play an active role as "watchdogs" for their interests. Conversely, only active civic workers who fulfilled their responsibility to the community through a participation in local organizations were acknowledged the right to criticize policy makers and to hold them accountable. Thus, the populist sensibility reflected in the political culture of Queens reinforced—and was reinforced by—a keen understanding of the residents' civic duties. Populism and civic republicanism were traditions that complemented each other in Queens.[15]

In Chapter 5, I examine the relationship between Queens citizens and their municipal government in the context of the citizens' battles for public services such as schools. Here I argue that at the core of the political struggles of middle-class citizens was a belief that the state (in this case, the municipal government) had a responsibility to deliver the good life that they had come to expect. Specifically, Queens residents expected policies to guarantee that adequate public services would be provided to match the rapid pace of residential construction. They demanded better planning of metropolitan development and a financial commitment that matched the needs that they most acutely felt as residents of the new "suburban frontier." The absence of a consistent, balanced, and adequately funded policy of metropolitan development was crucial in defining their relationship to their government. Seen in this light, Queens citizens embraced the main tenet of New Deal liberalism, that of the state's responsibility toward its citizens.

The relationship between middle-class citizens and the state, including their expectation of governmental responsibility to the needs of their residential community, is further illustrated by a close analysis of the strategies and arguments that Queens activists used in their political battles. Residents' correspondence to city officials and the local newspapers' reports on their activities reveal a fundamental assumption that policy making was a rational process, based on the objective gathering and assessment of information. Decisions, they assumed, should be made following consultation with informed citizens who, because of their familiarity with local problems, were best positioned to provide expertise on the matter. Their expertise on local needs was based on the gathering of "hard and cold statistics" through neighborhood-based surveys (surveys of the local school-age population prepared by housewives, for instance). Like the policy makers whom they were trying to sway to their views, Queens community activists spoke the language of "facts and figures" and rationality. In brief, at the core of their understanding of citizens' and state's responsibility was the belief that an informed and rational citizenry, presenting reasonable demands backed by documented evidence, should be heard by policy makers. Throughout the 1950s, in spite of evidence to the contrary, civic leaders remained remarkably (even naively) confident that reasonable bureaucrats and elected officials would respond to their factually supported demands.

That this type of argument was voiced by full-time housewives, who constituted the majority of community activists, both highlights the importance of their appeals to rationality, and raises interesting questions about women's public consciousness in the age of *The Feminine Mystique*. It also brings us to the question that framed this research in the first place.

This study began as an attempt to trace the public and political involvement of white middle-class women in the 1950s and, because of the centrality of the home to these women, who were mostly full-time housewives, community politics was an obvious choice. Given the prominence that maternalist politics has had historically (as a form of political language based on women's maternal responsibilities), I was expecting middle-class women of that generation to put their maternal responsibilities at the center of their political strategy.[16] But as we will see in Chapter 6, research greatly complicated my initial assumptions. It revealed that women were indeed central to community activism, yet their self-identification as political actors and citizens was characterized by an uneasy relationship to their culturally prescribed gender roles. The use of maternalist argument was not totally absent from the repertoire of Queens community activists, as the case of baby carriage parades illustrates. Yet this spectacular form of direct action, which centered on the dissonant image of the disorderly mother, was neither their typical nor their preferred form of political action. It was used as a last resort strategy, when lobbying through conventional means had failed to bring about results.

Although undoubtedly conscious of the power that their maternal role could yield politically, and in spite of the physical and cultural association that women had with the local community by virtue of their domestic responsibilities, female community activists chose to downplay their feminine identity when entering the public and political arena. Not only did they present themselves as "rational" citizens, therefore operating on the basis of objective knowledge as opposed to maternal instinct. But, as is evident in the battle to improve local schools, female activists insisted on the communal and parental rather than the feminine nature of the struggle: "Parents" rather than exclusively "mothers" were concerned for the well-being of community schools. In general, female activists, in accord with the men in their communities, seemed to have conceived of community activism as a gender-neutral field.[17]

In Part III, I depart from a strict analysis of the case of northeastern Queens to reflect on its implications for our understanding of postwar history. Going beyond this case study will show that the experience of this particular group of suburbanites was not unique but shared by fellow middle-class Americans. More specifically, I will argue that the emphasis on rationality and process that was so central to Queens citizens was also a major component of the era's political culture. This section aims to provide a renewed vision of gender and middle-class identity in the 1950s.

Chapter 7 pursues the analysis of women's public and political roles introduced in Chapter 6 by turning to the Volunteers for Stevenson, a national organization of citizens who took an active part in the 1952 and 1956 presidential elections. Not only was its significant contribution to the Democratic Party's campaign based on the work of female volunteers, but in an effort to win women's votes, the group drew explicit connections between housewives and rational, independent voters. This parallel between the Volunteers' strategy and that of Queens community activists illustrates the larger significance of this case study for our understanding of postwar political culture. The emphasis on active, critical citizenship which we found at the local level, and which was embraced by women as well as men, was also prominent on the national political scene.

A second interesting parallel to the conclusions that I have reached regarding the housewives' view of themselves as independent and critical citizens is provided by Betty Friedan in some of her pre-*Feminine Mystique* writings. There, Friedan offered a positive assessment of volunteerism as a forum where housewives could hone their political skills, which contrasted sharply with her criticism of this particular form of public involvement as meaningless in her 1963 classic. These writings also portray housewives from northeastern Queens, where Friedan was living at the time, as challenging the authority of male experts—an attitude that was very much at odds with the submissiveness that Friedan attributed to her generation in 1963. It is beyond the scope of this study to elucidate what led Friedan to her rejection of community-based volunteerism in *The Feminine Mystique*. But rediscovering the meaning that this important form of public activity had for women before its fall from grace is an important part of our reassessment of the 1950s—and, ironically, Friedan's writings are useful for that purpose.

In the eighth and last chapter, I draw out some of the implications that this case study raises for our assessment of middle-class antiliberalism in postwar America. The defense of residential communities that constituted the basis of middle-class suburban citizenship has drawn attention mostly for its inherent and, at times, explicit racism; an early manifestation of the white working- and middle-class opposition to liberalism which has been more commonly associated with the 1960s.[18] Extending my analysis to the debates over school and residential integration that took place in New York City in the 1960s and in which Queens suburban citizens took part, I address more specifically the question of whether the history of Queens community politics in the 1950s was part of this simmering "crisis of liberalism," which has permeated the history of northern metropolitan areas since World War II. I answer yes to the question, although I point to other factors than race to explain the growing resentment that local residents felt toward New York City politicians.

The richness of this case study lies in the absence of conflicts over race in the 1950s, which makes it easier to see and analyze the tensions that nevertheless existed between Queens community activists and their policy makers. These tensions were constant in the two decades following World War II, and they set the stage for the residents' negative reaction toward the integration plans devised by New York City officials for their communities in the late 1950s and 1960s. They were based on their municipal government's failure to coordinate metropolitan development to ensure adequate services to their communities, as well as its disregard for citizens' input in the decision-making process. Without the overshadowing presence of overt racial conflicts for most of the period under study, these dynamics which had frustrated local residents from the very beginning of suburban expansion come to the fore. They continued to be present when racial integration became an issue in the 1960s. This case illustrates that two decades of frustration with elected officials and bureaucrats who failed to provide the most basic elements of a promised "good life" and who failed to listen to the reasoned arguments of well-intentioned "good citizens" led to a growing disenchantment with the state.

The experience of Queens suburbanites profoundly challenges our image of postwar middle-class life. The Alley Pond citizens who met in the comfort of their backyard and discussed the Korean War effectively belied the academic wisdom on the period. Their example forces us to discard old stereotypes. But realizing that middle-class Americans were not Greek idiots is only the beginning. More challenging is the task of understanding their political views and reassessing the period in light of that new knowledge. This book will, I hope, contribute to this endeavor.

The model of citizenship embraced by middle-class citizens, I argue, was based on the assumption that one has a right to a residential community of quality and that both citizens and the state were obligated to the community's welfare. This legitimate goal brought them to take an active part in the civic and political life of their residential communities. It also constituted the gauge by which they measured the performance of policy makers. In line with the era's liberal ethos, which was predicated on a dual emphasis on individual rights and state responsibility, Queens suburbanites expected the state to help them build a healthy living environment. That the New York City government (as, no doubt, other metropolitan governments) failed to meet the residents' expectations ultimately weakened their faith in responsible and rational liberalism. Listening to the hopes and disappointments of these men and women is important, not only because it is our obligation as historians to recapture the richness of the past but also because it is our obligation as citizens to be respectful of our fellow citizens.

Part I
The Formation of
Suburban Queens

Chapter 1
"Queens Has a Street Named Utopia"

In 1950, Barbara Lee, journalist for the community newspaper *Meadow Lark*, captured in these words the atmosphere of northeastern Queens at a time when it was in the midst of a profound transformation. "Fifteen years ago, the land was tilled by a few lone farmers. . . . Then, in the middle 1930's the placid countryside was plunged into a building fever that is yet to be quieted. Small compact communities shot up. Here, in the shadow of New York skyscrapers, a 'small-town' life was bustling into activity." The "small town" that she described was, in fact, a series of neighboring communities, each "steeped in its own distinctive character" and bearing its own name: "A stranger trying to find his way around this neighborhood would meet more than his share of confusion if he were guided solely by the names of local communities, Cunningham Crest, Hollis Hills, Flushing Manor." Yet these neighborhoods had a common feature: their newness. In Lee's terms, "It is a welded community taking its first steps on its own." Also located "in the shadow of New York skyscrapers," on northeastern Queens's rapidly vanishing farmlands and golf courses, they had a common identity as "suburbia within New York City." It is to these new neighborhoods that thousands of young families moved between the late 1930s and the late 1950s to become "suburban pioneers."[1]

"The growth of Queens since the turn of the century has been nothing short of colossal," wrote a senior member of Mayor Wagner's administration in 1955.[2] Since the late nineteenth century, Queens County had experienced a series of developments that transformed it from a collection of rural villages and townships to a mix of urban and suburban neighborhoods. From the 1860s through the 1930s, the western part of the county hosted most of the development: The opening of

Table 1. Population of New York City and Its Boroughs, 1930–1957

	1930		1940	
The Bronx	1,265,258		1,394,711	(+10%)
Brooklyn	2,560,401		2,698,285	(+5%)
Manhattan	1,867,312		1,889,924	(+1%)
Queens	1,079,129		1,297,634	(+20%)
Richmond	158,346		174,441	(+10%)

	1950		1957	
The Bronx	1,451,277	(+4%)	1,424,367	(-1.9%)
Brooklyn	2,738,175	(+1.5%)	2,602,433	(-5%)
Manhattan	1,960,101	(+3.7%)	1,794,069	(-8.5%)
Queens	1,550,849	(+19.5%)	1,762,582	(+13.6%)
Richmond	191,555	(+9.8%)	212,020	(+10.6%)

Source: Based on Wallace S. Sayre and Herbert Kaufman, *Governing New York City* (1960; New York: Russell Sage Foundation, 1965), table 1, 18. Reprinted with permission.

the Long Island Railroad terminal at Hunters Point in 1861 fostered the growth of middle-class railroad suburbs. The completion of the Queensboro Bridge connecting the borough to Manhattan in 1909, and the subsequent extension of the city's mass transit lines to Queens in the 1910s and 1920s, fostered a second wave of development as garden apartments and small detached bungalows sprung up along the elevated lines. Between 1900 and 1930, the population grew from 150,000 to over 1 million.[3] This demographic expansion continued during the 1940s, when Queens increased its population by 20 percent. As Table 1 shows, between 1950 and 1957, at a time when all the other boroughs except Staten Island registered a net loss, Queens's population again rose by almost 14 percent.

Local boosters made no effort to conceal their enthusiasm for this phenomenal growth. In August 1936, lauding the rapid construction of a development of single-family homes, Bayside Hills, the editor of the community newspaper, *Bayside Times*, could find no better comparison to the expansion of this section of Queens than the myth of uninhibited expansion of the old frontier. "If that is not the nearest approach to a modern 'Covered Wagon procession' with the building of a town going on while one watches it, then we miss our guess."[4] Queens is "New York City's largest borough," it is the "fastest growing homeowner borough," it is "one of the most populous [counties] in the country," boasted the Chamber of Commerce during the 1950s and 1960s.[5]

In contrast with the early part of the century, when most of Queens development was concentrated in the western part of the borough, the largest part of the demographic expansion from the 1930s on took place in the northeast where large tracts of wooded land, farms, and golf courses proved fertile grounds for the surge in residential development (see Figure 1). The opening of the TriBorough and Whitestone bridges in 1936 and 1940, and the construction of their accompanying networks of expressways throughout the 1940s and 1950s, provided New Yorkers with direct access to this area.[6] In 1950, 44 percent of the housing stock in northeastern Queens was recent construction, built since 1940.[7] Between 1950 and 1957, while the population of the older, more densely settled communities in western Queens increased only slightly or decreased, northeastern Queens increased its population by 55 to 60 percent. (The population of Flushing and Bayside alone had already increased by 46 percent between 1940 and 1948.)[8] It was in the areas located south of Northern Boulevard, and especially between Horace Harding and Grand Central Boulevards, in Bayside, Hollis Hills, Bellerose, and South Flushing, that the bulk of the midcentury migration to Queens was concentrated. A large number of these newcomers were young families.[9]

Although the area was located within the limits of New York City, developers and journalists emphasized the suburban qualities, especially the pastoral and child-centered environment, that the borough's neighborhoods offered. As one could read, for instance, in the *World Tribute and Sun* in 1963, "The big lure to Queens traditionally has been the suburban quality of the borough. It's a place where parents could buy a back yard for the kids and a swatch of land for growing roses or tomatoes; a place far removed from the teeming sections of the city they were glad to leave behind; suburbia without a crushing commuting burden."[10] Also typical of the publicity that the "Borough of homes" received in metropolitan newspapers was a 1948 *World Telegram* article, "Queens Has a Street Named Utopia," in which Utopia Parkway, Bayside, was praised for offering the best of both worlds. "Neither urban nor rural, its one-family houses reflect idyllic living," read the headlines. "There are the hard city streets of homes and the far-distant suburban retreats, and in between are the outlying city sections combining many advantages of city and country." The article further described "a street of pretty, one-family houses, of back yard tomato patches and front yard flower gardens, of television sets in the living room and automobiles in the garages." Recent development had not destroyed the pastoral qualities of the environment: "Less than two decades ago, the section was farmland. It is still

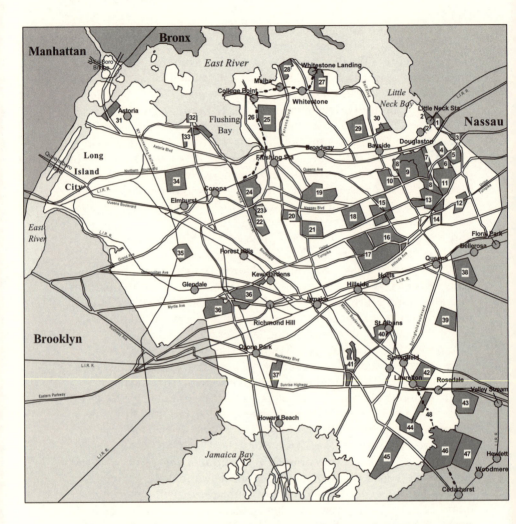

Figure 1. Centers of Active Development in the Borough of Queens, 1932. *New York Times*, January 31, 1932, Section 11, 2:2, "Queens Borough (General) 1950s and Pre-50s," Vertical Files, Municipal Reference and Research Center, New York City.

1. Large tract of land to be developed by Cord Meyer Corporation
2. Land around Little Neck Railroad station to be developed by Lewis Development Company
3. Land being developed by Yale Land Company on which some new English-type houses are being built
4. Tract of land being developed by Bryce Rea of Little Neck
5. Brenner property
6. Marvin Farm of thirty acres purchased by William Lawson
7. Land assembled by F. W. Lewis of Little Neck for apartments overlooking Alley Park
8. Large tract of land purchased by the city of New York
9. Oakland Golf Course
10. Queensboro Golf Course
11. North Hills Golf Club developed by William Lawson of New York
12. Land being developed by William Lawson
13. Matawok land sold by Lewis Development Company to syndicate and later bought by city
14. Land being developed by Mezick
15. Richards Farm bought by city
16. Hillside Park purchased by the city
17. Old Wigan-park Land Company property
18. Fresh Meadow Golf Course
19. Kissena Park
20. Parental Home-proposed civic center
21. Pomonok Golf Club built by Lewis & Valentine Co.
22. Area proposed for new park on Flushing Meadows
23. Housing project of garden apartments owned by William Lawson of New York, consisting of forty-four acres
24. Brooklyn ash removal land now made into a golf course
25. New York City Airport
26. Whitestone line taken over by city for subway
27. Clearview Golf Course
28. City park
29. Cord Meyer development and golf course
30. City park
31. Astoria park
32. Curtis Wright Airport
33. City park
34. Jackson Heights
35. Juniper Swamp-Rothstein property purchased by city for a park
36. Forest Park
37. Aqueduct race track
38. Belmont race track
39. Proposed golf course owned by Central Airport of New York, Inc.
40. St. Albans Golf Course
41. Baisley Park
42. Laurelton houses on site of Laurelton Golf Course
43. Curtiss Airport
44. Land proposed by Queens Planning Commission for a park
45. 100 acres proposed by the city for purchase to provide a waterfront park golf course
46. Proposed industrial section in connection with Jamaica Bay dredging
47. Proposed golf course
48. Suggested LIRR re-arrangement to replace Rockaway Line

reminiscent of open fields ablaze with black-eyed Susans; of crickets chirping at dusk and woodpeckers a-pecking in the morning." As for the "Utopians" that Taylor interviewed, they seemed "content to be peaceably provincial"—nicely fitting contemporary images of suburbanites.[11]

The neighborhoods described here offered detached single-family houses, a type of dwelling that represented 41 percent of the built environment in northeastern Queens in 1950. Another 13 percent of all dwelling units consisted of owner-occupied attached houses. An example of these were the Tyholland Homes, built in 1947 near Horace Harding Boulevard—123 brick houses "with six pleasant, spacious rooms" were available for the price of $10,700 each. This price was at the bottom end of the market for single-family houses, either detached or attached, in northeastern Queens. In 1950, 48 percent of all owner-occupied houses in the area were valued at between $10,000 and $15,000, 39 percent were worth more than $15,000, and only 13 percent were available at less than $10,000. Hence, only a marginal part of the market in Queens was competitive with the basic Cape Cod models available in nearby Levittown, Long Island, for as low as $7,500 in late 1947.[12]

Queens's reputation as "the borough of home owners" accurately reflected the higher proportion of home ownership in Queens in comparison to the other boroughs of New York City. In the postwar era, however, the balance between home owners and renters was slowly tipping in favor of the latter. (This contrasts with the national trend, which saw the rate of home ownership increase in the postwar period.) In the borough as a whole, tenants represented 54 percent of the population in 1950 and 56 percent in 1960; in the northeastern section of Queens, tenants were still a minority (39 percent) in 1950, but the construction of a number of large-scale garden apartments in the early 1950s would soon increase the proportion of tenants in the area.[13] Built by banks and insurance companies in the immediate postwar period and sponsored by the Federal Housing Administration after 1949 (under Section 608, the multifamily division of the Housing Act), large-scale rental developments mushroomed on Queens vacant land in the late 1940s and early 1950s. Although featuring a higher density than the neighborhoods of single-family houses, these "suburban apartments" were praised for their pastoral and child-centered qualities.[14]

Perhaps the best known of northeastern Queens's garden apartments was the New York Life Insurance Company's Fresh Meadows, which opened for occupancy in 1949. According to urban critic Lewis

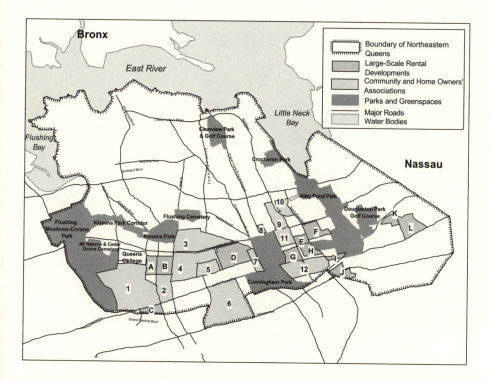

Figure 2. Northeastern Queens, 1960. The boundaries of community and home owners' associations have been determined from the associations' papers, when available, and from community newspaper accounts. For the large-scale rental and cooperative developments, see Ira S. Robbins and Marian Sameth, eds., *Directory of Large-Scale Rental and Cooperative Housing* (New York: Citizens' Housing and Planning Council of New York, 1957).

Community and Home Owners' Associations:

1. Queens Valley Home Owners' Association
2. Flushing Suburban Civic Association
3. Harding Heights Civic Association
4. Flushing Heights/Horace Harding Civic and Improvement Association
5. Fresh Meadows Civic Association
6. Jamaica Estates Civic Association
7. North Cunningham Heights Home Owners' Association
8. Tyholland Civic Association
9. Bayside Hills Civic Association
10. Oakland Hills Civic Association
11. Cunningham Heights Home Owners' Association
12. East Cunningham Park Civic Association

Large-Scale Rental Developments:

A. Pomonok
B. Electchester
C. Parkway Village
D. Fresh Meadows
E. Bell Park Gardens
F. Oakland Gardens
G. Windsor Park
H. Windsor Oaks
I. Alley Pond Park
J. Bell Park Manor and Terrace
K. Grand Central Apartments
L. Glen Oaks Village

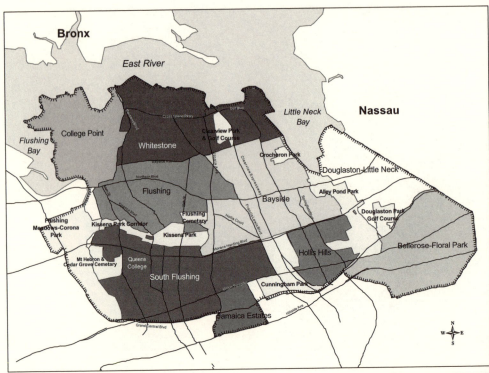

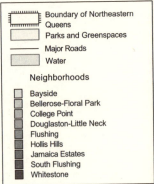

Figure 3. Neighborhoods of Northeastern Queens, 1960.
The exact boundaries of Queens neighborhoods vary slightly
from source to source. This map is based on the divisions
adopted by the Community Council of Greater New York in
1958 and by New York City in 1967. Hollis Hills was designated as such by developers of tracts of single-family homes
around Union Turnpike in 1948. I have chosen to separate it
from Bayside because of its distinct postwar character. The
boundaries of Jamaica Estates are those established by the developer and home owners' association when the area was
built in 1929. The 1960 Census Tract Map has been used to
produce this map. See, respectively, *Queens Communities: Population Characteristics and Neighborhood Social Resources* (New
York: Bureau of Community Statistical Services, Research
Department, 1958); "New York Neighborhoods," *New York
Sunday News*, October 22, 1967, 15, "Queens Borough, General, 1961–1969," Vertical Files, Municipal Reference and Research Center, New York City; "Hollis Hills Designated," *New
York Times*, December 12, 1948, Section 8, 4; Thomas J.
Lovely, *The History of the Jamaica Estates, 1929–1969* (Jamaica,
N.Y.: Jamaica Estates Association, 1969); Bureau of the Cen-
sus, *U.S. Census of Population: 1960* (Washington, D.C.: Gov-
ernment Printing Office, 1961).

Mumford, the development, adjacent to Cunningham Park, offered the best of family and community suburban living. It had an "air of pastoral composure and peace, with children running about freely and safely." Apart from the misgivings Mumford had for the two thirteen-story apartment towers that stood in the middle of the large complex, which was composed of residential buildings of one, two, and three stories, a nursery center, and the first suburban branch of Bloomingdale's department store, he had nothing but praise for the "community carpeted from end to end with lawns." As he described in the *New Yorker* in October 1949, "order and comeliness and charm pervade the design." The "plentiful verdure against a restful background of brick walls" and the "great pools of domestic quiet behind the long, irregular, widely spaced rows of three-story apartment houses and two-story dwellings" impressed him especially. Although more than 3,000 families were now housed on the former Fresh Meadows golf course, the site had maintained its pastoral character. Wrote Mumford:

[It] provide[d] for the comfort and the aesthetic satisfaction of the inhabitants from the time they wake up, after a night of peaceful sleep, and put their small children on the lawn behind the houses—where they scamper about with reasonable safety on the grass while the mothers go shopping at the nearest marketing center—until everyone goes to bed again. Fresh Meadows is not just more housing; it is a slice of the City of Tomorrow.[15]

Albeit on a more moderate tone, *Architectural Record* also praised the planners for creating an environment hospitable to families with young children:

The buildings are disposed in small groups, each group informally outlining a neighborhood, a comfortable unit of this world that a small child can grasp and accept. Each little group has its own play yard, with equipment, its own stretch of lawn with benches and trees, its own limited vista, its little private terrace gardens, and no doubt its own neighborhood gossip.[16]

Child-centeredness, pastoral environment, privacy and neighborhood life—Fresh Meadows had many of the major features of the ideal suburban community.[17]

These features were also those noted by residents of Fresh Meadows, who were asked by the *Long Island Star Journal* in 1949 how they liked their new home: "I think this is an ideal place to live and a perfect location for people raising families," stated a housewife. In the opinion of a professional woman, a model: "I like it because it is close enough to Manhattan for people going to business or any social engagements and because it is far enough away to ban the Manhattan

crowds and give you a feeling of suburban living." Concurred a salesman: "I think Fresh Meadows is the best project in Queens and an
ideal place for a family. You have every facility for your daily wants
and still you are not in a crowded city." Moving away from the crowds
and congestion of the city, yet remaining at a commuting distance from
it—also an essential part of the suburban dream—was as important
as finding an environment congenial to family life for these young
professionals.[18]

Smaller than Fresh Meadows, but featuring a similar approach to
suburban rental, was Parkway Village, a 685–unit development built
by a consortium of fifteen savings banks in 1948. Parkway Village had
the distinction of housing employees of the United Nations (delegates
and staff from various nations), as well as American professionals
and high-level managers—including Betty Friedan and her husband,
Carl, who lived there between 1950 and 1956. (When they moved
to Parkway Village, Betty was employed as a reporter and writer for
UE News, a position which she held until 1952. In 1950, Carl was running a theatre, but switched to his own public relations and advertising firm during their stay in Queens.) Later, she would remember
their first home outside of Manhattan with fondness: "It was almost
like having our own home: The apartments had French doors opening on to a common lawn where the children could go out and play by
themselves, instead of having to be taken to the park." Friedan's comment reflects the pastoral character of the development, which featured 110 attached two- to three-story buildings, colonial style; more
than 80 percent of its forty-acre site was devoted to green space.[19] As
Table 2 indicates, compared with large-scale rental developments built
in Manhattan at the same time, which featured high-rise buildings
and higher land use, Fresh Meadows and Parkway Village were attractive to families with young children.

After 1949, the construction of large-scale garden apartments accelerated when the Federal Housing Administration (FHA) extended
its guaranteed loans to builders of rental housing. Attracted by the
generous terms of Section 608, builders flocked to the rental market.
(As revealed by a Senate investigation in 1956, builders routinely over-
estimated their costs, land prices, and fees when applying for a low-
interest FHA-guaranteed mortgage, making windfall profits out of the
deal—$500 million, in total.)[20] In northeastern Queens only, seven-
teen developments were built between 1949 and 1953 under this lucrative agreement. They ranged in size from 300 units to close to
3,000 units and added more than 14,000 rental units to the housing
stock (see Table 3).

TABLE 2. Large-Scale Rental Developments Built by
Banks and Insurance Companies, 1947–1949,
Queens and Manhattan

Name Date built	Number of units	Rent per room (in 1957)	Number and height of buildings	Coverage (percentage)
Queens				
Fresh Meadows	3,008	$28 u	2b 13s	15
1949			137b 2, 3s	
Parkway Village	685	$30 u	110b 2, 3s	18
1948				
Manhattan				
Peter Cooper Village	2,495	$34 u	21b 15s	24
1947–49				
Stuyvesant Town	8,755	$21	35b 12, 13s	25
1947–49				

Source: Ira S. Robbins and Marian Sameth, eds., *Directory of Large-Scale Rental and Cooperative Housing* (New York: Citizens' Housing and Planning Council of New York, 1957). Note: Coverage: percentage of land covered by residential buildings; b: buildings; s: stories; u: includes utilities.

The Gross-Morton Corporation, developer of Glen Oaks Village, in Bellerose, and Windsor Oaks and Windsor Park, in Hollis Hills, Bayside, was among the first to avail itself of the opportunity offered by Section 608. (It was also among those who benefited from the lucrative Section 608, making a profit of $4 million on Glen Oaks Village alone.)[21] Although the percentage of land covered in its two-story building developments (Glen Oaks and Windsor Oaks) was slightly higher than at Fresh Meadows and Parkway Village (respectively, 22, 20, 15, and 18 percent), the promotional material highlighted their familial and pastoral qualities. As one could read in an ad in a Long Island daily, Glen Oaks Village, with its 175-acre site, was "A child's paradise of broad green lawns, paths, gardens and playgrounds where youngsters can romp safe from traffic . . . and in plain view of mother in her beautiful apartment."[22] A young mother concurred: "I love it out here . . . fresh air, sunshine, room for the kids to play . . . friendly people."[23] As for Windsor Park, one of the rare developments in northeastern Queens to feature six-story buildings, it was reported that efforts were being made to keep the Hollis Hills developments "countrified." The promoter insisted that only a small portion of the

TABLE 3. Large-Scale Rental Developments Built under
FHA, Section 608, 1949–1953, Queens

Name Date built	Number of units	Rent per room (in 1957)	Number and height of buildings		Coverage (percentage)
Alley Pond Park 1950	550	30.50 u	31b	2s	35
Arrow Brook Gardens 1950	326	27.00	14b	2s	25
Auburndale and Oak Tree Villages 1951	788	26.00	n/a		34
Bayside Manor Park 1951	462	27.50	9b	3s	25
Campus Hall Apartments 1952	930	27.00 u	38b	2s	22
Glen Oaks Village 1949	2,904	26.00 u	134b	2s	22
Grand Central Apartments 1952	400	23.00 u	20b	2s	22
Grand Central Parkway Gardens 1951	386	30.00 u	20b	2s	19
Jewel Gardens Apartments 1949	388	23.00 u	16b	2s	40
Kew Gardens 1953	1,008	28.00 u	11b	6s	n/a
Kew Gardens Hills 1950	1,269	24.00	53b	3s	50
Kew Terrace Apartments 1950	360	25.00	n/a		n/a
Langdale Apartments 1951	360	25.00 u	21b	2s	50
Oakland Gardens 1949	1,588	24.00 u	38b	2s	23
Queens College Gardens 1951	402	24.00 u	17b	2, 3s	25
Windsor Oaks 1951	898	26.00	52b	2s	20
Windsor Park 1951	1,668	27.50	19b	6s	11

Source: Ira S. Robbins and Marian Sameth, eds., *Directory of Large-Scale Rental and Cooperative Housing* (New York: Citizens' Housing and Planning Council of New York, 1957). Note: Coverage: percentage of land covered by residential buildings; b: buildings; s: stories; u: includes utilities.

TABLE 4. Large-Scale Cooperative Developments,
1950–1954, Queens

Name Date built	Number of units	Rent per room (in 1957)	Number and height of buildings		Coverage (percentage)
Bell Park Gardens 1950	800	250 dp 15.49	39b	2s	23
Bell Park Manor and Terrace 1951	847	250 dp 15.00	50b	2s	20
Electchester 1952–54	2,225	470 dp 14.72–16.91	36b	3, 6s	18

Source: Ira S. Robbins and Marian Sameth, eds., *Directory of Large-Scale Rental and Cooperative Housing* (New York: Citizens' Housing and Planning Council of New York, 1957). Note: Coverage: percentage of land covered by residential buildings; b: buildings; s: stories; dp: down payment.

land would be occupied by the nineteen buildings: 89 percent of the site was to be "devoted to landscaped gardens, lawns, play areas and wooded parks. Existing trees, to the greatest extent possible, are to be preserved in their natural state." Its location, directly across the street from the 500-acre Cunningham Park and within a few blocks of the 464-acre Alley Pond Park, no doubt compensated for its relatively urban character.[24]

In addition to owner-occupied single-family houses and privately owned garden apartments, an innovative and controversial form of cooperative housing, sponsored by the New York State Limited-Dividend Housing Program, was also available to the new migrants to northeastern Queens.[25] In keeping with the environment where they were built, these cooperatively owned garden-apartment developments maintained a relatively low density (see Table 4). They included Bell Park Gardens as well as Bell Park Manor and Terrace, both in South Bayside.

The two-story attached brick buildings of Bell Park Gardens, for instance, covered only 23 percent of its six-acre site. (It was comparable to its neighbor, Oakland Gardens, a Section 608 development also built in 1949 on the site of a former golf course. Both had slightly less than 40 buildings and the same land coverage.) Each apartment faced onto an internal courtyard, and playgrounds were available for children. As described by Herman Stichman, the New York State Housing Commissioner, "maintain[ing] the open spaces so desirable in a residential community" was crucial to the project's promoters.[26] Bell Park Manor and Terrace was built on the same design.

Also part of the limited-dividend program was Electchester, located in South Flushing. Although it had buildings as high as six stories on a fifty-seven-acre site (part of the former Pomonok Country Club), it was also designed on the model of the garden apartment, with enclosed garden courts and broad avenues. Its location, however, next to Pomonok Houses—a public housing project for moderate income families built in 1951—gave it a more urban character. Pomonok's 2,071 apartments were divided among thirteen three-story and twenty-two seven-story buildings. Although it included facilities congenial to young families—a community center provided various activities for the family, and a children's center housed a nursery school and after-school program—keeping the construction costs low was more important than investing in green space. The area of South Flushing where Electchester and Pomonok were located was one of only two small districts in northeastern Queens to be classified, in 1969, as "high-medium density residential"—a zoning classification that allowed for apartments higher than six stories.[27]

With its combination of single-family homes, garden apartments (either rented or cooperatively owned), and, occasionally, more urban developments such as Pomonok Houses, northeastern Queens was a diverse environment, but not an unusual place. Indeed, the area encompassed in one geographical location a variety in the built environment that was, in fact, typical of postwar suburbs.[28] But for residents of northeastern Queens, the element that most clearly distinguished the area as a suburb was not whether they owned a single-family house or rented in a garden-apartment complex. Rather, it was the pastoral quality of their environment. Although they were within the city's administrative jurisdiction, their neighborhoods, situated on the outskirts of the built urban environment, had a pastoral, even rural, character. Developers and observers praised the green open spaces that the area, still recently covered by farms, public parks, private country clubs, and golf courses, had maintained. Residents who moved to the new areas of Queens were struck by the undeveloped nature of their new homes. At the time the first families moved to Bell Park Gardens, recalled one of them, the surrounding area was still wooded.[29] Journalists and observers, such as Lewis Mumford, often wondered at the existence of this oasis in the midst of the great metropolis. To be sure, the suburban nature of Queens was relative. The area was greener and more spacious than the urban neighborhoods of Manhattan, Brooklyn, and the Bronx that many of the migrants were leaving, but less so than the more distant suburbs of eastern Long Island or Westchester County. As an "inner suburb," northeastern Queens offered a relatively low-density and pastoral environment within the administrative limits of New York City.

As was also typical of postwar communities, the residential neighborhoods of suburban Queens were occupationally diverse. Indeed, as David Halle has argued convincingly, debunking the myth of the homogeneous suburb, a number of factors including income overlap between better-paid blue-collar workers and lower-echelon white-collar workers (such as clerical workers, accountants, retail managers, and teachers), and the widespread availability of cars, ensured the formation of occupationally mixed residential neighborhoods after World War II.[30] In Queens, better-paid blue-collar workers and civil servants lived next door to lower-echelon white-collar workers and professionals.

Like Park Forest, Illinois, the suburban community that William H. Whyte analyzed in *The Organization Man*, the percentage of college-educated professionals and managers in such garden apartments as Fresh Meadows, Glen Oaks Village, and Oakland Gardens was high—in fact, significantly higher than the average for northeastern Queens (see Tables 5 and 6). Only a few neighborhoods of home owners, such as Douglaston, were of comparable upper-middle class status. More common in northeastern Queens were families whose male breadwinner was employed in a blue-collar occupation, such as craftsman or operator, or in the lower-echelon white-collar occupation, as in the clerical, sales, and service sector. (A large number of Queens residents were municipal service workers: families of policemen, firemen, sanitation workers, who were barred from living outside of the city.)[31] Each of these two categories, which formed what would come to be called the lower middle class, included 28 percent of the male population. The majority of residents had a high school education (43 percent) or less (31 percent). As in other middle-class communities in the postwar era, the proportion of women in the labor force was low (26 percent in 1950), but increasing (34 percent in 1960); 47 percent of them were employed as clerical workers.[32]

Like the majority of suburbs in the postwar era, northeastern Queens was almost exclusively white.[33] In 1950, African American residents were concentrated on a few blocks in the old sections of Bayside and Flushing.[34] Still in 1957, New York City's special census of population revealed that, of all the boroughs of New York City, Queens had the largest proportion of all-white census tracts: 61 percent, as compared with Manhattan, which had the lowest proportion with 8 percent. This figure, which includes neighborhoods in the southwestern part of the Borough (Hollis, St. Albans, South Jamaica, and Springfield) where

TABLE 5. Occupation and Education, 1950: Renters

		Occupation of men[1]			Education[2]		
	Women in labor force (percentage)	Professionals and managers (percentage)	Clerical and sales (percentage)	Craftsman, operators, and service (percentage)	Elementary school (percentage)	High school (percentage)	College (percentage)
Fresh Meadows	21.1	65.8	24.9	8.0	9.2	35.3	51.9
Glen Oaks Village	22.6	48.3	31.0	19.2	10.0	46.5	37.4
Oakland Gardens	22.5	55.5	27.4	16.0	13.3	45.1	39.9

Source: U.S. Census of Population: 1950, table 2, "Age, Marital Status, and Economic Characteristics, by Sex, by Census Tracts."
Note: These three garden apartments were selected because they were occupied before 1950 and because their corresponding census tract is easily identifiable: 1,347 for Fresh Meadows, 1,551 for Glen Oaks Village, and 1,377 for Oakland Gardens.
1. The balance is composed of "laborers," "private household workers," and "occupation not reported."
2. The balance was "not reported."

TABLE 6. Occupation and Education, 1950: Home Owners

	Women in labor force (percentage)	Occupation of men[1]			Education[2]		
		Professionals and managers (percentage)	Clerical and sales (percentage)	Craftsman, operators, and service (percentage)	Elementary school (percentage)	High school (percentage)	College (percentage)
Bayside							
1,081	23.7	24.4	31.1	42.4	45.4	50.0	0.0
1,399*	21.0	40.5	32.4	24.6	8.3	44.0	16.6
1,403	21.6	38.0	26.5	33.1	29.6	46.3	22.8
1,409*	22.0	28.4	28.5	39.0	34.6	51.0	12.0
1,417	24.6	30.9	26.4	39.0	34.6	50.9	13.2
1,429	23.6	34.3	27.4	34.0	38.7	48.2	12.9
Bellerose							
1,301	26.3	32.3	27.4	36.0	39.5	44.3	14.6
1,617	26.6	25.1	32.4	38.1	45.4	40.3	11.8
Douglaston							
1,483*	24.0	63.0	22.8	10.4	17.0	32.1	50.5
1,507*	24.0	43.0	28.0	29.0	26.3	38.3	30.5
Flushing							
1,141	26.6	47.9	29.2	21.0	24.4	47.4	26.2

	Women in labor force (percentage)	Occupation of men[1]			Education[2]		
		Professionals and managers (percentage)	Clerical and sales (percentage)	Craftsman, operators, and service (percentage)	Elementary school (percentage)	High school (percentage)	College (percentage)
Flushing Suburban							
1,257	31.4	16.5	25.7	49.4	54.45	37.2	5.2
Jamaica Estates							
472*	28.2	59.4	21.4	17.8	31.6	40.6	24.4
1,273*	22.3	71.5	18.5	8.9	37.4	39.4	17.4
1,275*	22.1	72.4	16.5	9.0	22.8	50.4	25.9
South Flushing							
809	16.1	52.9	25.2	19.8	30.1	40.3	17.4
837	27.1	31.0	28.6	37.8	39.3	44.2	13.7
1,247	20.2	47.5	26.9	22.0	26.1	48.8	20.0
1,267	17.8	35.1	28.7	34.4	18.2	19.0	8.43
1,269*	21.0	34.9	24.2	37.8	33.3	49.2	14.2
1,333	18.1	52.3	27.3	18.6	32.5	39.3	26.8
1,339*	22.5	43.9	29.0	25.4	33.7	46.2	20.2
1,341*	19.3	43.6	24.9	27.9	42.4	38.4	16.3
Whitestone							
997*	19.0	20.8	56.7	19.5	23.5	55.3	18.9

Source: *U.S. Census of Population: 1950*, table 2, "Age, Marital Status, and Economic Characteristics, by Sex, by Census Tracts."
Note: Only the census tracts that were at least 80 percent owner-occupied were selected. An asterisk indicates a tract that included 80 percent or more single-family detached homes. The rest include single-family detached, one-attached, and semi-detached dwellings.
1. The balance is composed of "laborers," "private household workers," and "occupation not reported."
2. The balance was "not reported."
3. An unusually high percentage of the respondents (54.5 percent) did not report their level of education.

substantial black communities lived, would be higher if the northeast alone were considered.[35]

The only significant transformation in the racial composition of northeastern Queens to occur during the 1950s took place in South Flushing, in a neighborhood of modest single-family houses located just south of Electchester and Pomonok. (Since Pomonok Houses was a public housing project for moderate as opposed to low-income families, only 9 percent of its population was black in the early 1950s.)[36] Known as Flushing Suburban, this small area of older homes saw its black population increase from 7.5 to 50 percent between 1950 and 1960.[37] In spite of a partial "white flight" following the arrival of black families, the neighborhood remained racially integrated.[38] In 1960, of all northeastern Queens neighborhoods, Flushing Suburban had the largest proportion of low-skilled workers (21 percent of its male population were operatives) and the greatest proportion of women in the labor force (46 percent of the total female population), but also a small proportion of professionals, managers, and clerical workers, which reflected the existence of an emerging black middle class. (The lower economic status of this area, compared with other parts of northeastern Queens, is also reflected in the 1950 census, as reported in Table 6.)[39]

Although the postwar migration did not significantly change the racial makeup of northeastern Queens, it did introduce a fair degree of cultural diversity as many Jewish families decided to make northeastern Queens their new home. As Deborah Dash Moore documented, American Jews undertook an important migration after World War II, from the New York City's boroughs of Brooklyn, the Bronx, and Manhattan to suburban outskirts and cities of the sunbelt.[40] The migration to Queens was part of this phenomenon. Although no data is readily (or systematically) available on the geographical or cultural origins of the migrants to Queens, it seems likely that many were Jews moving out of New York City's more urban boroughs. Between 1930 and 1957, the percentage of New York City's Jews living in Queens increased from 5 to 20 percent. (During the same period, the proportion living in Brooklyn and the Bronx decreased from 46 to 40 percent and from 32 to 23 percent, respectively. By then, only 16 percent of New York City's Jews lived in Manhattan.)[41] As a result, certain neighborhoods— such as South Flushing, Fresh Meadows, the Bell Park-Oakland Gardens area in South Bayside, and Glen Oaks in Bellerose—had a sizable Jewish population.[42] This cultural diversity is also reflected in the large proportion of first- and second-generation immigrants who resided in northeastern Queens as a whole. In 1960, the census listed 15 percent of the population as foreign-born and 38 percent of foreign-born parentage.

They were, predominantly and in roughly equal proportions, from Eastern Europe, the USSR, Germany, and Italy.[43]

In the years immediately following World War II, the northeastern section of the borough of Queens offered developers and builders a vast territory in which to expand. In line with the established character of the area, large tracts of single-family homes (either detached or attached) were added to the built environment. In 1950, home owners represented 60 percent of the area's population; socioeconomically, they ranged from the low to the high end of the middle class. Increasingly so, however, large-scale garden apartments made their appearance in the "borough of home owners." As the name indicates, this particular form of rental housing (in contrast with the urban, high-rise apartment building) was designed to maintain a relative pastoral environment attractive to young families—internal courtyards, play areas, and low buildings (usually two stories) were typical features of these projects. Most garden apartments built in suburban Queens after the war were developed and owned privately, with the assistance of the Federal Housing Authority after 1949; they catered to families of professionals, managers, and white-collar workers who could afford their relatively high rent. In addition, a few cooperatively owned projects were built. Although featuring an architectural style similar to the privately owned garden apartments, these cooperatives offered affordable housing to families of low-echelon white-collar workers and blue-collar workers, thanks to fiscal exemptions from both the city and the state governments. Finally, as was typical of the postwar suburban migration, the majority of the families who moved to Queens after the war were white and a significant minority were Jewish.

In this chapter, we have surveyed the landscape of northeastern Queens as the area went through a process of demographic growth and residential development in the immediate postwar period. Although the area was located within the limits of New York City, it represented an attractive suburban option for thousands of young families who were looking for a relatively low-density and pastoral environment. In some neighborhoods, the conventional single-family dwelling dominated the built environment, but large garden-apartment developments (either privately or cooperatively owned) also housed many newcomers to the "wilds" of Queens. The diversity of the built environment in Queens, like that of its population, is an important reminder of the heterogeneity of postwar suburbia. It highlights the fact that these communities were immensely more dynamic and complex than the image of the "mass-produced suburb" conveys. Indeed, as we examine in the next chapter, the transformation of northeastern

Queens that we have surveyed here generated intense political debates over issues as crucial as the accessibility and quality of residential neighborhoods and the responsibility of the state to provide affordable suburban housing. It is to these debates that we now turn.

Chapter 2
Housing and Access
to Middle-Class Status

During World War II, the United States entered a period of relative prosperity. Wartime industrial production, assisted and supplemented by massive governmental intervention, revamped a national economy that had reached an unprecedented low during the Great Depression of the 1930s. Among the groups that most expected to partake of the newfound prosperity were white, working-class families. Thanks to a combination of factors—including the virtual elimination of unemployment and the working-class militancy that led to major gains in job security and social benefits—their income level increased substantially. Between 1939 and 1951, the median income for white men increased from $1,100 to $3,300.[1] Even when adjusted for inflation, the increase was significant. As historian Nelson Lichtenstein estimated, the average weekly earnings in manufacturing leaped 65 percent during the war; real wages (adjusted after inflation) increased by 27 percent.[2] Combined with the accumulation of wartime savings and the increased participation of married women in the workforce, this higher income level boded well.

For the families of these relatively privileged members of the working class, access to middle-class status was in sight. Yet many were frustrated in their quest for what they considered their rightful due: an affordable home, in a location congenial to their young families. The debates that surrounded the construction of publicly assisted housing for moderate-income families in northeastern Queens in the late 1940s and early 1950s illustrate the forces that shaped and restricted access to affordable suburban living. As seen in the success of the real estate and building industry in halting a promising program of moderate-income housing, a middle-class citizen's right to the good life, defined in this case as "a decent home at a reasonable cost," was pitted against another defining principle of American political culture: the private industry's right to the housing market.

The class identification of unionized blue-collar workers—or "Affluent Workers"—has been the subject of much scholarly debate. Not only since World War II but ever since the late nineteenth century, qualified and unionized blue-collar workers have enjoyed higher wages and more security than other working Americans, allowing their families an income level sufficient to gain access to certain standards of living associated with a middle-class lifestyle. As historian Michael Kazin has argued, working people and their union representatives (especially the American Federation of Labor) commonly referred to themselves as members of "the middle class," or other synonymous terms such as "the average citizen," "the average American," or "the American people." "Lumping a majority of Americans into a 'middle class' may be analytically imprecise," concluded Kazin, "but for at least forty years most workers have seemed content to do so and to include themselves in it."[3]

David Halle and other scholars have shed more light on the process of class identification that Kazin alludes to here. Their studies show that, rather than unambiguously embracing a middle-class identity, workers have maintained a dual identity, or "dual consciousness." As reported by Stuart Blumin, citing Steven Ross, during the early twentieth century, well-paid manual workers "continued to see themselves as members of the working class with reference to the relations of the workplace, but also came to see themselves as middle class with reference to consumption and their lives away from work." Halle, in his study of the class consciousness of a group of blue-collar workers in the 1970s, came to a similar conclusion. As he and others have suggested, while maintaining a strong identity as workers, they felt that their integration in the middle class was to be accomplished through their activities away from work—in the realm of home and local community.[4]

In the immediate postwar period, however, many aspiring members of the middle class faced one of the most serious housing shortages in U.S. history. Interrupted by the Depression, residential construction was lagging. As discharged servicemen and former war workers were coming back to their hometowns by the hundreds of thousands, newly reunited or married couples were doubling up with in-laws and other relatives or haunting funeral parlors to get the addresses of recently vacated apartments. In December 1945, *Life* gave national coverage to an advertisement published in an Omaha newspaper: "Big icebox 7 by 17 feet inside. Could be fixed up to live in." *Life* reported that in 1946, the United States needed a minimum of 3.5 million new homes; only a fraction of these—460,000—were expected to be built that year. According to Gwendolyn Wright, "Senate investigations found hundreds of thousands of veterans living in garages, trailers, barns, and even chicken coops."[5] In Queens, in 1947, the shortage of housing was such that the borough president, James A. Burke, and the American Legion encouraged home owners to convert their attics or basements for rental to veterans.[6]

Not only was housing difficult to find, but what was being built in the immediate postwar period was beyond the means of many families. In the words of historian Nathaniel Keith, families of craftsmen, clerical workers, and sales workers, whose 1951 annual income was three times what it had been in 1939, "could afford radios, televisions, washing machines, and automobiles, but [they] could not afford new houses at prevailing prices."[7] By lengthening the amortization period of the home mortgage, and hence decreasing monthly payments, the insurance programs sponsored by the Federal Housing Administration (FHA) and the Veterans' Administration (VA) did make home buying more attractive for many families of moderate means. Similarly, the accumulation of wartime savings allowed many families a respectable down payment on a new house. As a result, the number of home owners rose by 71 percent between 1940 and 1950—"the largest increase for any decade on record," noted housing reformer Nathan Straus.[8] Yet, as critics such as Stuart Chase, John Dean, and Straus also noted, the democratization of home ownership was far from complete.[9]

Given the rule of thumb that a family should not buy a house costing more than twice its annual income, middle-income families in the late 1940s and early 1950s could afford a house in the price range of $7,000 to $8,000—for example, one of the 17,000 two-bedroom houses built by William J. Levitt on Long Island between 1947 and 1952. According to Rosalyn Baxandall and Elizabeth Ewen's recent analysis of postwar suburbia, Levitt's success story set an example that many builders followed. Yet, as they also noted, "the average house cost between $12,000 and $15,000" in Nassau County in 1950, and property values continued to rise not only on Long Island but nationwide. This raises the question: Were affordable houses built in sufficient number to provide for the hundred of thousands of families who aspired to join the ranks of the home owning middle class? Evidence from a variety of sources suggest not. In Queens, where real estate costs were higher than in Nassau, the *Long Island Daily Press* advertised the first "1,000 . . . Bungalows to be Sold for $9,000" in 1949. Older houses were no doubt available for a low price, although the 1950 census counted only 13 percent of owner-occupied houses in northeastern Queens that were estimated at less than $10,000. In the New York–New Jersey metropolitan area as a whole, the *Wall Street Journal* reported in mid-1951 that only 5 percent of the houses being built then were expected to sell for under $7,500. Indeed, nationwide, the typical new home purchased with the help of an FHA long-term, low-interest mortgage in 1953 was valued at $10,000. The "typical" buyer of an FHA-insured house had an annual income of $4,880. As these figures suggest, a significant number of "respectable, hard-working" families were hard-pressed to find affordable housing in the mid-1940s to mid-1950s.[10]

Families seeking homes faced a number of options. They could, of course, continue to live doubled-up with friends and relatives. They could rent a flat, but considering the shortage of rental housing in the immediate postwar period, its prohibitive costs, and the limited space that it offered families with children, that option was limited.[11] They could also, as New York senator Herbert Lehman put it, "mortgage their souls" and join the ranks of the growing army of "small home owners." In Queens, as in the rest of the country, many did. Interviews conducted with 170 families who had moved into recently completed homes in that borough in mid-1947 revealed that three-quarters of them claimed they had been "forced to buy in order to have a decent place to live."[12] Queens College sociologist John Dean, a student of the well-known housing reformer Charles Abrams, estimated in 1945 that at the national level "probably not less than one out of every six [home-owning] families would prefer not to have bought a home." In a study conducted in two middle-sized cities in 1951, he found that the percentage of those who had bought because no other shelter was available had risen since 1946, especially among skilled workers.[13]

A final option to circumvent the shortage of housing was to add a second income through the paid labor of the wife and mother. The irony of having to sacrifice one of the cardinal values of postwar "respectable" family life in order to secure a home of one's own did not escape the attention of contemporaries. Consider, for instance, the drama of a homeless family, as recounted by Idaho senator Glen Taylor during a congressional debate over middle-income housing in 1950: "I have a brother in California who is in the middle-income group which we seek to help here today. Naturally, he and his wife wish to live decently." Taylor explained that, after having been forced to live in a converted chicken coop, his brother managed to buy a real house. But this did not put an end to the disgrace forced upon the "family man." "To show how desperately people crave a decent place in which to live, in order to pay for the home, my sister-in-law is working in a hospital. . . . She should not have to do that, to leave her girls, who are growing up, without the constant care of a mother. But in order to try to hang on to this house, she is doing what I have recounted."[14]

The problem of the group "caught in the middle," as they came to be known, had a solid foundation in the logic of postwar housing reforms. The results of the housing legislation adopted under the Roosevelt, Truman, and Eisenhower administrations, in close cooperation with the private real estate, building, and mortgage lending industries, are well known.[15] Through a combination of slum clearance, urban development, restrictive covenants, blockbusting, and a panoply of other strategies, private interests and public agencies fostered the creation of a racially segregated "dual" housing market. This polarized market was dominated, at one end, by subsidized public housing where a disproportionate number of African Americans and Puerto Ricans lived and, at the other end, suburban communities exclusively reserved to whites.[16] Less well documented, however, is the effect this joint private-public effort had on families of blue-collar and low-echelon white-collar workers, or families of moderate income, as they were then called.

From the beginning of federal intervention in the housing field in 1934, Congress had specifically required that a substantial margin be left between the spheres of public intervention and the private market. As explained by the chief economist of the Federal Public Housing Authority in 1946, "In order to avoid any possible competition with private enterprise, it has long been the policy of the [Authority] that public housing should admit as tenants only families with incomes at least 20% below the lowest level being reached by [the] . . . supply of adequate housing [provided by private industry]." While, from the economist's perspective "the 20% gap leaves a large field open for the expansion downwards of private enterprise to markets not yet reached by it," this buffer zone maintained to avoid federal intrusion in the market also left thousands of families struggling for a decent shelter.[17] As noted in 1949 by Catherine Bauer, former executive secretary of the Labor Housing Conference, federal housing legislation "still leaves a large no man's land in the housing market: the families who are ineligible for subsidized public housing but who cannot afford the ordinary speculative home as currently produced."[18]

In order to remediate the situation, housing reformers and representatives of organized workers lobbied the federal government to provide financial and technical assistance to nonprofit corporations and cooperatives for the construction of middle-income housing (on the model already adopted in New York State in 1927, for instance). As described by Gail Radford, the first of such efforts was led by the Labor Housing Conference, a lobbying group established by the Pennsylvania Federation of Labor in 1934. Under the pressure of a conservative Senate and the active lobby of the private housing industry, the section on nonprofits and cooperatives was one of the first to be abandoned in the negotiations that led to the gutting of the Wagner Housing Bill of 1937.[19] After World War II, the American Federation of Labor (AFL), the Congress of Industrial Organizations (CIO), and all the major veterans' organizations (the American Legion, the Veterans of Foreign Wars, the American Veterans of World War II, and the American Veterans Committee) pressured Congress to adopt a program of technical and financial aid to housing cooperatives. Considered as an amendment to the Housing Act of 1949, the program would have allowed the federal government to offer a long-term low-interest loan to housing cooperatives and other nonprofit corporations for the construction of multiunit rental projects. The program was never brought to a vote in 1949; it received presidential support in Truman's State of the Union address in January 1950 and was debated in Congress that year (although again defeated). A middle-income housing program generally along the lines of the bill rejected in 1950 was reintroduced as part of the Housing Act of 1957 and again defeated. Finally, the Housing Act of 1961 included provisions for low-interest housing loans for lower-middle-income families.[20]

The debates that surrounded the middle-income housing bill of 1950, paired with the position of the AFL on housing as advocated in its publication, *American Federationist*, offer a glimpse at the importance that "a decent home at a reasonable cost" had for postwar Americans. As many observers have noted, home ownership was considered a mark of middle-class status.[21] In the words of sociologist John Dean, "For many families of modest income, home ownership today represents a step up into middle-class respectability."[22] The middle-class property owner was, in turn, ascribed inordinate civic and political virtues. "When a man owns his home, or when he owns his share of his apartment building," insisted a Democratic senator defending the federal bill in 1950, "he has a stake in our system of private property. He is then willing to defend the right of private property because he owns some of it. When we promote the concept of home ownership we strengthen our democracy."[23]

In their letters to the House of Representatives expressing their support for the bill, the presidents of the two major national labor organizations used a similar language. "Congress can make a substantial contribution to the stability of our economy and the preservation of our American system through passage of the middle-income housing bill," wrote Philip Murray of the CIO. "Our free democratic form of government will be made more secure if the masses of the people become home owners," concurred AFL president William Green. Themes reminiscent of the environmentalist arguments of decades of housing reforms also permeated the debate. According to Democratic senator Herbert Lehman of New York, "In a civilized and highly integrated society, adequate housing is one of the keys to social and political health. Slums and congestion breed not only crime and disease, but social unrest and instability. Inadequate housing is as much a threat to national progress and national health as is illiteracy, epidemic, or immorality." Republican senator Ralph Flanders of Vermont agreed: Children who grew up in slums were not only "easily attracted into lives of crime, but still more easily, and still more importantly, [became] easy recruits to communism."[24] These arguments, celebrating the civic worth of home owners and the importance of adequate housing to a stable, democratic (i.e., noncommunist) society, were at the center of the rhetorical strategy used by the promoters of publicly assisted middle-income housing.

The supporters of the middle-income housing bill endorsed the virtues associated with a propertied middle class to sell their program. But they did so without losing sight of the economic imperative that sustained their initiative. Most significantly, indeed, they insisted that home ownership should be available at a price and convenience amenable to wage earners. It was because the cooperatives seemed "a realistic and workmanlike housing plan," affordable to the working family, that it was endorsed. In the words of Louisiana senator Russell Long:

We must . . . recognize that, for a large proportion of our middle-income families who work and serve in our offices, plants, and stores in high-cost metropolitan areas, the prospect of the free-standing vine-covered cottage of a half century ago is still inviting but no longer practical. Their only present hope for decent housing lies in a well-planned, multiple-dwelling type of housing project, accessible to urban employment and served by schools and other community facilities, and with space for their children to breathe and play and grow. . . .

I am firmly convinced that housing cooperatives furnish an efficient, effective, and economical method for assisting many middle-income families to avail themselves of the privileges of home ownership.[25]

This "practical" perspective was one shared by the AFL, whose postwar housing program not only included long-term low-interest loans to cooperatives but also called for the construction of a greater supply of rental housing. "Many veterans do not want, at this time, to buy homes," one could read in the *American Federationist* in March 1946. "They prefer to rent until they are more certain where their future jobs and homes will be."[26] The AFL postwar housing program also asked for a reform of the FHA system of mortgage financing, pointing out that home buyers, not only mortgage lenders, should be protected by the insurance program. One of the measures that they demanded was a grace period or moratorium on payments in cases of default due to unemployment.[27] As these demands illustrate, their endorsement of the American dream of home ownership was tailored to the particular situation of workers. "Labor's housing goal," argued the AFL's Housing Committee, "is a good home for every American family, a home which it can enjoy and a home which it can *afford*."[28]

Although the federal government failed to act, municipal and state governments took the initiative to address the plight of the "caught in the middle"—especially in a state such as New York, where a strong tradition of housing reforms existed. In June 1946, Edmund J. Butler, chairman of the New York City Housing Authority, recommended that the city intervene more actively to provide apartments for those "living in the gap." He claimed that 300,000 were ineligible for subsidized public housing but could not afford rents charged in privately owned apartments. In early September, he submitted to Mayor O'Dwyer a plan for the construction of apartment buildings without the cash subsidy involved in current public housing projects. The projects, he insisted, would be built at no cost to the taxpayers. The sale of city-guaranteed bonds would cover construction costs, which would be kept to a minimum thanks to the lower interest rate made possible by the use of government credit, a partial tax exemption, and the use of vacant land. Rental fees would be sufficient to absorb all operating expenses and debt service.[29]

Among those who favored the Authority's proposal were, of course, veterans who would be given preference in the new moderate-income housing projects. The left-wing American Veterans Committee (AVC) was one of the most vocal supporters of the program, praising the benefits this represented for " 'middle-class' wage earners."[30] Since April 1946, in fact, the municipal authorities had been pressed by a number of groups to intervene to alleviate the critical housing shortage. Housing Action—a group composed of 45 organizations, including the American Veterans Committee, the Catholic War Veterans, the Jewish War

Veterans, the Congress of Industrial Organizations, the International Ladies Garment Workers Union, the Citizens Housing Council, and the Urban League—had presented a plan for the construction of 50,000 moderately priced garden apartments that contained some of the main features of the Butler proposal. The "Straus plan" (named after the chairman of the group, Nathan Straus, former administrator of the United States Housing Authority) included a direct subsidy of $1 million by the city.[31] The American Legion, which had decided not to join Housing Action because it included "left-wing elements," sponsored its own group, Operation Housing, and proposed a similar plan.[32]

In spite of the urgency of the situation, New Yorkers would have to wait almost two years before the O'Dwyer administration announced the adoption of its "No-Cash-Subsidy" program—a program in most respects similar to the Butler plan, which would eventually provide 17,000 units for moderate-income families. The average rent ($16.59 per room per month including all utilities) was substantially more than that charged in fully subsidized projects for low-income families ($9) but cheaper than any comparable accommodations in the metropolitan area.[33] Here was "a type of public housing never before attempted in this country," boasted the New York City Housing Authority, a "courageous and ingenious use of the City's powers to finance housing" on behalf of "the 'caught-in-the-middle' group, the forgotten men of the housing crisis."[34] Of the twenty projects built through this program, only the last one was located in northeastern Queens: Pomonok Houses was completed in 1951. The fact that the Housing Authority received 12,000 applications for the 2,072 apartments available there reflects the urgent need for moderate-income housing in the metropolis.[35]

In many ways similar to the No-Cash-Subsidy program was the New York State Limited-Dividend Housing Program. Starting in 1926, New York State authorized the formation of limited-dividend housing companies which could ask their municipality to grant a long-term exemption from real estate taxes (usually covering the period of the mortgage) in exchange for agreeing to limit their profits. In addition to this tax exemption and no-profit policy, a number of mechanisms were used to reduce the cost of construction, including a total waiver of state taxes, reduced interest rates on mortgage loans, and close supervision of the building operations by state inspectors to ensure building at cost.[36] The goal, as explained by New York governor Alfred Smith in 1926, was to provide an alternative for wage earners of moderate income (unionized workers, for instance) who had difficulties finding adequate accommodation at a price they could afford.[37] In exchange for a modest down payment (which could be financed at a low interest rate) and a monthly fee (approximately half of the rent charged in private garden apartments), the "owner-tenants" purchased stocks in the housing company and acquired ownership of their apartments. Any significant surplus accumulated by the housing company (above 6 percent) had to be reinvested in the development or used to lower the rent. After the war, in the context of an acute housing shortage, state housing commissioner Herman T. Stichman encouraged groups "that appear able to manage their investments efficiently" to take advantage of this program. Labor and veterans' organizations did.[38]

In Queens, where vacant land was still available, three projects were built. The United Veterans Mutual Housing Corporation (a group formed by the AFL-affiliated Uniformed Firemen's Association, the Brooklyn and Queens chapters of the American Legion, and the Veterans of Foreign Wars of Queens) sponsored Bell Park Gardens and Bell Park Manor and Terrace, both located in South Bayside and each housing 800 families. A much larger project was the 2,225–unit Electchester, sponsored by the Local 3 of the International Brotherhood of Electrical Workers (AFL) in cooperation with employers' associations. Other housing cooperatives built garden-apartment developments in the 1950s—the Queens and Brooklyn chapters of the Disabled American Veterans, for instance, sponsored the construction of Clearview Houses in Whitestone (2,013 units)—but denied the exemption from real estate taxes granted to the first three projects they were unable to match their low rent.[39] Like the No-Cash-Subsidy program, these projects were immensely popular. The 800–unit Bell Park Gardens, reported the sponsors in early March 1948, "without advertisements but only through their own [labor and veterans'] organizations, have received in excess of 2,500 applications before they stopped taking them."[40] (Only veterans of World War II were eligible in the Bell Park projects.) In spite of the popularity of these projects, however, the use of state assistance for middle-income housing was attacked by powerful forces.

It had been a long-standing policy for public housing authorities "not to compete" with private developers, either in the selection of sites or in the clientele targeted. In both the No-Cash-Subsidy and Limited-Dividend programs these axioms were violated. Not only was the government appropriating scarce vacant land for its projects, thus temporarily departing from its policy of slum clearance, but it was tapping into the middle-income market as opposed to targeting low-income families only.[41] (In 1948, a suit filed by John Neufeld Jr., a long-time member of the Bayside Taxpayers and Improvement Association, argued that the Public Housing Law, devised to provide housing for low-income families, did not authorize the NYCHA to intervene in the moderate-income market. The claim was dismissed by the New York Supreme Court, which supported the NYCHA's contention that a low-income family was one that "cannot afford to pay enough to cause private enterprise in their municipality to build a sufficient supply of adequate, safe and sanitary dwellings." One's location in a given housing market, not a fixed dollar figure, was the criterion used to determined eligibility to public assistance.)[42] Departing from its usual practice, the O'Dwyer administration touched a sensitive nerve in the relationship between the state and the private housing industry. The willingness of liberal reformers such as Herman Stichman to criticize publicly the private enterprise's failure to "meet the demand of lower middle income families" only added fuel to the fire.[43] Resisting the shrinking of a potential market and the use of valuable vacant land, private builders and realtors vigorously opposed the programs. Through a well-crafted and efficient public campaign, which mobilized many Queens residents, they transformed the city's and state's housing programs from a wage earners' and veterans' blessing into a symbol of injustice and oppression for the small home owner. The debate that raged between 1948 and 1950 illustrates the hostile ideological context in which the right to affordable housing was asserted.

The battle of public opinion began in the borough of Queens in March 1948, when O'Dwyer's program was submitted to the Board of Estimate for approval. As Stichman and NYCHA chairman Thomas Farrell insisted that the need for moderately priced housing was too great to be further ignored, small home owners and their self-proclaimed representatives launched an aggressive attack to discredit the programs. The reasons why many local residents joined the fight were complex, but one thing was clear: The right to affordable housing was a contentious proposition.

Leading the opposition against "Tax-Free Housing" was Norman Newhouse, publisher of two daily newspapers: the *Long Island Daily Press* and the *Long Island Star-Journal*. According to Farrell, Newhouse had a personal interest in defeating "the housing program . . . [which] would interfere with [his] father-in-law's firm's private building program." On at least two occasions, Newhouse contacted the O'Dwyer administration to pressure for cancellation of the program. More publicly, though, it was through a battery of front-page articles and alarmist editorials that the dailies ignited the flame of public opinion.[44]

Local builders and realtors were also prominent among the programs' opponents and were instrumental in bringing many civic and home owners' associations to join the campaign. For instance, as soon as the Board of Estimate had approved O'Dwyer's program in March 1948, George F. Young, leader of the Central Queens Allied Civic Council and himself a real-estate broker, urged the fifty civic associations affiliated with the Council to "deluge" the mayor with telegrams to "let him know how Queens feels about this monstrous scheme."[45] Three weeks later, on April 21, 1,000, "indignant members" of civic associations, representing between 50 and 100 groups (depending on the source), gathered at the Newtown High School auditorium to protest the No-Cash-Subsidy program.[46] Again, when in March 1949 the United Civic Council, representing home owners' and civic associations in central Queens, joined the fight, the connection with local representatives of the real estate and building industry was unmistakable. A. Edward MacDougall of Jackson Heights, vice president of the Long Island Real Estate Board, was one of the guest speakers who on the invitation of Leon A. Katz, housing chairman, UCC vice president, and himself a builder, convinced the delegates to do so.[47]

Finally, representatives of the two major parties also allied themselves with the programs' opponents. The presence of eleven state assemblymen, senators, and city councilmen of the Republican and Democratic Parties at the Newtown High School rally testified to the popularity of the protest, as local politicians were always attuned to their constituents' sentiments. Although Republican officials were especially vocal in the campaign, the Queens County Democratic Party, renowned for its conservatism, also pledged its support. As explained by a party official, "The Democratic Party of Queens will not hesitate to differ with our national, state or city party when the interest of the 300,000 Queens home owners is involved. Our citizens in Queens will always come first—the party second."[48]

There is no doubt that the anti-public housing campaign in Queens was linked to the campaign then carried nationwide by the private housing industry. In the immediate postwar period, the real estate lobby (a loose group of about sixteen national organizations related to the private housing industry) had developed an elaborate system of communication linking its central organizations in Washington to realtors, builders, and their allies throughout the country, including local chambers of commerce, newspapers, and home owners' associations.[49] The Washington-based public relations departments of the National Association of Real Estate Boards and the National Association of Home Builders were especially active in this regard, distributing thousands of leaflets, "suggested" news releases, editorials, letters to the editor, and even scripts for radio programs and speeches to be delivered before local clubs. (Their propaganda was not limited to the local press, but also targeted schools, where pamphlets outlining their objections to public housing were distributed.)[50] The fact that the lobby's "information kits," produced in Washington, contained an article published in the *Long Island Star-Journal* on March 15 attacking the No-Cash-Subsidy program and information about the lawsuit filed by John Neufeld illustrates the close links that existed between the Queens campaign and its national counterpart.[51]

In their campaigns, both the *Daily* and the *Star* adopted a definite populist tone, which also reflected the strategy adopted by the national real estate lobby. "It would help tremendously if we could parade in a few small property owners from around the country, a little bedraggled and run down at the heel looking," a correspondent wrote to Herbert U. Nelson, executive director of the National Association of Real Estate Boards, on January 17, 1949.[52] Or, as summarized by Samuel O. Dunn in *American Builder:* "It is difficult to make the man on the fence move away from the public housing side because of what a builder has to say, but no one can gainsay the motives of the little home owner."[53] A related technique favored by the Washington-based news service was to personalize the issues: "Undoubtedly persons aggrieved in this manner are known to the board members. Why not contact them and ask them to give the facts about their individual situations in their own words to editors of local newspapers? This would present the public with concrete evidence, fully documented by the injured parties themselves, and could be most persuasive." The *Star* had its "Mark Nelson of 27–15 27th Street, Astoria, a photographic supply salesman . . . who does not make over $4,000 a year" and would be deeply hurt by the proposed programs.[54] Creating the image of a widespread popular protest could only have a snowballing effect.

Reflecting the fact that, unlike most public housing projects, the O'Dwyer and Stichman programs involved no "threat" of racial integration—they were directed at families of unionized workers and veterans, the majority of whom were white—the usual references to "racial invasions," "mixed housing," or "Negro housing" were absent from the Queens campaign.[55] As illustrated by the image of a couple watching white families moving into a two-story attached apartment, the real estate lobby had no difficulty adapting its opposition to public housing to cases when no black or low-income people were involved. The presence of a car and baby carriage in the illustration reinforces the middle-class and respectable character of these families.[56] Similarly, the anticommunist argument that was so prominent in the attack on public housing at the time played no prominent part in the local campaign, perhaps because of the fact that the programs' beneficiaries were World War II veterans whose patriotism could hardly be called into question. Thus devoid of the usual racial and ideological lines of attack, the opponents' arguments centered around monetary and fiscal issues.

More specifically, the campaign against middle-income public housing focused on the income of the prospective tenants, higher than the ceiling ordinarily allowed in low-income housing, and on the additional fiscal burden imposed on the small home owners, who were likely to be in the same income bracket as those to be housed by the program. Ironically, it was against the extension of governmental assistance to families "like themselves" at their own expense that Queens home owners were encouraged to fight. Through a well-crafted rhetorical strategy, the program's opponents succeeded in replacing the image of the "forgotten man of the housing crisis," that is, a respectable wage earner and veteran, unable to afford a decent home for his family, by that of the financially overburdened small home owner-taxpayer.

On March 15, the *Star* set the tone of the opponents' campaign in a front-page article: "After a weekend of thinking it over, Queens home owners realized with a shock today that they are being asked to help pay the rent for more than 5,000 families earning as much as $5,900 a year (nonveterans) and for veterans making as much as $7,900 a year."[57] The prospective tenants, claimed columnist Charles Hall, were in an "income group" that does not require tax exemption: "Who's going to gain? The poor? The underprivileged? The one-third who are ill housed? Hardly! The 5,320 families who'll move in at Queens' expense are people whose income 'doesn't exceed $7,900 a year!' "[58] Of course, $7,900 was much more than the average Queens home owner could claim for a year (in 1949, the median family income in Queens was $4,121).[59] But as City Housing Authority executive director James England reminded his opponents in late March 1948, the figure of $7,900 was the technical maximum income authorized by the New York State Public Housing Law.[60] Given the dire need for housing, and since priority was given to families with the lowest income, the majority of those actually admitted would not be high-income families as the opponents alleged. Nevertheless, Norman Newhouse continued to insist personally that no family earning more than $3,000 should be allowed in the moderate-rental projects. Unwilling to pay the political price for what was becoming an increasingly unpopular program, the O'Dwyer administration pressed its Housing Authority to lower the income ceiling, bringing it to par with that imposed on fully subsidized public housing projects ($3,984). In doing so, it had disregarded the opinion of New York City Housing Authority chairman Farrell that such a ceiling would exclude "a veteran with a large family" and had given the opponents their first victory.[61]

A related theme that dominated the protest was the "cost to the tax-payer" that the exemption represented. As the legislative director of the National Association of Home Builders had suggested to its local associations in July 1949, a waiver of taxes could be interpreted as "the equivalent to authorizing a local subsidy to be obtained by increased taxes on local property owners." In a later memo he further explained, "Since public housing pays very little taxes, it is always startling to compute the amount of taxes that the projects in your area would have paid if they had been taxed on the same basis as other real property. Make the computation and then send a press release to your newspapers charging failure to pay and cite the tax loss."[62] Echoing this advice, the *Star* editorialized, "[These families] would pay no taxes . . . instead, their share would be apportioned by other tax-payers, among them the home owners of Queens, most of whom do not earn anywhere near that figure."[63] The assurance given by the programs' promoters that the lost revenue occasioned by the exemptions did not automatically translate into an increase in property taxes was to no avail.[64] In early December 1949, the protest escalated when the *Star* announced that state housing commissioner Stichman was considering "fifty applications for additional limited-dividend state housing projects within the city," all of them to be built on vacant land. City construction coordinator Robert Moses' own press release denounced "some very foggy ideas" about the allocation of public funds and protested that "Stichman has no right to give away huge sums of city taxes for many years to come without the city's approval." (The granting of tax exemption was under the Board of Estimate's authority, not Stichman's.) Moses supported the opponents' argument that a "snowballing" increase of "tax-free housing" would have a disastrous effect on the taxpayers' pocketbooks.[65]

At stake here were financial considerations. But equally important was the fear that the values of self-reliance and independence, which had long been part of the cultural makeup of the American middle class, were now threatened. This moral argument was made early in the debate by Louis C. Moser, vice president of the North Queens Home Owners' Association of Jackson Heights, when the Board of Estimate first approved the No-Cash-Subsidy program. (The first project, Woodside Houses, was to be built in Jackson Heights.) "Our organization, who are your taxpayers, your own American citizens, your own voters, are you trying to drive us away from the proper democratic way of life? We had the courage to invest in the bad times and carry on and pay your taxes. Now you want to saddle us with additional taxes." At the same occasion, Queens borough president James A.

Burke, casting the sole negative vote, spoke against the program in these terms: "These home owners [who "bought their homes out of the savings of a lifetime"] are not rich, but they are self-respecting, law-abiding citizens of our city and country. They pay their taxes faithfully each year."[66] Middle-class respectability and independence, not only their pocketbooks, were threatened.

Throughout this attack on the middle-income housing programs, the opponents insisted that theirs was a popular cause—a people's crusade against mismanagement. Speaking against the granting of a tax exemption to Electchester in the name of the UCC and the Central Queens Allied Civic Council, Daniel Russo argued that it was a case of "People versus Pomonok" ("Pomonok" then referred to Electchester). As quoted in the community newspaper *Meadow Lark*, "We were abruptly told that the city was 'committed' to Pomonock [sic] at the home owner's expense. How many more such 'commitments' have been made—agreements that bypass the people?"[67] That many home owners' associations indeed joined the opposition is confirmed by the letters they sent to the New York City Housing Authority and to the mayor's office, as well as by the reports of community newspapers who, in contrast with the dailies, remained neutral in this debate. The arguments presented by those Queens residents who opposed the projects (insofar as they can be distinguished from those of the real estate lobby, which is not always an easy task) partly reiterated those found in the dailies, albeit with a special emphasis on the issue of responsibility. Not only was the responsibility of middle-class folks, like themselves, at stake; so was that of the state. Adding an element that was absent in the real estate lobby's arguments, they put the housing debate in the broader context of the state's responsibility to provide public services that matched the rapid pace of residential expansion.

Already in the early stages of the protest, allegations that people "like themselves" were being offered public support at their expense had a special resonance for them. Wrote a member of the Bowne Park Civic Association to Mayor O'Dwyer on April 12, 1948:

Home owners living in this area feel that they should not be required to support public services by increased taxation in order to provide low cost housing for families that are in higher income groups than themselves. Police protection, sewers and sanitation facilities, fire protection, and all other services included and paid for by city taxes collected must be borne in part by our members. . . . By no stretch of the imagination are we able to understand how a plan that is founded on the basis of such unjust principles of taxation can be permitted at the expense of the taxpayers. . . . No, your honor, we do not believe that it is right to pick out families from the same income groups and have some pay for the services of the group while the others are tax free.[68]

Concurred the president of the Little Neck Community Association, "It seems utterly unreasonable to expect the taxpayers to support families making the same or larger incomes than themselves. The plan of the Housing Authority discourages all initiative when it gives families modern housing . . . without requiring them to raise a finger. It is no wonder that home owners with all their trials and tribulations can't see any merit in the plan." Although he opposed the City Housing Authority's No-Cash-Subsidy program, he supported Bell Park Gardens: "At least there the veterans are putting a sizable down payment, . . . and actually doing something to help themselves. . . . They deserve it, but not others who would like a free ride at public expense."[69] If the income was the same, then the difference separating them from the potential beneficiaries of government largesse must be a question of character. As a member of the Flushing Manor Civic Association wrote to Mayor O'Dwyer,

Once again we wish to call upon you and demand that you limit Commissioner Stichman's authority . . . to helping the persons who need housing, whose incomes are below $4,000 maximum. Anyone with an income above that figure can well afford to buy his own home or pay a higher rental than these projects would provide, and also share in the cost of government the same as any other small home owner who had the courage and gumption to go out and borrow money on his own to buy a piece of property and maintain a home on it.[70]

The Oakland Hills Civic Association, which regularly wrote to city and state officials, expressed the same outrage at being asked to pay for those who "assume no responsibility."[71] In the opponents' view, not only the financial stability of the property-owning and taxpaying lower middle class was under fire, but its core values, too. The qualities that made it "respectable" were sold at discount price and, adding insult to injury, at their expense. Small home owners had shown the courage, the initiative, and the boldness to buy property on their own, so why should they pay for "free-riders" who refused to do the same?

Related to this concern about the distribution of governmental resources was the problem of the housing shortage itself—and here the myths of the democratization of home ownership and of the relative prosperity of the postwar "affluent" workers came into play. While sponsors and proponents of state-supported middle-income housing argued that at least 150,000 affordable homes were still needed in New York City, others simply could not comprehend the thought that "a wealthy group" such as the unionized electricians was in need of assistance. In June 1949, writing in anticipation of the granting of a tax exemption for Electchester, a reader of the *Daily* expressed his bewilderment: "As a new home owner, I object to paying taxes to subsidize the electricians. Why they need this assistance, only they know."[72]

It is clear that the ordinary citizens who spoke against the projects, either individually or through their civic associations, had reasons to be concerned. When the O'Dwyer program was announced in early 1948 and during the two years that the protest lasted, residential construction, which had been interrupted during the war, had resumed with a vengeance. A number of private housing developments, some promising to attract more than 2,000 families, were under construction: Fresh Meadows, Glen Oaks Village, Oakland Gardens, among others. As early as August 1946, the United Civic Council, which then represented thirteen home owners' associations, had expressed its fears that their cherished environment would be destroyed by the rapid demographic growth. They pressed for "revised zoning to protect their neighborhood against undesirable construction."[73]

In addition to these concerns were worries that already overburdened public services, such as traffic regulations or schools, would be further taxed. The *Star* echoed a sentiment shared by many residents when it cited the objections of a Bellerose housewife: "If this project [Bell Park Manor and Terrace] is approved 88th Avenue will become a main traffic thoroughfare, and the lives of our children will be endangered."[74] As also expressed by the members of the Flushing Manor Civic Association, "We've fought hard for [the public] school [that] is scheduled to be built next year. But if Clearview Houses materialize, there won't be enough room in it for our children."[75] In December 1949, Edward Sharf, president of the Queens Valley Home Owners' Association, was most explicit about the need to balance residential development and adequate public services when he sponsored a resolution adopted by the United Civic Council. "Mammoth housing projects," it stated, "are responsible for a large portion of overcrowded conditions in Queens public schools." He asked the municipal administration "to allow for adequate school facilities before granting permits for multi-family developments."[76] As we will see in Chapters 5 and 6, this rapid influx of population was not followed by a corresponding investment in public services. The lack of school seats and of adequate traffic safety regulations, in particular, were sore points between residents and city officials. The increasing frustration that Queens residents felt about inadequate public services could easily be redirected against public housing.

Although the programs' opponents claimed to speak in the name of all Queens citizens, public opinion was far from unanimous. In 1948, a few voices within civic circles supported the programs and protested that "many misleading statements" were dominating the debate. "I hope that your readers will make an effort to learn the issues involved in this public housing proposal," wrote Joseph Friedman, a Fresh Meadows tenant, to the *Meadow Lark*. "Too much confusion has been added to this situation by uninformed sources." Friedan was a member of the Americans for Democratic Action (ADA) and, by his own account, "closely associated with public housing."[77] Especially in February and March 1950, at a time when several civic organizations were trying to convince the Board of Estimate not to grant the tax exemption promised for Bell Park Manor and Terrace, representatives of organized workers and veterans attempted to remind their neighbors of the rationale for such projects. These included members of the ADA, Jewish War Veterans, and Liberal Party who had recently moved to Bell Park Gardens. For its part, an affiliated member of the Building and Construction Trades Council of Greater New York, which was cosponsoring Electchester along with the International Brotherhood of Electrical Workers, assured Mayor O'Dwyer that the majority of their members, who were workers *and* home owners, favored the programs. The opposition to the program, he continued, was "attributable to the exaggerated, and in many instances, fallacious statements that have been issued in the local press, seeking to frighten the average taxpayer into believing that the cost of this program will prove an excessive burden upon them."[78] In Bell Park and Oakland Gardens, the local ADA branch also intervened. In the words of Leon Potash, its spokesperson:

The factor generally overlooked, is the inability of the vast majority of veterans to afford private housing at today's inflated prices. We were not fortunate enough to have been able to purchase homes in the 1930's when they were selling for $5,000 to $6,000. The cost of comparable housing today is at least two to three times as great and consequently well beyond the means of practically every veteran. After five years of tents and foxholes, we were rewarded with another five years of Quonset huts, reconverted barracks and other "emergency" accommodations which were supposedly temporary in nature, but now show little sign of being replaced. Bell Park Gardens represents the first decent housing we have had in a decade.[79]

This was the experience of Peter Walkman, a member of the Bell Oak Jewish War Veterans Post who had organized a motorcade of twenty-seven automobiles and 175 veterans from Bell Park Gardens: "I, like most of Bell Park's residents, came from crowded, unsatisfactory quarters. We needed a decent place in which to live but were unable to afford the high rentals of postwar apartments or the excessive carrying costs of a house of our own. Tax-exempt housing, which gave us Bell Park Gardens, is the only solution to the problem."[80] The same sentiment was expressed by Mr. and Mrs. Irving Katz, residents of Middle Village, who asked city construction coordinator Robert Moses about the delay in the construction of Bell Park Manor and Terrace. In October 1949, they had placed a $1,200 down payment on an apartment for which they had been promised occupancy in eight months. In early March 1950, they began "wondering what [had] happened to [their] money." The construction had been delayed because the Board of Estimate had yet to approve the tax exemption. "We hope you will use your good offices to rush the building of this much needed veterans housing project. As in most cases, we have been living doubled up since the end of the war, and we need this apartment very badly."[81]

In spite of the virulent opposition that the city administration encountered, the No-Cash-Subsidy program went ahead. In March 1948, Queens borough president Burke was the sole member of the Board of Estimate to vote against its adoption. Similarly, the protestors were unable to force the Board to withdraw the tax exemption it had already granted for the last two of Stichman's projects—Bell Park Manor and Terrace and Electchester—before the decision was made public at the end of 1949. They did block, however, the granting of further exemptions—namely, for Clearview Houses, a limited-dividend project sponsored by the Queens and Brooklyn chapters of the Disabled American Veterans—thereby rendering the New York State program of aid to housing cooperatives dormant once more.

Perhaps the most lasting impact of this campaign was to limit city and state intervention in the middle-income housing market. Through a well-orchestrated "grassroots" campaign, private builders had reappropriated "their" territory—not only symbolically but literally by monopolizing the borough's vanishing vacant lands. The problem of the "caught-in-the-middle" group, however, was far from being solved. In 1954–55, various New York City agencies and officials noted the still-widespread need for middle-income housing. Wrote the Wealth and Health Council of New York City: "Perhaps the most serious housing need of all is for the families in the lower middle-income brackets."[82] The Mayor's Committee for Better Housing, a group of prominent citizens assembled by Mayor Robert F. Wagner to study all aspects of the housing problem in 1954, made similar observations.[83] It insisted that not only families concerned but the city itself had a vested interest in housing this "indispensable element of our population":

To preserve New York's vitality, housing for middle-income groups must be provided in substantial volume. These middle-income families make up the heart of the productive working force of the city. They should, if they choose, be able to live near their places of employment. They should be interested in and proud of their city. They make the operation of our great enterprises possible. They carry on our municipal services. They are our shopkeepers, our artisans, our policemen and firemen, our teachers and a hundred other indispensable elements of our population.

About one-fifth of the 500,000 families whose annual income ranged from $4,500 to $7,500, the subcommittee estimated, lived in substandard dwellings in 1954; an additional 10,000 lived doubled-up or overcrowded in housing not classified as substandard; finally, as many as 20,000 families faced displacement from dwellings not classified as substandard.[84] The 25,000 apartments or so that O'Dwyer's and Stichman's programs had built had been insufficient to solve the postwar housing shortage in New York.[85]

The virtues of moderate-income housing were obvious according to its defenders: With a little assistance on the part of the state, the families of average wage earners would not only find adequate accommodation but would become respectable property owners. During the 1940s, their annual income had tripled. After the war, they were demanding that the promises of American prosperity be carried a step further. Bringing a "decent" house within the financial reach of "middle-income families" was "a hard-earned right," argued the representatives of organized workers and veterans.[86] This conviction was shared by postwar liberals such as Herman Stichman and Connecticut governor Chester Bowles, who, in 1948, championed a state-sponsored program similar to that discussed in Congress. In his opinion, "the American people have become firmly convinced that good housing is a fundamental human right in a democracy. They have increasingly shown that, wherever good housing cannot be financed through usual or private means, the job of developing other means is a responsibility of their government."[87]

In contrast to Bowles's assessment, however, the legitimacy of government intervention in the field of housing was by no means established. The virulent opposition that the supporters of moderate-income housing faced in New York City is representative of the obstacles that housing reformers encountered nationwide. As historians Robert Griffith and Elizabeth Fones-Wolf have shown, conservative forces resorted to ingenious methods, such as manufacturing grassroots campaigns, in their efforts to restrict the scope of New Deal liberalism in the immediate postwar period. In northeastern Queens, evidence suggests that the individuals and organizations with close links to the private housing industry at both the national and local levels were instrumental in shaping the virulent campaign that ultimately gutted what appeared to be a promising solution for those "caught in the middle."

As this debate illustrates, the postwar middle class was an eclectic group, as were those claiming to speak in its name. On one side were liberal reformers who wanted to push the limits of New Deal liberalism and carry the government's responsibility for its citizens to the field of housing. On the other side were the defenders of private industry who envisioned the ordinary taxpayer as the victim of state expansion. In this debate, Queens middle-class citizens sided with both. As a group, they were profoundly divided on the issue. Indeed, as we examine in the next chapter, this divergence of opinion is only one example of the ideological diversity of the Queens citizenry.

Chapter 3
Suburban Radicals

According to traditional accounts of the 1950s, suburban domesticity offered Americans a retreat from the turmoil of politics. From C. Wright Mills's scathing description of "average men" as "strangers to politics" to Betty Friedan's equally sweeping criticism of family life that "took the place of politics," contemporary critics have bemoaned the apolitical nature of the postwar suburban middle class.

Historians have reinforced this image by reasserting the "private" nature of suburbia and explaining this private retreat to an apolitical world as a response to the tumultuous political world of World War II and the cold war. In *Homeward Bound*, Elaine Tyler May argued that *Life* magazine's famous 1959 photograph of the "sheltered honeymoon," which showed newlyweds kissing as they descended into their backyard bomb shelter for two weeks of "unbroken togetherness," should be considered a fair representation of the mood of the time. "For in the early years of the cold war," May explained, "amid a world of uncertainties brought about by World War II and its aftermath, the home seemed to offer a secure private nest removed from the dangers of the outside world." Although the "self-contained home" was a vulnerable construction that needed constant ideological reinforcement, it "held out the promise of security in an insecure world."[1]

Among the family-centered men and women of the postwar generation were the residents of Queens's suburban neighborhoods. While many of them no doubt lived the private life that contemporary critics and historians have described as typical of their generation, many others do not fit the mold. As we examine in this chapter, Queens residents took part in a number of heated political debates: over the quality and cost of rental housing, racial and religious integration, cold war militarism, and the McCarthyist violation of civil liberties. Along with the housing controversy, these debates feature a highly politicized and divided citizenry. They also illustrate how issues of national and inter- national relevance were discussed in the very heart of suburbia. Indeed, it was in local PTAs and community associations, in the area's Jewish Community Centers and, sometimes, in the residents' own homes, that these debates were carried. The home and residential neighborhoods were not a shelter from the troubling "outside world" but a forum from which it was assessed, discussed, debated, and ultimately acted upon.

The issues that we examine in this chapter have one thing in com- mon: They were issues central to the agenda of the postwar political left. Although Queens had long been a bastion of conservative politics, its ideological makeup was transformed with the post–World War II migration. This new ideological pluralism is evident in changing elec- toral patterns and in the debates that took place in community organi- zations themselves.

Many of the actors that we will encounter in the following pages were Jewish. Similarly, many of the neighborhoods where progressive politics was especially noticeable had a significant Jewish population. That this was the case reflects the strong tradition of radical activism in the New York Jewish community. After the war, many Jewish fami- lies moved from Manhattan, Brooklyn, or the Bronx to Queens. That they brought with them the concern for social justice that had long characterized their communities should come as no surprise.[2]

Before we proceed, a word about the most famous of these Queens radicals is in order. Betty Friedan moved to Parkway Village, a garden apartment in northeastern Queens, in 1950, where she lived until 1956. As Daniel Horowitz recently described, Friedan was hardly the naive, apolitical housewife that she later claimed to have been. Her in- volvement in the Parkway Village rent protest in 1952, which reflected a concern for both economic and racial justice, was not an isolated event but reflected the experience of her radical neighbors.

Also fascinating about Friedan's radical past is the pain that she took to conceal it. Horowitz discusses this delicate problem in his book, and it is not my intent to speculate on the issue here. Interesting for our purposes, however, is the depiction of the relationship between inter- national and community politics that she later presented. For one who was so intimately involved in both, it is fascinating to see how she mis- leadingly presents them as opposite. In "The Way We Were—1949," she wrote that the type of political involvement many of them em- braced in their new suburban communities, in "school boards and zoning and community politics," seemed "somehow more real and secure than the schizophrenic and even dangerous politics of the world revolution. . . . Suburbia, exurbia, with the children as an excuse—there was a comfortable small world you could really do something about, politically." As described here, her generation's geographical move to the suburb was accompanied not by a process of depoliticization (as she suggested in *The Feminine Mystique*) but by a shift in the nature of their political involvement: from international and radical politics, to community politics. This may reflect her own disillusionment with the former, but it is at odds with the experience of many of her generation. Suburban radicals of the 1950s married "politics of the world revolution" with the political involvement that they undertook "with the children as an excuse." They did not replace one with the other.[3]

As we saw in Chapter 1, Queens underwent a significant demographic growth and cultural diversification in the fifteen years following the end of the war. This had a noticeable impact on the electoral makeup of the borough. Dominated since the turn of the century by the Republican Party, Queens County saw its electoral pattern significantly altered by the postwar migration. While the older, well-established neighborhoods continued to vote solidly Republican, the recently developed areas lent their support to the Democratic Party and, to a lesser degree, to left-wing third parties such as the New York Liberal Party and the American Labor Party.

In 1932 and 1936, Queens County had followed the national trend and cast a plurality of its vote for President Franklin D. Roosevelt.[4] As soon as 1940, however, it had returned to the Republican camp (Table 7). But between 1948 and 1952, the construction of several large-scale housing developments and thousand of homes in the Eighth Assembly District had the potential to reverse the situation. The weekly press conveyed especially well the suspense that surrounded each election during this period:

Bayside and surrounding areas are front and center in the political picture, and party workers will be watching every straw in the wind from now to election day, . . . for indications of the local vote. . . . In the three Election Districts designated this year for Oakland Gardens and the veterans co-op alone [Bell Park Gardens], over 1,600 voters registered. How will they vote?[5]

Increasing the impact of the new "mystery area" was the remarkably high level of registration in the district. "The political pundits have witnessed our registration figures with mingled emotions," commented the *Meadow Lark* in 1950. "They simply don't know how the most populous district in the boro will cast its ballots."[6] Again in 1952,

TABLE 7. Presidential Elections, 1920–1960

	Queens County vote		National popular vote	
Year	For Republican candidate (percentage)	For Democratic candidate (percentage)	For Republican candidate (percentage)	For Democratic candidate (percentage)
1920	68.7	25.7	60.3	34.1
1924	53.6	31.0	54.0	28.8
1928	45.9	53.4	58.2	40.8
1932	34.3	61.5	39.6	57.4
1936	33.0	64.9	36.5	60.8
1940	52.7	47.0	44.8	54.7
1944	55.3	44.4	45.9	53.4
1948	50.6	42.0	45.1	49.6
1952	57.1	41.9	55.1	44.4
1956	59.9	40.1	57.4	42.0
1960	45.1	54.7	49.5	49.7

Source: Richard M. Scammon, *America at the Polls: A Handbook of American Presidential Election Statistics, 1920–1964* (Pittsburgh: University of Pittsburgh Press, 1965).

observers noted the absence of an obvious voting pattern in Queens. "Pre-campaign reports and surveys of past voting records indicate that while the Democratic plurality in the other four boroughs of New York City and Republican upstate plurality can be determined to a fair degree of accuracy, Queens County remains the number one mystery."[7] With an all-time registration record (78.1 percent of its eligible voters) and an increase of 20.1 percent since 1948 (from 666,370 to 811,630), the fastest-growing county in the state was closely watched. As explained by a local observer, "Both major parties were claiming the increased Queens enrollment as Heaven-sent for their particular cause." The GOP based its case on the fact that, except for the New Deal interlude, Queens had been voting Republican since 1940; its opponent counted on the migration from the other heavily Democratic boroughs to play in its favor.[8]

The 1952 election results give a good idea of the area's pulse. That year, the Republican incumbents for the state Senate, state Assembly, and House of Representatives returned to their seats, but the opposition that they faced revealed the electoral diversity that now characterized northeastern Queens. When examined by electoral districts, a pattern becomes clear: While the oldest neighborhoods to the north of the borough (northern Bayside and northern Flushing) voted solidly Republican, the area south of Northern Boulevard, where recent developments were concentrated, supported the Democratic Party and, to a lesser degree, its alternatives to the left, the Liberal and American Labor Parties.[9]

Seeking reelection to the state Senate was Seymour Halpern, an insurance broker from Kew Gardens now running for his seventh two-year term in the Fourth District. From his beginnings with the fusion reform movement of Fiorello LaGuardia in 1933 to his alliance with Mayor John V. Lindsay in 1965, Halpern had a solid reputation as a moderate Republican. Thanks to his active legislative record in a variety of areas, he could count on the support of a cross-section of the community. By 1954, after fourteen years in the state Senate, he had sponsored 232 laws, including 54 in his last term. As chairman of the Civil Service Committee, he won wage increases and pension reforms for state employees, sponsored the initial legislation that created the New York State Division of Veterans' Affairs, and supported his constituents' struggles for additional schools and other municipal services. In 1952, he won the endorsement of groups as diverse as the Central Trades and Labor Council of the American Federation of Labor, the New York City CIO Council, veterans' organizations, civic and home owners' associations, and the Queens Chamber of Commerce.[10]

Running against this formidable opponent were Democrat and Assistant District Attorney Lawrence T. Gresser Jr., Liberal Party candidate Simon Mollin, a Flushing teacher, and Arnold J. Olenick, Kew Gardens Hills resident and candidate for the American Labor Party. Of Halpern's three opponents, only Gresser made a strong showing, winning 30 percent of the vote against Halpern's 60 percent (Mollin garnered 6 percent and Olenick 2 percent of the vote). Among the areas that gave a greater percentage of their votes to Halpern were those located in northern Bayside: the districts surrounding Little Neck Bay, among the oldest neighborhoods of northeastern Queens, registered between 70 and 86 percent of the vote for the Republican candidate. In Jamaica Estates, another long-established neighborhood, Halpern won approximately 70 percent of the vote. In contrast, areas such as Electchester and Pomonok Houses in central Queens denied Halpern his majority: While only 34 percent of the voters in Electchester cast their ballot for Halpern, 44 percent supported the Democratic candidate, 11 percent the Liberal Party, and 4 percent the American Labor Party. (The distribution was similar in Pomonok Houses.) Gresser also made a strong showing in Windsor Park and Windsor Oaks, two garden-apartment developments built in 1950 in eastern Bayside (where he won between 41 and 49 percent of the vote).

The race for the state Assembly also illustrated the challenge that the new migration posed to Republican incumbents. Jamaica Estates

Republican Samuel Rabin, a practicing attorney for twenty-five years, was running for his fifth term as state assemblyman on an anti-tax campaign. He swore to use his office to keep city hall in line: "Everybody over there burns the midnight oil dreaming up new taxes, but nobody ever thinks about ways to economize."[11] Rabin's main opponent was Edward Sharf, a resident of Kew Gardens Hills for ten years and president of the Queens Valley Home Owners' Association. His campaign pledges emphasized liberal themes, such as extending the rent control law to cover tenants in apartments built after 1947. (As we will see shortly, this issue was pressing for many new residents.) Sharf was endorsed by the Central Trades and Labor Council (AFL) and the Americans for Democratic Action.[12] Also in the run were Herbert J. Lipp and Laurence I. Seidman, candidates for the Liberal Party and the American Labor Party, respectively. Once more, while Rabin won a solid majority of votes in older neighborhoods (between 70 and 80 percent), his support dwindled in recently developed areas. In the districts south of Northern Boulevard, in Bayside and Flushing, his majority decreased to between 50 and 65 percent; in the garden apartments of eastern Bayside (Windsor Oaks and Windsor Park) and in Central Queens, Sharf led with more than 50 percent of the vote and the Liberal Party candidate gained approximately 10 percent of the vote. In the Eighth Assembly District at large, Rabin won with 54 percent, against 35 percent for Sharf, 6 percent for the Liberal contender, and 2 percent for the American Labor Party candidate.

By far the most polarized campaign in 1952 was that for the congressional seat. Queens Village Republican and incumbent congressman Henry J. Latham, a former Navy officer, was running against Joseph J. Perrini, listed on both the Democratic and Liberal Parties' tickets. Typical of the tone of the campaign was Latham accusing his opponent of collusion with "two 'left-wing' groups, the Americans for Democratic Action and the Liberal Party. I wouldn't touch them with a 170–foot-pole."[13] Among the issues that distanced Perrini from Latham was his pledge to work for the repeal of the anti-union bill, the Taft-Hartley Act.[14] Latham received only 50 percent of the district vote, Perrini followed with 44 percent. The contrast between neighborhoods to the north of the borough (75 percent Republican) and central Queens (65 to 70 percent Democratic-Liberal) was stark. Most of the home-owning areas between Horace Harding Boulevard and Union Turnpike in south Flushing, as well as east Bayside, gave a majority vote to Perrini.

The results of the 1952 election revealed that the postwar migration had indeed changed the configuration of the area. The oldest neighborhoods of upper Flushing and upper Bayside, as well as Whitestone and Little Neck–Douglaston, voted solidly Republican. In contrast, the area south of Northern Boulevard, where recent developments had occurred, turned to the Democratic camp and, to a lesser extent, to third parties on its left. (This excludes Jamaica Estates, one of the oldest and wealthiest neighborhoods, which remained Republican.) Overall, although coming short of defeating the GOP trio of Rabin, Halpern, and Latham, the new residents had introduced a significant electoral diversity in the Eighth Assembly District.

Increasingly, the new Queens electorate was made up of young, progressive Democrats looking for a political home in an environment that was traditionally conservative. As noted in a discussion among New York State Democratic Party strategists in 1952, "Queens has 2 registered Democrats for every one Republican, but the voters are maverick." That they were "maverick" was partly due to the conservative nature of the Democratic Party organization in Queens County. As revealed by the same source: "Most of the Democratic organization is Irish-led. Other ethnic groups have been largely ignored. If they were not ignored, and if there were a liberal and representative Democratic organization in the County, we should have no worries in New York State."[15] Among the other ethnic groups that he mentioned were Jews and Italians.

The pattern established in 1952 continued in the rest of the decade: newly developed parts of the borough became home to a reenergized Democratic Party, led by young and progressive figures, while key Republican figures, some moderate and others conservative, continued to dominate.

The formation of a new assembly district for the 1954 election (the Tenth) illustrates the vibrant presence of liberal Democrats. Representing the new and largely Jewish communities of Fresh Meadows, Bell Park Gardens, Oakland Gardens, Bell Park Manor and Terrace, and Glen Oaks Village, Louis Wallach was elected to the state Assembly in 1954 and stayed in office until he was appointed judge in 1964. Only thirty when first elected, this veteran of World War II was an attorney, practicing in Jamaica, Queens, and Jewish. Prior to his election, this part of the Ninth Assembly District had been carried by a Republican.[16] The reconstituted Eighth Assembly District, which now included mostly older communities, continued to be a Republican stronghold. (Republican John DiLeonardo replaced the incumbent Samuel Rabin, who was elected to the state Supreme Court in 1954.)[17]

The more moderate member of the 1952 Republican trio, state senator Seymour Halpern, continued to be an active figure in Queens politics, although he left his seat in 1954 to run for Congress.[18] With Halpern's departure, the Republicans' hold of the state Senate seat proved to be less secure. (This senatorial district was also reapportioned and changed from the Fourth to the Fifth for the 1954 election.) After the four-year tenure of Bayside resident Walter McGahan between 1954 and 1958 (McGahan was a former city councillor and a Republican to the right of Halpern), the seat went to the Jewish and liberal Democrat Jack Bronston, who was one of Wallach's close political allies.[19] Ironically, only the reactionary Republican Latham kept his hold of the Fourth Congressional District against the challenges of young, liberal Democrats (Thomas Dent in 1954 and Joseph Perrini in 1956 and 1958).

Throughout this electoral activity, liberal Democrats played a prominent role. Whether successful in their bids or not, they proved the pundits right: the future of the Democratic Party in Queens County lay with these energetic young men, most of them Jews, lawyers, political neophytes, and self-proclaimed reformers. The 1954 Democratic ticket, for instance (and the opposing camp in the primary), was dominated by newcomers. In addition to Louis Wallach, elected in the state Assembly, was Leon Beerman, who opposed McGahan for the state Senate. Beerman, a thirty-eight-year-old attorney, veteran, and liberal Democrat, had won the Democratic primary against the "regular" candidate, Fred Rosenberg. Both were Jewish. Also in 1954, Thomas Dent, a thirty-five-year-old Bayside attorney and an "independent" Democrat, challenged Representative Latham unsuccessfully; he had also won a contested primary against two other newcomers, both self-proclaimed reform candidates: Jacob Orenstein, a Flushing attorney, and Julius Feigenbaum, a lawyer practicing in Manhattan and Flushing. In the 1956 election, only the state senate seat was contested among Democrats: Leon Finz lost the primary to "regular" candidate Jack Bronston. Both were Jews, attorneys, and in their early thirties. In 1960, Bernard Helfat, a liberal Democrat and Douglaston lawyer, challenged Halpern's congressional seat. These political neophytes, all with deep ties to the network of community activists, revealed a vibrant Democratic Party.[20]

The prominence of Jewish lawyers in the politics of northeastern Queens was also visible in the multiple rent protests carried out by the residents of newly built garden apartments.[21] However, in this case, much more than electoral or legal means were used by Queens residents. The political struggles led by tenants reflect the variety of strategies—from mass protest to legal and political action—that was typical of grassroots community politics.

Among the issues that concerned this new generation of Queens residents was, indeed, the cost and quality of rental housing. A substantial minority of Queens citizens were renters in the early 1950s, and a majority among them were families of white-collar workers and professionals who had moved into garden apartments built in large number after 1949. With the exception of the New York Life Insurance Company's Fresh Meadows, where middle-class families seemed to have found the quality of life promised by builders and promoters, the tenants of most large-scale garden apartment developments in northeastern Queens engaged in collective protests during the 1950s. Indeed, as buildings constructed after February 1947 were excluded from the New York Rent Control Law, and as the FHA, who underwrote the mortgages, did little to supervise the quality of housing thus subsidized, owners systematically raised rent even as they neglected the most basic maintenance. As their suburban dream appeared to be in jeopardy, the tenants attempted to redress what they perceived as blatant examples of economic and social injustice.

A case in point is the Windsor Park rent protest of 1952. Only two years after having moved into their new homes, more than 1,500 families from this garden-apartment complex built and owned by the Gross-Morton Corporation protested against what they claimed were unfair rent increases that threatened their middle-class status. "We protest the arbitrary and unethical manner in which Gross-Morton is treating us," wrote Stanley Taxel, a member of the Windsor Park Civic Association, to Adolph A. Berle Jr., state chairman of the Liberal Party in 1952. "The dream, shared by some 1,668 families, had been to bring up their children in the development which had been advertised in 1950 as 'Park Av. apartments in a woodland garden setting,' " he recalled. These were "empty phrases in newspaper ads and salesman's glib tongues. . . . We have been deceived into believing that we are to live in a quiet and peaceful atmosphere. Their action is an affront to our intelligence, dignity, self-respect and most of all, to our POCKETBOOKS." The source of Taxel's anger was the rent increase of approximately 20 percent which had recently been forced upon the tenants. "These increases," explained Taxel, "will cost the families here anywhere from $175.00 to $225.00 a year. It could represent a clothing [sic], savings, vacation, entertainment." The tenants of all Gross-Morton developments, he told Berle, "want to know what you are going to do about it, before they vote. Let us hear from you."[22]

Turning to the Liberal Party in October 1952 was the tenants' last resort. Led by a coterie of young attorneys but strengthened by the support of the whole tenancy, the Windsor Park Civic Association was in the third month of its rent protest. Since August, after it had appeared that direct negotiations with Gross-Morton would bring few results, 1,100 residents had gathered at the Hollis Hills Jewish Center and enthusiastically endorsed the Civic Association's recommendations to take the matter to court. Shortly, using an elaborate structure of building delegates and floor captains to contact every tenant, a $5,000 "war chest" was raised. When, at the end of the month, 1,500 tenants met again at the Oakland Jewish Center—in a hall that was made to accommodate half that number—it was decided that they would try to secure a Supreme Court injunction restraining the Gross-Morton Corporation from evicting a first group of eighteen tenants who refused to renew their lease at the increased rent. The families involved in this case were those who had signed leases effective September 1, 1950, but whose apartments had not been ready for occupancy for months after that. In court, the tenants argued that the eviction, which would force them out of their apartment before the full two years of their original lease, was illegal.[23] The landlord's attorney, for his part, pointed to paragraph 13 of the lease, which specified that late occupancy could not be used to extend the length of term. The leases, concurred the judge, were "clear and intelligible," and therefore there was no basis for an injunction. After two subsequent appeals, the tenants lost their struggle.[24]

This was neither the first nor the last time that the Gross-Morton Corporation was confronted by its tenants. In 1952, and again in the spring of 1954, tenants of Glen Oaks Village (the second-largest garden-apartment development in northeastern Queens, after Fresh Meadows) fought rent increases unsuccessfully.[25] In light of these conflicts, the tenants were especially outraged to learn in 1954 that their landlord, who was one of the largest builders in Queens and the first to take advantage of the FHA's guaranteed loans for rental projects, had made a substantial profit on the construction of their project.[26]

In addition to rent increases, the tenants often protested against their landlord's neglect for the maintenance of their property. According to the tenants of Grand Central Apartments, for instance, the following conditions prevailed in the six-month-old development:

dirty laundry rooms, with washing machines that seldom work; mud roads to and from the parking areas which make it impossible for cars to pass without ruining tires and springs . . . ; cellars which remain flooded for many weeks after a heavy rain; the lack of promised play areas for the children; unpainted baseboards which were left months ago and have not as yet been completed; and the many attics which have not been insulated, making the houses excessively cold throughout the winter months.

In order to force the management to assume its responsibilities, more than 200 tenants (about half of the residents) withheld payment of their rent in February 1952. According to the community newspaper, the *Glen Oaks News*, it was "the first time in Queens history that an association has employed this method in dealing with owners." (This strategy would be used again shortly in Parkway Village.) "This step was taken as a desperate one and certainly not as a mild action," emphasized the members of the Grand Central Tenants Association. Again in 1956, they complained of insufficient heat, maintenance, and landscaping.[27]

Likewise, in May 1954 the Jeffrey Gardens Tenants League appealed to Mayor Robert F. Wagner Jr. and Queens borough president James A. Lundy to urge the owners of their 225-family development to solve the various maintenance problems which had plagued the complex since 1950. Their grievances ranged from "improper heat and hot water" to "crumbling sidewalks, stoops, and stairways due to lack of repairs" and "broken basement windows." Still, in 1956, they continued to "demand justice."[28]

Finally, in the winter of 1953–54, the tenants of the 1,588-unit Oakland Gardens, with the help of Bayside attorney Milton Levin, sued their landlord (then Springfield and Hill Development Corporation) for failing to repair a malfunctioning heating system. Although the case was settled in their favor on July 1, 1953—the Court then imposed a fine on the owner—the problem continued; he was fined again in 1954–55 and sentenced to thirty days in the workhouse.[29]

Faced with rent increases and lack of maintenance, the tenants used legal recourses but continued to hope for a political solution. They were supported in their effort by the New York Liberal Party and liberal Democratic Party candidates who lobbied for an extension of the New York State Rent Control Law to include all apartment developments constructed after 1947.[30] In 1952, for instance, both the Liberal Party and the Kew Gardens Hills Democrat Edward Sharf put this issue on their platform. That Assemblyman Louis Wallach, a liberal Democrat who had himself been a tenant at Langdale Apartments in the early 1950s, launched a similar campaign to extend the Rent Control Law ten years later, in July 1962, shows the longevity of the problem. Although ultimately unsuccessful, his battle on behalf of middle-income tenants received an overwhelming response from the residents of many Queens garden apartments: Windsor Park, Windsor Oaks, Alley Pond Park, Glen Oaks Village, Bell Park Gardens, Oakland Gardens, Fresh Meadows, Grand Central, and Langdale Apartments. Wallach's contention that "tenants are in a squeeze, receiving fewer services and paying higher rents" no doubt spoke to the experience of thousands of tenants. Families who had moved to the garden apartments of Queens in the immediate postwar years pleaded for "governmental protection in the fixing of reasonable rents and the maintenance of essential services."[31]

The history of tenants' activism in suburban Queens belies standard interpretations that associate the suburban migration of the postwar era with a decline in political action. Middle-class tenants did not "withdraw to the preoccupations of child rearing" when they moved to their suburban garden apartments, as Joel Schwartz argued in his study of the New York City tenant movement.[32] They organized collectively and engaged in political action to ensure an environment of quality for their families. That they would have to do so might have come as a surprise for these middle-class families, but in fact they did not hesitate to agitate for what they considered their right to a promised standard of living.

The numerous rent protests organized by middle-class tenants also puts in a new light Betty Friedan's involvement in a similar event in Parkway Village in 1952. The Parkway Village rent protest that we examine now was not isolated, but it reflected the experience of many progressive families who spoke against unregulated corporate practices. Particular to this case, however, was a combination between the struggle for economic justice, on the one hand, and a virulent defense of cultural and racial integration, on the other. The latter aspect reflected the concern for intercultural and interracial "brotherhood" (as the term was then used) that many Queens residents shared.

Parkway Village, where the Friedans lived between 1950 and 1956, opened for occupancy in 1948. It was build to house the employees of the United Nations, which was then establishing its headquarters in New York City. With residents from all over the world, and a small number of American families, it had a truly international character. At a time when the New York metropolitan area was sharply segregated along racial lines, Parkway Village was unique in offering its residents the chance to live in a culturally and racially mixed community.

Ironically, the creation of this distinctively integrated community was a direct result of the discriminatory practices that characterized postwar metropolitan development. Shortly after New York City had succeeded in attracting the United Nations' headquarters to its land—on the site of the 1939 World's Fair, in Flushing Meadows Park, Queens—the city, and the nation as a whole, faced a potentially embarrassing situation. As the United Nations delegates and staff sought accommodation in the metropolis, they faced the harsh reality of residential segregation. In late 1946, the UN started negotiating with the New York Life and Metropolitan Life companies to rent a block of apartments for its personnel in Fresh Meadows and Peter Cooper Village in Manhattan. By April 1947, however, the companies' discriminatory policy led to a cancellation of their rental agreements with the UN. (UN employees vehemently protested against the humiliation to which they were subjected and the flagrant violation of the principles

racism
UN -
employee

of the UN Charter that such policy entailed.) By the time other accommodations were found, including Parkway Village, some UN employees had been forced to move several times and had lived in temporary shelters for more than a year.[33]

Forced to intervene directly to ensure that its employees would be able to find convenient accommodation, the UN negotiated an agreement with Parkway Village Incorporated, a consortium of fifteen savings banks, by which the international institution rented the garden-apartment development in its entirety, then sublet suites to its employees. Acting as intermediary between the landlord and its employees, the UN guaranteed that none of them would be refused tenancy. It also absorbed part of their rent. Hence, when it opened for occupancy in 1948, families from forty-five countries moved into Parkway Village; the remaining apartments were rented to American families—veterans, professionals and high-level managers who could afford the relatively high rent.[34]

The rent protest began on June 3, 1952, when the residents received notice that upon expiration of the rental agreement between the UN and Parkway Village Incorporated on September 30, their rent would increase by an average of 24 percent. The increase, argued the Parkway Village Community Association, would force many of the families of UN employees out of the development. The hardship and cost of relocation would be especially taxing for African and Asian families, whose options were severely limited by discriminatory practices. Also at stake was the survival of the United Nations International Nursery School, which faced a substantial rent increase because it was housed in four apartments in Parkway Village.[35]

Most important in the eyes of the community association, however, was the preservation of their unusual multicultural community. As explained by Dr. Djalal Abdoh, representative of Iran to the UN and chairman of the Parkway Village Community Association, much was at stake in maintaining intact their model community: "Because we have been able to live together—citizens of at least fifty countries, all races, religions, beliefs—in a friendly atmosphere, our children are growing up with no prejudice at all. It is proof that a future can be built on the basis of equality, understanding and cooperation of all people, and it is worth fighting to keep it that way."[36] The preservation of their cherished culturally and racially integrated community was at the center of the rent protest that residents of Parkway Village carried out in 1952.

Between June and September 1952, the community association encouraged tenants to withhold renewal of their leases while they protested the rent increase. They hired as counsel the lawyer and housing expert Charles Abrams, who was then renowned for his fight against racial discrimination at Metropolitan Life's Stuyvesant Town.[37] They appealed to politicians at every level—from Mayor Vincent Impellitterri to Governor Thomas Dewey, President Harry Truman, and Mrs. Franklin D. Roosevelt, then a member of the U.S. Human Rights Commission—to "uphold the honor of the United States and the hospitality we have offered to the United Nations."[38] Their protest was assisted by a citizens' committee who acted as an intermediary between the owners and the tenants. Dedicated to the preservation of this "world community," this committee included, among other prominent citizens, former United States Housing Authority Commissioner Nathan Straus, Representative Jacob Javitz, and Dr. Ralph J. Bunche, United Nations officer and former resident of Parkway Village.[39] A negotiated settlement was finally reached in September when the owners agreed to lower their request for rent increases from an average of 24 percent to an average of 16 percent per rental unit.[40]

Among the active participants in the tenants' protest was Betty Friedan, then editor of the *Parkway Villager*, the Association's monthly newsletter. Although her later reflections on that stage of her life make no mention of those tumultuous few months, the copy of a speech delivered at a tenants' meeting during the protest, found in her papers, suggests that she played an active role in the event.[41] In that speech, probably delivered on June 17, Friedan condemned the rent increase for the threat that it represented to their culturally and racially integrated community: "We believe that such an increase can have been asked only to force out of the village the UN people and especially those of minority groups. . . . We feel that [Parkway Village] has been and that we must strive to keep it an international community in which our children can grow up in an atmosphere of equality, friendship and understanding of all peoples." Their community, she continued, "truly reflects the spirit of the United Nations and symbolizes the brotherhood and cooperation which is the hope of the world."[42] Through her active involvement in the rent protest, which was framed by the protesters as a struggle for racial as well as economic justice, she was clearly continuing the progressive politics that had characterized her work as a labor journalist in the 1940s.[43]

That the experience of intercultural exchanges that Parkway Village offered was important to Friedan and her neighbors is further evidenced by an unpublished article that she wrote during her stay at Parkway Village, "They Found Out 'Americans Aren't So Awful, After All!' " In this glowing description of Parkway Village's cultural pluralism, Friedan describes how "a large 'minority' of ordinary American accountants, advertising men, engineers, lawyers and salesman, from Iowa and Texas, Brooklyn and the Bronx," and "foreigners from fifty different countries" lived side by side in mutual neighborly respect despite "the difference of language and customs" that separated them. How friendship and "good neighborliness" may act to counter prejudice is the gist of this essay: "When you do become friends, you simply stop thinking of people in terms of their nationalities." In this account, mundane social events—such as the picnic at the beach where the Friedans and an Indian couple shared roasted corn on the cob and "exotic sweet-and-peppery tidbits"—offer the residents an occasion for cultural exchanges. So does the day-to-day supervision of community affairs. As she wrote in her description of the internal dynamics of the village's numerous committees: "International protocal [*sic*] is strictly observed when an Iranian minister plenipotentiary, a Pakistani official, a Swiss lawyer and an urbane French diplomat debate garbage collection and baby carriage storage with outspoken American housewives."[44]

The "exotic" nature of Parkway Village—indeed, an exceptionally culturally diverse community—was noted by others in Friedan's neighborhood. For instance, Julia Schreier, columnist for the community newspaper *Kew Hills News* and a recent arrival from Manhattan, published a similar article in 1955, celebrating the "spirit of brotherhood" that permeated the area:

Just the flash of an Indian sari disappearing through the door of a supermarket as I entered, aroused my interest. A fresh-complexioned English girl requesting a book at the library desk, in clear, clipped accents, brought my head up. A charming Frenchman stressing surprised syllables made my head swim a little. A young Negro girl walking down my street on her way home from work, proud and beautiful, made me turn back to my dinner on the stove with a light heart. This was beginning to look like the kind of place I wanted my child to grow up in.

The multicultural and multiracial nature of Parkway Village and its immediate surrounding was central to the residents' definition of community.[45]

That South Flushing was so receptive to racial and cultural diversity is to be understood in the context of the demographic makeup of this area of northeastern Queens. In addition to being the home of a large number of white home owners in Kew Gardens Hills (represented by the Queens Valley Home Owners' Association, which was chaired by the liberal Democrat Edward Sharf), South Flushing had one of the largest Jewish populations of all northeastern Queens. It also hosted a racially integrated group of home owners (represented by the very active Flushing Suburban Civic Association) and a sizable unionized population in Electchester (one of the controversial moderate-income projects built under the New York State Dividend Law). All of these diverse groups (and more, including the Pomonok Tenants Council) took an active part in the neighborhoods' progressive politics.

Concern for issues of racial justice was manifested, for instance, in the community newspapers. In 1955, the *Flushing Guide*, the Flushing Suburban Civic Association's newsletter, celebrated the desegregation of schools in the nation's capital and denounced the "barbarous" murder of Emmett Till. Julia Schreier in the *Kew Hills News* condemned the "frenzied mobs" of Little Rock, Arkansas, in 1957, and expressed her wishes that children in her predominantly white home-owning community of Kew Gardens Hills would "feel a natural revulsion toward the goons who were violating basic human dignity." She also denounced racist violence on the occasion of the bombing of the Birmingham Sunday School, which killed four girls in 1963.[46]

One should not be surprised that the struggle for freedom then raging in the South reverberated in the local papers, considering that the area was the home of civil rights leaders of national reputation: Roy Wilkins, executive secretary of the National Association for the Advancement of Colored People, lived in Parkway Village and Mabel K. Staupers, who led the struggle to integrate black women nurses into the Army and Navy Nurse Corps during the war, resided in Flushing Suburban.[47] Direct action in support of the movement's protest against segregation was also taken in the neighborhood. For instance, in April and May 1960, on the occasion of the sit-ins, the local branch of the NAACP picketed the Woolworth store in South Flushing: fifty people participated in the action.[48] Still in August 1963, residents of Kew Gardens Hills joined the March on Washington after having organized their own public mass meeting for civil rights (the meeting, held at the local public school, was sponsored by twenty local organizations).[49]

Closer to home, the first flare of racial politics came up in 1952 when the residents of Kew Gardens Hills protested the discriminatory policy of a local developer and owner of a recently built garden apartment, Harry Osias. In July, a community newspaper reported that over 100 residents attended a meeting called by the "Committee to End Discrimination in the Osias Development." Representatives of the American Jewish Congress, the Jamaica branch of the NAACP, and the International Nursery School of Parkway Village supported the committee's work "in bringing brotherhood into their community by its efforts to eliminate discrimination against Negroes in the renting of apartments."[50]

Two years later, residents in the area continued to tackle issues of discrimination in housing and employment policies through the

Neighbors for Brotherhood. The group was formed in 1954 following a forum on "Teaching Brotherhood to Our Children" sponsored by the Garden Hills Nursery School. It paid visits to local merchants to discuss employment and service practices. The new Safeway Supermarket was among the establishments visited; the manager assured the delegation that it had a policy of nondiscrimination in employment. Also, the new stores being built at Electchester were visited "to convey the organization's interest in having democratically selected personnel in all our community's stores." In the fall of 1954, and again in 1956, a public forum on discrimination in housing was held at which it was suggested that Neighbors take a survey of the landlords in the Kew Gardens Hills area to determine their policy regarding restrictive housing.[51]

In addition to this work, the Neighbors for Brotherhood was committed to promoting interreligious and interracial integration through social and cultural events. As explained at its first meeting in June 1954, "Neighbors for Brotherhood hopes to foster brotherhood by helping us meet our neighbors and exchange experiences. Learning about the cultures of our neighbors will develop mutual respect and understanding among the people of this area. Understanding will help us see and feel the injustices that some, unfortunately, are subjected to in our community and country, and will inspire us to join in combating the evils of bigotry and prejudice."[52] Toward that end, the organization, along with a number of other community associations in South Flushing, sponsored an annual Brotherhood Festival. The evening event, featuring brief speeches by religious leaders and people of different nationalities, took place each February during "Brotherhood Week," the celebration of religious and racial tolerance sponsored by the National Conference of Christians and Jews. In February 1955, for instance, Doris Griss, president of the local chapter of B'nai B'rith, headed a committee formed by twenty community organizations, including, in addition to the Neighbors for Brotherhood, local branches of the American Jewish Congress, the NAACP, the Urban League, Hadassah, Workmen's Circle, the Knights of Pythias, and the Jewish War Veterans as well as various home owners' and tenants' organizations, PTAs, and churches. In 1958, the Brotherhood rally was organized by African-American Aldean Moore, president of the Flushing Suburban Civic Association. Every year, until at least 1964, when the tenth annual Brotherhood Festival was held, this celebration continued to be very popular in the community.[53]

In Fresh Meadows, an area where neighborhoods of single-family homes coexisted with the giant New York Life Insurance Company's garden-apartment complex, the residents were also actively involved in the celebration of "Brotherhood Week."[54] A case in point is the "Mass Brotherhood Rally" organized in December 1950 by the Fresh Meadows Community Association along with representatives from the Unitarian, Lutheran, and Episcopal churches, the Hillcrest Jewish Center, the National Council of Jewish Women, Hadassah, B'nai B'rith, the American Jewish Congress, Kiwanis, and the PTAs of P.S. 26 and P.S. 173. The activities consisted of an opening ceremony of Brotherhood Week at the auditorium of P.S. 46 on Wednesday night with a keynote speech by the assistant secretary general of the United Nations, Benjamin Cohen, an "interracial program" at P.S. 173 on Saturday featuring a basketball game between the Harlem Metropoles and the Bell-Oak Jewish War Veterans, and an interfaith service held at the school auditorium.[55] In 1954, the celebration of interfaith and intercultural brotherhood was held for the fifth consecutive year in this predominantly white but religiously integrated community.[56]

Finally, a strong progressive voice was also found in Glen Oaks, another area that included a large representation of Jewish families. Abner Kohn and Roberta Strauss, editor and associate editor of the *Glen Oaks News*, made their own contribution to intercultural tolerance by virulently denouncing anti-Semitism. Beginning on July 3, 1952, in a column titled " 'Hate' Campaign," they attacked such publications as "Headlines," an ultraconservative, red-baiting, and anti-Semitic tract.[57] In August, the subject of their wrath was "Common Sense," another hate publication which a reader had brought to their attention.[58] In July and August 1952, the *News* also published a series of front-page articles on religious and racial bigotry based on the pamphlet "Civil Rights in the United States," published annually by the American Jewish Congress and the National Association for the Advancement of Colored People.[59]

The active support that residents of South Flushing, Fresh Meadows, and Glen Oaks professed for racial justice and the respect of religious and cultural diversity reflected the existence of strongholds of progressive citizens in northeastern Queens. That these were areas where a substantial Jewish population lived should come as no surprise. With a great number of Jewish families leaving the urban core of Manhattan, the Bronx, and Brooklyn for newer areas, the left-wing politics with which the New York Jewry has been historically associated migrated as well. Although these suburban radicals raised issues that probably would not have been raised otherwise, it is good to remember that their views were not necessarily shared by the majority of their neighbors. This became clear when progressive citizens touched on issues related to the role of the United States internationally and their domestic corollaries. At the height of the cold war, debates over peace, nuclear escalation, civil defense, and civil liberties generated vehement conflicts among neighbors.

The reality of international politics inhabited the lives of Queens middle-class suburbanites in a most immediate fashion. This is illustrated, for instance, by the promotion for bomb shelters in the local community. In 1950, the *Bayside Times* reported that the Gross-Morton Corporation, one of the biggest builders in Queens, offered the underground garages of its 1,600–family garden-apartment development, Windsor Park, to the local Civilian Defense committee for use as a bomb shelter. "The eight garages will be ventilated, have two exits, and can be emptied of cars on short notice," reported the weekly. "They comprise 160,000 square feet of area safe from all but direct hit—and nothing is safe from that."[60] In May 1951, the *Times* advertised a ready-made bomb shelter, "suitable for small homes," on display at the corner of 223rd Street and Northern Boulevard. The ad claimed, "Constructed to withstand the effects of an atom bomb beyond 2,500 ft. radius, the shelter can comfortably hold seven adults and can be purchased and installed for less than $1,000."[61]

The civil defense program then currently under way in the nation as a whole was also active in Queens.[62] From time to time, air raid drills sent pupils hiding under their desks and adults seeking refuge in the basement of Bloomingdale's. The campaign had its opponents, as illustrated by the protest of the Women's Committee for Peace that air raid drills in public schools were dangerous to the mental health of children.[63] Housewives were also regularly bombarded by appeals to join the ranks of their local Civil Defense committee. Whether they did so is another matter. "Citizens have stalled, and preparations have crawled, far too long in the Civilian Defense mobilization," deplored the *Bayside Times* in January 1951. Indeed, in early 1953, Civil Defense leaders reported that 95 percent of the sixty associations affiliated with the Flushing Council of Woman's Organizations, one of the oldest civic organization in Queens, had not joined in its activities.[64]

Evidently no clear cold war consensus existed in northeastern Queens. The nuclear escalation, as well as the need to protect American democracy from the Communist evil, had its defenders and its detractors in the network of community organizations. Among Bayside's vigilant cold warriors was the Bayside Women's Club, represented by Mrs. Ella Streator at the Flushing Council of Woman's Organizations (FCWO). On December 12, 1946, Streator recommended at a meeting of the council that they congratulate the United States Chamber of Commerce "on their invaluable service rendered in the preparation and circulation of the pamphlet 'Communist Infiltration in the U.S.' " At the same meeting, a motion was carried to commend President

Truman for the instigation of loyalty oaths. The FCWO also supported the Board of Education for its "firm stand . . . to dismiss Communist teachers from our public schools." Again, in December 1948, during Freedom Week, Mrs. Streator "urged us all to guard most zealously our American Way of Life."[65]

Defenders of civil liberties had a public voice as well. In June 1950, the Queens Citizens Committee against the Mundt Bill was organized to defeat this "anti-subversive" measure. First introduced in Congress in 1948 by Republicans Karl E. Mundt and Richard M. Nixon, the bill provided internal security measures, including the registration of Communist-action and Communist-front groups, the emergency detention of persons believed likely to commit espionage and sabotage, and the tightening of laws against sedition and espionage. It became law in 1950 (as the McCarran Internal Security Act) over the veto of President Truman, who maintained that it "adopted police-state tactics and unduly encroached on individual rights."[66] Truman's opposition was echoed at a meeting of the Queens Citizens Committee, attended by representatives of the American Jewish Congress, the Jamaica branch of the NAACP, the Kew Gardens Hills Jewish Center, the Jewish War Veterans, and the Flushing Society of Friends. As described in the *Meadow Lark*, in mid-June the group "launched plans for a boro-wide campaign to mobilize community sentiment against the legislation, which, the committee charges, 'would transform the nation into a police state, on the pretext of controlling subversive activities.' " Three weeks later, 200 residents had announced their intention to "convene a city-wide protest against the measure and organize a mass lobby to Washington as soon as possible."[67]

In the summer of 1953, the *Glen Oaks News* added its voice to the defense of civil liberties by openly criticizing Senator Joseph McCarthy's investigations. As editor Abner Kohn explained as he launched a new series, "Joe McC: His Life and Affluent Times," he regarded McCarthy as "a terrible menace to our society" and resented his unethical attack on the reputation and integrity of dissenters. Reprinting excerpts from the Senate investigation of McCarthy's finances was his way of serving the senator a small dose of his own medicine.[68] At the occasion of the Army-McCarthy hearings of 1954, the *Glen Oaks News*, whose ownership had passed to Robert and Sue Barasch in October 1953, celebrated the counterattack on the Wisconsin senator as "democracy in action."[69]

It was, however, in the veterans' community of Bell Park Gardens that the most virulent cold war debate occurred in the early 1950s. On June 29, 1950, just as the United States was about to send ground troops to Korea, Bell Park Gardens was stirred by a heated controversy over the circulation of a petition urging President Truman to ban the atomic and hydrogen bombs. Two weeks earlier, more than forty people—housewives and mothers—had attended the initial meeting of the Bell Park Residents for Peace. In view of the upcoming meeting to be held in the home of Judith Green, the group's temporary chairperson, Hilda Ellison, urged all men and women to join the effort to "combat forces bent on destroying mankind in our time." Although ostensibly part of a larger campaign organized by the left-wing American Labor Party (ALP) to protest the American intervention in Korea and the ongoing nuclear escalation,[70] the local organizers insisted, "We seek no partisan advantage. We deeply hope that peace activity will transcend any existing differences of a political, religious, racial or ideological character." The Stockholm Peace Petition, which the members of Bell Park Residents for Peace were asking their neighbors to sign, called for "the outlawing of atomic weapons as instruments of intimidation and mass murder of peoples," demanded "strict international control to enforce this measure," and stated that "any government which first uses atomic weapons against any other country whatsoever will be committing a crime against humanity and should be dealt with as a war criminal."[71] Launched by the Soviet Union and endorsed internationally by Communist parties, the Stockholm Peace Petition gathered 1,350,000 signatures in the United States.[72]

No sooner had the housewives started circulating their petitions in the veterans' cooperative than they encountered resistance from neighbors. In the weeks following the announcement of the group's petition drive, local members of the so-called non-Communist Left—including the Liberal Party (LP), the Americans for Democratic Action (ADA), the American Veterans Committee (AVC), and the Jewish War Veterans (JWV)—launched a counterattack, soon to be joined by the conservative segment of the Bayside community, including the editor of the *Bayside Times*, the American Legion, the Bayside Woman's Club, and the Bayside High School Parents' Association.[73] The debate reached a climax on July 20 when, mobilizing almost as many people as the peace group had, their opponents stormed into the apartment of Beatrice Schutz, where the peace activists' meeting was being held. With about seventy persons attempting to crowd into Schutz's living room that night, the cold war took a dramatic turn in Bell Park Gardens: "Though the meeting did not break up into a riot as a similar one in the Woodside Veterans Houses did last week, it was stormy," reported the *Times*. Amid jeers and calls for order—"Red-baiter," "Disrupter," "Mister, please sit down"—the peace activists were nevertheless able to keep control over their meeting.

Predictably, the opponents' attack focused on the pacifists' alleged association with the "international fifth column." In the first public denunciation of the group, Edward Kramer, resident of Bell Park Gardens and LP member, set the tone of the opponents' argument: "Rip the cloak of red totalitarianism away from this so-called peace drive and an ugly truth remains," he charged. "The sole purpose of this campaign is to sap the will of the American people to fight unbridled Soviet imperialism and to combat unprovoked Communist aggression."[74] The following week, on July 20, both the *Bayside Times* and the *Meadow Lark* endorsed Kramer's and the ADA's denunciation of "the latest propaganda trick of the Kremlin." In a front-page editorial titled, "There Is No Peace," the *Times* clearly sided with the opponents.[75] In spite of the Bell Park Residents for Peace's assertion the same day that no common ideological alliance outside of peace motivated their action—"Most met each other for the first time. No one asked the other his political opinion or his religious belief. The objective that brought them together was to keep our country at peace"— they were by then thoroughly identified as Communist sympathizers and puppets of the Kremlin.[76]

Throughout the summer and fall of 1950, political meetings were still being held in private homes, although, after the stormy meeting in Beatrice Schutz's living room on July 20, the pacifists clearly appreciated a little privacy. As described by the *Times* on August 10, "The critics who disrupted the July 20 meeting of the Bell Park Residents for Peace missed last Thursday evening's meeting when it was switched from the Oakland Jewish Center to a private home, and members were tight-lipped about the new address." The *Times* estimated that while 25 critics showed up, in vain, at the Oakland Jewish Center, 70 people attended the meeting of the Residents for Peace at the home of Mr. and Mrs. Milton Kaufman. Meanwhile, many other groups were carrying on their own political meetings in the Jewish Center, such as the one organized jointly by the AVC and the ADA to discuss the U.S. support of the Spanish dictator Francisco Franco. As reported by the *Times*, this event represented an effort by the non-Communist Left "to take the initiative in political action in the area, and take from any 'peace' groups the opportunity of crying 'reactionary' at all other groups."[77] A meeting held by the local chapter of the Jewish War Veterans to discuss the issue of peace and Soviet aggression had filled the Jewish Center to capacity a week earlier.[78] Finally, when in the fall of 1950 the opponents launched their own counterpetition, the Declaration of Freedom, sponsored by Generals Lucius D. Clay and Dwight E. Eisenhower, they brought the debate to sites as varied as the Fresh Meadows branch of Bloomingdale's, local churches, and the Bayside High

School Parents' Association. Three hundred and twenty-five people reportedly signed the Declaration of Freedom in the area.[79]

In one of the last public notices of the Bell Park Residents for Peace's activities, on November 2, eight men protested against the violation of their late evening privacy by their political opponents' "fly-by-night tactics." "For months now," they complained in a letter to the editor of the *Times*, "[peace activists] have been placing leaflets under our doors much to our annoyance and without any recourse on our part since a number of these missiles were distributed after ten thirty at night."[80] By November 1950, the opponents had successfully driven the group underground, or forced its dissolution, as no further mention of it appeared in the local press.

Just as pacifists were about to be silenced in Bell Park Gardens, residents of Fresh Meadows launched an attack on an alleged subversion of their local PTAs. In September 1950, Burton Bendiner, leader of the Fresh Meadows branch of the ADA and a member of the PTA of Rufus King Public School (P.S. 26), charged that the PTA's executive committee was being infiltrated by Communists: "A well organized clique [was] determined to pervert the purposes of the organization for its own ends." The PTA was being used, Bendiner claimed, not "for the improvement of our children's schooling" but "as a political football." The event that provoked Bendiner's accusations was the adoption at a recent membership meeting of a resolution protesting the Board of Education's condemnation of the Teachers' Union (TU) for its Communist sympathies. Bendiner accused Arthur Goldway, president of the PTA and active TU leader, of having "railroaded" the resolution. "Many of us are prepared to stand up and protest the misuse of our local PTA. We are not going to be intimidated or silenced. We do not want to wake up one morning and find that perhaps our PTA has gone on record as naming the United States as the aggressor in Korea."[81]

A similar attempt at red-baiting also occurred in the Bell Park–Oakland Gardens area, as Marianne Brecher, a member of the Oakland Area School Committee, bitterly complained. Her organization, she insisted in a letter to Heinz Norden, chairman of the Bell Park Gardens Community Council,

is a non-sectarian, non-political organization devoted solely and wholly to improving school facilities in the . . . area. It has come to our attention through a worker of the membership committee that malicious rumor with obvious intent to discourage a growing membership has been spread by several members of the Bell Park Gardens School Committee to the effect that the Oakland Area School Committee is a Communist organization. It is my privilege as chairman of the liaison committee . . . to ardently deny any such possibility. It is my privilege as an American citizen to demand proof of these insidious charges. . . . If no proof is forthcoming, then the community will accept the accusation for what it is worth and will consider the source.[82]

In the Bell Park–Oakland area and in Fresh Meadows, parents did not rally behind the red-baiting crusade in PTAs. Brecher's letter was the last word published on the matter in local newspapers. Bendiner's charges were unanimously contested by both the members of the executive committee, who defended Goldway's "impartial handling" of the matter, and PTA members, who gave Goldway a vote of confidence.[83] Still in May 1951, when Peter Chanko, head of the Fresh Meadows Civil Defense Committee and member of the PTA's nominating committee, initiated an inquisition among the candidates for the upcoming election to the PTA's executive, the red-baiting tactic was once more rebutted. Of the 22 candidates, only 6 answered Chanko's questionnaire, which inquired whether they were Communists or Communist sympathizers, supporters of the Stockholm Peace Petition, opposed to Civil Defense drills in the public schools, and favorable to the employment of Communists as teachers. The majority of the candidates, many of them founding members of the group, issued a joint statement "reject[ing] this inquiry as irrelevant to the central purposes of the PTA; as calculated to divide the community and to reduce the effectiveness of the PTA as an organization; and as an intrusion into the field of individual conscience." Leo Margolin, chairman of the nominating committee, insisted that Chanko's initiative had been disavowed not only by the four other members of the nominating committee but by the general membership as well. By electing the candidates who had refused to comply with Chanko's red-baiting tactics—including president Arthur Goldway—the membership once more asserted its continuing support for its leaders.[84]

In February 1952, the PTA of P.S. 26 was confronted one last time with cold war ideological struggles. This time, it was Thelma Bearman, vice president of the PTA of P.S. 173 and leader of the Kew Meadows Committee (an umbrella organization formed in the fall of 1950 to coordinate the activities of six PTAs in Fresh Meadows and in the neighboring Kew Gardens Hills area), who was accused of using parents' organizations to promote her ALP-backed candidacy for the upcoming congressional election. Just a week earlier, when Bearman had announced her independent candidacy on a "Better Schools ticket," the *Long Island Herald* had praised her effort to carry the "active work in behalf" of the local school problem in Washington.[85] When the ALP endorsement was made public, though, all of Bearman's efforts on behalf of the school battle could not attenuate the outrage that the editorialist felt. Parents had been victim of a "political fraud," the *Herald* dramatically claimed:

> Last week parents throughout this area thought they had finally found a representative.
> Last week community newspapers, quick to back truly civic-minded citizens, thought they had found a prime example of such citizens in Mrs. Thelma Bearman.
> Last week our community found out what it is to be hoodwinked by unscrupulous political aspirants.

Claiming to have uncovered Bearman's true political colors, Harold Feldman, then publisher of the *Herald*, violently withdrew his support for Bearman's candidacy:

> Mrs. Bearman claims that she is running for Congress in order to fight for better schools.
> Schools, however, are not the only problem confronting our legislature.
> And how would Mrs. Bearman vote on innumerable national and world wide questions which would come before her in Congress?
> Surely she would vote as the American Labor Party directed.

The critics alleged that Bearman had hidden her "political affiliation throughout her civic activity and early political campaign." But even more reprehensible were the ALP leaders who, the editorial concluded, were now "claim[ing] as their own the valuable contributions which Bearman had made toward improving school conditions in this area."[86]

Although Bearman herself quickly disappeared from the public eye, controversies continued to rage in the area PTAs over the integrity of the leaders of the Kew Meadows Committee. In the PTA of P.S. 26, although a dozen members attempted to gain control over the executive committee and to convince the group to withdraw from the "thoroughly discredited" Kew Meadows Committee, the move was repudiated.[87] However, the PTAs of P.S. 164 (Kew Gardens Hills) and P.S. 173 (Hillcrest), believing that the Kew Meadows School Committee "knowingly or unknowingly, was following the ALP and Teachers Union lines," withdrew from the Committee against the recommendations of their leaders.[88]

Except in the cases of Bearman's ALP candidacy, community newspapers in the Fresh Meadows and Kew Gardens Hills area did not feed the red-baiting mill as the *Bayside Times* had done during the Bell Park Gardens peace debate in 1950 and 1951. In fact, in October 1950, shortly after the Bendiner episode, ALP Queens County leader Arnold J. Olenick congratulated the editor of the *Meadow Lark* for "publishing something that is rapidly becoming a museum-piece; an honest newspaper."[89] The *Lark*'s editor during these events seemed indeed more concerned with the effects that sensationalist accusations of Communist infiltration might have on the "hard and continuing work in behalf of the school, the children and the community" than with the danger of a potential infiltration. Commenting on the October 26 meeting, which Feldman called "a freak meeting that drew the crowds," he expressed his fears: "Now that the political charges and counter-charges have been aired openly—and most democratically— we wonder whether future meetings devoted to such 'dull' matters as more school facilities will be as well attended."[90] In fact, PTA members themselves were worried that these debates would be "recklessly destructive of a necessary and effective community effort to improve the local school situation." In the context of a serious shortage of schools, a lot was at stake in disturbing "the orderly workings of the finest P.T.A. in the city."[91]

The groups that apparently sparked cold war ideological debates in community associations—the ALP and its opponents, the LP and ADA—had only a small following in northeastern Queens. The Bayside Hills club of the ALP, for instance, which recruited in both Bell Park Gardens and Oakland Gardens starting in December 1949, increased its membership from 22 to 55 from February to August 1950. In December 1950, the four ADA branches in northeastern Queens (Central Queens, East Queens, Fresh Meadows, and North Shore) had, respectively, 88, 39, 28, and 59 members.[92] Regardless of their relatively small membership, however, the turmoil they created had wide local visibility—no doubt because sympathy for the issues that they raised went beyond their official membership. The popularity of these contentious issues is illustrated by the large attendance at meetings where they were discussed. As described in the community newspapers, for instance, meetings of the PTA of P.S. 26 during the controversy over the alleged Communist infiltration were "crowded to the rafters." (The same expression was often used to describe attendance at the Brotherhood Festival.) The PTA's ranks had swollen from 500 to 1,800 at the time of the controversy.[93] Finally, the weekly press, which was itself a participant in these debates, gave them extensive coverage. Suburban radicals may have been a minority among northeastern Queens citizens, but they were a vocal and visible one.

In this chapter we have seen suburbanites rushing in one of their neighbors' living room to disrupt a political meeting or protesting the violation of their late-evening privacy by pamphleteers slipping "missiles" under their doors. This clearly calls into question the myth of a secure private nest removed from the political turmoil of the age. But more interesting perhaps to note is that not only the home, but the residential community, its institutions and public places (such as Jewish Centers, churches, shopping malls, and schools) were the sites of political debates. This was no accident but a deliberate strategy on the part of political groups. As explained by the Queens County ALP to its canvassers in 1950, targeting neighborhood public spaces could maximize the party's effectiveness: "Best results were reported where the peace ballots were used in front of food markets. . . . Continue going out on the streets with tables and clipboards. Try the supermarkets in your community during the day. Use the opportunity presented by meetings in your community such as Parents Association, etc."[94]

This connection between an effective political strategy and visibility in the residential community was not unique to the ALP. At the official reception marking the foundation of the new Bayside Post of the AVC, in March 1950, the 40 veterans in attendance were instructed to "maintain an active front in local civic endeavors."[95] The rationale behind it, however, was articulated most explicitly by an active member of the Liberal Party. Addressing an LP workshop in 1953, Edward Kramer, a lawyer and executive of the International Ladies Garment Workers Union and resident of Bell Park Gardens, gave a detailed account of the behind-the-scene strategies used to defeat their opponents. Gaining visibility in the community and ultimately control over its key institutions had been crucial to the party's struggle to assert its ideological and electoral presence in Bell Park Gardens.

In this case, the Board of Directors, responsible for the management of the cooperative housing development, and the Community Council, in charge of supervising civic activities, were targeted. As Kramer explained to fellow LP militants, "When we moved into Bell Park, many of us who are of the Liberal party, or who had a tendency to become members of the Liberal party, were really groping in the dark, none of us knew exactly how to proceed to start to organize a party club." After several preliminary exploratory meetings, he continued, "We came to a rather radical decision":

We decided that before we could attempt to build a club of the Liberal Party, we would work in the community first, and see what we could do and what we could accomplish in our development, and in our cooperative, merely as individuals working for the good of the community and home; and hoping that after we had proven our worth as members of the community, we could then be in a position to organize a party club.

Kramer further explained how the battle with their political rivals— "the 'comrades' whom we 'affectionately' call in Bell Park, 'The North Korean Gang' "—first interrupted their organizational work: "Before we had a chance to get into community work, we found ourselves locked in a battle, ideological warfare with the ALPer's, and subsequently 'The Stockholm Peace Petitioners.' " In effect, in 1950 and 1951, two slates of candidates "furiously campaigned" for the Board and Council seats. Drawing a turnout of almost all 600 stockholders, the LP slate was elected in both cases by "a narrow margin," according to Kramer's own account.[96] Acknowledging that the strategy of service to the community they opted for might "raise quite a discussion and argument," Kramer nevertheless went to a remarkable extent to explain to his fellow party members how crucial it was to pay attention to "such mundane things as painting the house, getting hot water, keeping the grounds clean, playground equipment, sewage and things like that."

The point I want to make is, that these people were not elected to the Board of Directors because they were members of the Liberal Party, but because they had shown the community that they were willing to devote the time and their energy for the good of the community in solving the many problems which arose. . . .

Those [mundane] things are not the type of things which require the official action of the Liberal Party, but you would be surprised how much of an impression on the community it makes when people are willing to go to bat for others living in the community on such ordinary questions as hot water and house painting. There I believe we as people who are interested in the Liberal Party can best accomplish our purpose by serving on those committees which have been established in the community to handle such problems.[97]

Having established its control over community institutions, the Liberal Party was also able to control the symbolic power conferred by one's belonging to "the community." In August, Heinz Norden, chairman of the Bell Park Gardens Community Council, had indeed denied the pacifists the stamp of "official" community approval: "I am instructed to advise you," he wrote to the editors of two local newspapers, "that the BELL PARK GARDENS COMMUNITY COUNCIL is the name of the official organization of Bell Park Gardens residents; and that the organization which calls itself Bell Park Gardens for Peace [sic] is in no way connected with the BELL PARK GARDENS COMMUNITY COUNCIL." Hence, when in early September the group changed its name from Bell Park Gardens Residents for Peace to Bayside Women for Peace—explaining that "women of the Oakland and Alley Pond Park areas as well as Bayside proper had joined in the activities of the group"—the *Bayside Times* was in a position to claim this as a victory for the anti-Communist camp.[98]

This chapter concludes our analysis of the physical and political

context of Queens community activism. As a recently expanded suburb, northeastern Queens offered young families a chance to live in a
relatively pastoral and child-friendly environment without divorcing
themselves from the major political debates of the day. As we have
seen in the last two chapters, Queens citizens were divided on issues as
varied as the role of governmental intervention in the field of housing
and U.S. cold war policies. Through their disagreements, however, an
issue of common concern emerged: the well-being of the residential
community. To be sure, different groups in Queens defined their community differently: Whether it should be composed only of home
owners and "respectable taxpayers" and whether it should be racially
and culturally integrated were among the major issues of contention.
Yet as political groups such as the real estate lobby and the Liberal
Party clearly understood, no "broader" political issue could be tackled
effectively in residential neighborhoods if divorced from the concerns
of citizens for their local community. Contemporaries understood very
well that framing their political strategies with the concerns of local
communities in mind, indeed working from within the community,
was key to their success. Historians who have for too long ignored the
political nature of 1950s suburban communities have stripped the period, indeed politics itself, of much of its richness.

Part II
Political Culture, Political Consciousness

Chapter 4
Active Citizenship and Community Needs in Queens

Ever since the early twentieth century, when Queens underwent its first major residential development, civic boosters had taken great pride in the area's "community spirit." They continued to do so in the postwar period. As the editor of the *Bayside Times* wrote in 1950, "Great changes have been wrought on the face of the community. Thousands of new homes are here, where acreage lay before. . . . [But] the passing of the old sites and topography is the surface change. It does not mean Bayside no longer has the local, friendly spirit and character of old. It can just as well mean a stronger community feeling, and resultant stronger community cooperation for achieving our common purposes."[1] In these efforts to proclaim the continuing survival of Queens's "local, friendly spirit" in the midst of a phenomenal and controversial growth, the editor was no doubt exaggerating the cohesiveness and unity of an increasingly diversified community. He was also understating the transformations that the recent demographic expansion had introduced. Nevertheless, this celebration of "the community spirit" remained the defining feature of Queens civic and political culture.

Centered around an active and expanding network of civic associations, Queens political culture was focused on the celebration of participatory democracy. The active citizen, informed and engaged, was the model praised in the pages of community associations' newsletters and weekly newspapers. Civic responsibility—or the citizen's duty to participate in the public life of his or her community—was presented as essential both to secure the community's urgent needs and to fulfill a higher ideal of responsible citizenship. Although a contradiction theoretically exists between the pursuit of private interests and the defense of a disinterested public good, civic leaders unabashedly embraced both.

Among the factors that strengthened the model of an active citizenry and provided an incentive to participate in the affairs of one's community were the very tangible needs created by the suburban migration. As noted by Stanley Elkins and Eric McKitrick in 1954, conditions on the "new suburban frontier" created a context favorable to citizens' involvement. The "time of troubles" that they described provided ample opportunities to get involved.[2] This active involvement to secure basic needs has been noted by other analysts of suburbia. As William Dobriner had described in the case of Levittown, Long Island: "A suburb of such size faces the enormous problem of developing an institutional structure quickly enough to meet the many needs of so large a concentration of people. The problem of water supply, garbage removal, street repair, recreational facilities, houses of worship, schools, and police protection were just some of the problems that had to be met, and quickly." The problems that the residents of northeastern Queens confronted from the late 1940s to the mid-1950s were not substantially different from those encountered by other suburban "pioneers."[3]

In addition to these factors, the positive attributes associated with "the community" in American political culture constituted a powerful incentive to local involvement.[4] The alleged purity and selflessness of civic workers who defend the "heartfelt" needs of a pristine community strongly reinforced their legitimacy, especially when contrasted with the corrupt and selfish "politicians." Indeed, along with the celebration of civic participation, Queens political culture was marked by a distinct disparaging of politics. Even though many elected representatives were themselves issued from the ranks of civic workers and continued to entertain close connections with the network of community organizations, the sphere of civic activity was considered distinct from politics—indeed, "above" it.

Unlike recent expressions of dissatisfaction with the electoral process, however, this disparagement of politics did not lead to a cynical withdrawal from it. To the contrary, the model of citizenship that prevailed in these middle-class communities encouraged an active engagement in the political process. Fulfilling one's duties as citizen by being involved in one's community in fact provided the authority to criticize elected representatives and to demand that they be responsive to their constituents' needs. Overall, the political discourse prevalent in northeastern Queens implied a mutual responsibility between citizens and their elected representatives. Only if informed and engaged could a citizen have the right to criticize his or her government; in return, elected representatives were expected to be accountable to their constituents and their needs.

The backbone of Queens political culture was its network of civic associations. In the mid-1930s, this network was already in place, although it would greatly expand in the years to come. The North Shore Civic Alliance, whose territory ran from the East River on the north to the Grand Central Parkway on the south and the Nassau County line on the east (that is, all of currently developed Bayside, Flushing, Whitestone, and Douglaston–Little Neck), comprised thirty affiliated home owners' or taxpayers' organizations in 1936.[5] In the 1940s, as the area's population increased, the network of home owners' associations grew. The United Civic Council (UCC), founded in 1940 to coordinate the work of such groups in the fast-growing sections of South Flushing, had thirteen affiliated in 1948, twenty-four in 1950, and thirty in 1957.[6] That year, UCC vice president Edward Costello spearheaded the formation of the Federation of Civic Councils, an umbrella organization that included five civic councils in addition to the UCC. It boasted of representing more than 180 home owners' and civic associations and speaking on behalf of 200,000 home owners.[7] In 1963, the office of the borough president of Queens reported a mailing list of 300 civic associations.[8] Still in 1974, the Federation proclaimed itself the largest local civic and home owners' organization representing 205 associations.[9] Many of these associations were short-lived, disbanding or forming anew as problems got solved and others arose. Several groups, however, were more durable and lasted for years.

Among the oldest and long active civic workers were also numerous women's voluntary associations, which pursued religious, philanthropic, and political goals. These included local chapters of national organizations, such as the National Council of Jewish Women, the Women's Democratic and Republican Clubs, and the Women's Christian Temperance Union, but also local groups such as the Flushing Peace Society. In 1928, thirty out of an estimated fifty women's groups in Flushing joined the Flushing Council of Woman's Organizations (FCWO), an umbrella organization that served as a forum for "coordinating the[ir] thought and action for community betterment" and encouraging women to embrace the "responsibilities of citizenship." "All women's groups today should work to meet the challenge to women to accept their responsibilities as citizens," stressed Ella Streator, FCWO president and member of the Bayside Hills Civic Association, in her address to the women's group in 1945. That year, its membership consisted of forty-six groups; in 1954, and still in 1973, the FCWO had sixty affiliates.[10]

Central to the expressed purpose of all civic and women's organizations was a commitment to securing the material needs of the community: to "improve" or to "protect" it, as the terms were often used. Also crucial to their mission was to encourage what was known as "good citizenship": a citizen's sense of responsibility for, and involvement in, his or her community. Reflecting the first aspect was a cartoon published in the pages of the community newspaper the *Meadow Lark*, in 1950, which illustrated civic associations "determined to ring the bell" when "vital needs"—traffic, parks, schools, sewers, buses, playgrounds, assessments—were thought to be neglected.[11] Also revealing of the philosophy of civic associations and community newspapers as watchdogs for the residents' special interests was the reception they offered newly elected borough president, Democrat James Crisona, as he was about to take office in December 1957. Robert J. Panaco, civic news editor of the *Home Town News*, submitted a "list of necessary services" to the attention of the borough administration, including improved police protection, road repair, better transportation, equitable distribution of sewer cost, and street cleanliness. He vowed "the cooperation of every civic leader and [community] newspaper provided [the new borough president] strives for and gets for the borough of Queens those services needed." He also assured the president-elect that they would "act as his conscience throughout the next four years by constantly reminding him of what the Queens taxpayer expects, should have and has been deprived of for many years."[12]

What these needs and services were vary according to the material circumstances of different constituencies. For home owners, for instance, the defense of their property investment was a central purpose of their civic involvement. This was unequivocally stated in the Bayside Hills Civic Association's monthly newsletter, the *Beacon*, in 1956: "Most of us have a good part of our life's savings invested in our home, and it is for our own benefit that we become deeply interested in our community."[13] The financial stake that home owners have in their communities, they argued, increased their sense of civic responsibility—"home ownership is conducive to good citizenship," as borough president James A. Burke reminded his constituents in 1949.[14] In fact, the defense of material interests and the promotion of civic responsibility went hand in hand in the literature produced by home owners' associations. For instance, in the 1953 version of its constitution, the BHCA defined its purpose as "to protect the homes of the members and inculcate a feeling of personal pride in the welfare of the community and *thus* develop a sound, vigorous, and enlightened citizenship."[15] The theme of "good citizenship" was also common in the *Beacon*. The editorial "Why Not Become Civic Minded?" is a case in point. Here, the editor describes how, in addition to "enabl[ing] one to discuss with his fellow neighbors and the community home owners as a whole . . .

government procedure which may affect the equity of their property," belonging to a civic association allows the individual to "lay the foundation for a career of public spirit." The article insisted that "the best way to prove your American citizenship in the community in which you reside, is by cooperating with and joining your local civic organization."[16] Similarly, among the "Ten Commandments for Better Community Spirit" identified by the Harding Heights Civic Association, one could find admonitions to "secure the blessings of democracy by being good public and civic minded citizens" along with the usual considerations of home owners' associations for their members' material welfare and suburban environment.[17]

Contrary to the belief that "home owners make better citizens," civic activism was by no means limited to them. Following the construction of many large-scale garden-apartment developments in the late 1940s, associations of tenants and community councils also proliferated. (The term *community council* was favored by residents of cooperatively owned garden apartments, such as Bell Park Gardens.) In addition to addressing the problems that they confronted with their own landlords (as in the case of the tenants' protests examined in the previous chapter), they collaborated with their home-owning neighbors on issues common to all.

One such organization was the Oakland Gardens Civic Association, which was formed shortly after the garden apartments opened for occupancy in February 1949. As described in the *Bayside Times*, which praised this "energetic and welcome addition to the civic life of the community," the residents of Oakland Gardens faced their own particular problems as the basic infrastructure was sorely lacking:

Beset by ankle deep mud, unpaved and unmarked streets, pitch blackness because there were no street lights, a corner telephone booth their only outside means of communication—Oakland Gardens tenants came to a mass meeting that wintry evening determined to form an organization that would secure these services for them with a minimum of delay.[18]

In addition to working to secure such basic services, the Association also joined its neighbors' struggle to improve transportation in the area. They coordinated social activities and provided services for the tenants—"a softball league, . . . dramatic society, book review club, photography club, and even baby sitting listings." Building a "spirit of community" among this transient population through leisure activities was an important part of their function.[19] Across the street from Oakland Gardens, the residents of the cooperatively owned Bell Park Gardens also formed a Community Council that remained active for years and fulfilled the same dual function: It acted as a lobby group to secure the residents' various needs and tried to foster a spirit of cooperation among them.[20]

The pride that Queens residents took in their active civic life was shared by a cross-section of the population: Older and newer residents, home owners and renters, conservative and progressive citizens displayed the same enthusiasm for a vibrant community involvement. The case of Kew Gardens Hills provides an example of how young, progressive, and newly settled families embraced the communal ethos prevalent in Queens. In 1963, on the tenth anniversary of the *Kew Hills News*, editor Robert Kenton noted the vitality of citizens' activism in his community in the 1950s. "A vital part of the area's growth in facilities and well-being," he reflected, "was the emergence of its many community organizations."[21] The Mid-Queens Community Council (MQCC), formed in 1955 under the leadership of Doris Griss, president of the local chapter of B'nai B'rith, coordinated the activities of the Hills's thirty organizations, including parents' associations, religious institutions, fraternal groups (B'nai B'rith, Knights of Pythias, Hadassah), and civic organizations (Women's Committee of Electchester, Queens Valley Home Owners' Association, Flushing Suburban Civic Association, Pomonok Tenants Council, Parkway Village Community Association).[22] Underlying the existence of this very active network of community organizations in Kew Gardens Hills were the same basic needs that beset any new development. As described by Kenton: "It seems but yesterday that people were moving in with roads unpaved, telephone booths out on the street, and civilization ending at Kissena Boulevard." Yet, as in other areas of northeastern Queens, there was more to civic life than these mundane issues. Again in Kenton's words,

When did this exodus from the city settle down and become a community? A community is far more than a group of houses or a number of people living in close physical proximity—it is a way of thinking about one's neighborhood. It took the time and effort of a number of organizations to transform the new raw area into a community in the best meaning of the term.

Joining neighborhood organizations was, in Kenton's view, the key to "transform[ing] the new raw area into a community in the best meaning of the term."[23]

Working in tandem with associations of home owners, tenants, and parents were the weekly newspapers, which boasted of representing "the voice of the community." The *Bayside Times* was first published in 1935, just as the county embarked on its modern era of expansion. After the war, four additional weeklies were published in northeastern

Queens: the *Pomonok News* (founded in 1952 and renamed the *Kew Hills News* the following year), the *Meadow Lark* (founded in 1949 and renamed the *Long Island Herald* in 1951), the *Glen Oaks News* (founded in 1948 and bought by the owners of the *Bayside Times* in July 1954), and the *Home Town News* (founded in 1948). As Morris Janowitz noted in his 1952 analysis of the community press in Chicago, these weekly newspapers, addressing themselves to relatively small geographic sectors, significantly increased after 1945. He attributed this postwar growth to greater economic resources, brought by the increase in advertising accompanying the growth of the shopping malls, and higher levels of literacy among the middle class.[24] The circulation of Queens weeklies—each printing 15,000 copies—was much smaller than that of the dailies' such as the *Long Island Daily Press* and the *Long Island Star-Journal,* which printed 275,000 and 92,000 copies, respectively, in 1959.[25] Community newspapers were typically operated by a small staff centered around a resident editor-publisher (in some cases, a couple). Distributed free or for a nominal fee in the neighborhoods, they relied almost exclusively on the sponsorship of local merchants for financial support. As noted by Leonard Kanter, "There is nothing hidden in the fact that we are able to publish the LONG ISLAND HERALD only through advertising support of the merchants in our community. . . . In supporting the local merchants, you support your local newspaper."[26]

To report and to encourage community life and civic duty was the raison d'être of the local weekly. As stated by the *Pomonok News* in its first issue, "This paper wants to be a forum in which news and opinions about our neighborhood will be exchanged."[27] One of the ways the publisher and associate editor of the *News,* Robert and Muriel Kenton, chose to be in touch with the neighborhood was by conducting "sidewalk chatters" with housewives. "What do you consider the improvements most needed in this community?" asked Muriel Kenton of her neighbors.[28] The Kentons were residents of Pomonok Houses at the time of their arrival in Kew Gardens Hills, but they continued to publish the *News* even after they moved to Bayside in 1958.[29] Like many community newspaper editors, the Kentons were actively involved in their local associations. Muriel served as vice president of the Pomonok Tenants Council during its first two years in 1953–55.[30]

Abner E. Kohn, editor-publisher of the *Glen Oaks News,* was particularly explicit about the role of the weekly newspaper when he compared it with the metropolitan or national daily, "which does not report the news and views of your community." As he wrote to his readers and neighbors: "We may disagree with you on politics and ball teams, but we obviously both agree that the strength of a wholesome nation lies in a healthy, well-knitted community." Unlike the Long Island dailies, which tended to be more sensationalist, the weeklies were tempered news carriers. As explained by Leonard Kanter, publisher of the *Meadow Lark*, this was essential to their goal of representing the views of a diverse community. "Recognizing that a community of 15,500 families is certain to represent diametrically opposed points of view on many matters, THE MEADOW LARK will hear and print opinions from all sides." Like community organizations, they strove to adopt a nonpartisan perspective. Only in a few exceptional cases, in fact, did the *Lark* and other weeklies depart from their guiding principles "to report the news fairly and impartially." As a whole, community newspapers operated as an integrative force—"the supplementary reading matter which ties the community into a whole," in Kohn's words—and reflected the diversity of voices expressed in a neighborhood.[31]

Along with civic organizations, weekly newspapers were vocal supporters of the value of an active citizenry. "No matter how capable the men now in office are—and we believe they are extremely so—they cannot do the job alone," one could read in the editorial page of the *Herald* after the inauguration of President Dwight D. Eisenhower in January 1953. "We, their constituents, must let them know our feelings on important subjects. We must believe in them, and obey the laws they write; but we must also offer our criticisms and suggestions as various issues arise."[32] The following October, and in the fall of each year, the *Herald* exhorted the "conscientious citizen" to be at the polls: "If you do not vote on Tuesday, we feel you are guilty of negligence not only to yourself but your neighbor as well. You are relegating your rights as a citizen into the hands of others who cannot possibly know of your wishes."[33] During the 1956 campaign, it also insisted that voters should be prepared to make an informed choice: "Cold as they are, facts and figures should be studied, as the election approaches, by every voter as he reads his newspaper and receives campaign literature in the mail." "Not to vote is morally wrong," one could read in an editorial published on November 1, "pulling down a lever . . . does not make us a good citizen. The fact that we consider and weigh facts is the important action in voting."[34] In a similar fashion, Kohn insisted that voting represented more than a passive delegation of power from citizens to elected representatives. Six weeks before the 1952 election, he emphasized, "Besides being a privilege, the right to vote is the opportunity for a citizen to select or reject the government in power. The citizen who does not vote cannot logically or morally criticize the government in power. The exercise of a right gives him the privilege to criticize."[35]

Active citizenship, of course, was not limited to the obligation to vote; above all, it included civic participation. "Don't sit back and let the girl upstairs or the fellow down the block do all the work," wrote the *Pomonok News*, inviting the residents to attend the meeting of their tenants' council at the beginning of the fall season.[36] "If you have faith in your country and your form of government," one could read in a front-page article published in the *Home Town News*, "you must take an active part in the operation of your community."[37] Acting collectively and expressing one's views through appropriate channels were crucial to responsible citizenship. As emphasized by Kohn three months before a public hearing of the City Planning Commission:

In the middle of October the public will be given an opportunity to express its views—as well as demands and denunciations—on the 1953 capital budget for New York City. . . . The residents of Queens must exercise their rights; they must fight for everything that will benefit the borough; and they must protect their interests at any public hearings. P-TA's, civic associations, and tenant groups must prepare now for the campaign in October.[38]

Expressing their opinion was presented here as a responsibility best fulfilled collectively.

Weekly newspapers and community associations were among the most prominent voices in the neighborhoods to encourage citizens' active civic and political participation. But they were not the only ones. National groups such as the League of Women Voters, whose very existence was predicated on promoting an "informed and responsible citizenry," also had a presence in northeastern Queens. Its three local branches were visible especially during registration and election time. In the last two days of the 1949 registration period, for instance, the members of the Fresh Meadows branch manned five booths on a busy thoroughfare, Union Turnpike, offering passersby information about registration. The October registration drive became an annual affair. And as Adeline Rubin, leader of the Glen Oaks branch of the League, noted, participating in the electoral process was only part of the citizen's duties: "Do you feel that your responsibility as a citizen ended for the year when you cast your vote at the polls? Or do you, like the League of Women Voters, consider good citizenship and active participation in your government a full-time job?" The League's message was similar to that expressed by Queens civic associations.[39]

Given the prominence that the ideal of participatory democracy held in suburban Queens, one is not surprised to find frequent references to the town meeting, symbol par excellence of citizens' collective participation in the affairs of their community and government. "Old-fashioned town meetings" were hailed in local newspapers as an example of "democracy on the local, community level."[40] "The old town meetings are being revived," read an invitation to attend the regular meeting of the Bayside Hills Civic Association in 1940.[41] Or, as reasserted by borough president James Burke in 1952, when he compared the town meeting to the contemporary civic association: "Both were formed to help solve problems of individual and community, for exchange of ideas, for closer relationship between the taxpayers and the officials of the government."[42] Again in 1958, Louis Wallach, Glen Oaks state assemblyman, culminated his campaign with a "legislative town meeting" to which he invited 300 leaders of civic, veterans, and parent-teacher associations. Hailed as an innovation in the Borough, the meeting was conceived as "a sort of community planning conference designed to come up with a legislative program to meet the pressing needs and desires of the residents of the Tenth Assembly District."[43]

As illustrated by the last example, an intimate relationship existed between Queens civic leaders and the area's elected representatives, especially the borough president and the area's state and congressional representatives. Indeed, throughout the years, elected officials of all parties, many of whom had risen through the civic ranks themselves, worked closely with civic associations. During his campaign for the state Assembly, Edward Sharf, president of the Queens Valley Home Owners' Association, expressed most explicitly the symbiotic relationship that many saw between the role of civic worker and elected official: "I believe that the job of an Assemblyman does not differ perceptibly from that of a civic leader except that his position enables him to act more effectively in promoting the needs of his community."[44]

Over the years, elected officials provided legitimacy to the primacy of community needs on which civic activism thrived. As reported by the *Bayside Times*, at a 1948 ceremony for the installation of the officers of the Bayside Hills Civic Association, Burke "emphasized the importance of active Civic Associations in bringing to the attention of city officials the needs of Queens residents. . . . The many revived and now active civic associations of the borough, keeping officials cognizant of the civic needs of Queens, are strong forces toward making Queens 'the place we want it to be.' "[45] In the late 1950s, as plans were being made for the establishment of the Queens Advisory Planning Board (later to become the Community Planning Board, a structure of communication between the borough president and the various residential communities), the cooperation between civic associations and the office of the borough president was reinforced. Writing to the North Shore Council of Home Owners' Associations, President James Crisona reassured civic associations of their continuing importance: "I have too great a respect for the vigor and vitality of our civic groups to fear . . . that they would be weakened by the organization of community planning councils."[46] Similarly, when in 1964 the Community Planning Boards were reenacted by the revised Charter, Crisona's successor, Republican Mario Cariello, reiterated, "The continuance of each and every civic association and home owners' group is vital for the continued growth and development of Queens." He also made a point of praising "their contributions in alerting, pinpointing and pressing for necessary planning and improvements."[47] While no doubt electorally self-serving, these statements provided an official stamp to the philosophy of community needs that sustained popular democracy in Queens.

The message that Queens residents received through their local newspapers and associations, as well as elected officials, was clear: Only by engaging actively in the civic life of their communities could they fulfill their duties as citizens and secure the various services and needs adequate to a middle-class residential community. The virtues of civic involvement were also emphasized through constant praising of civic leaders' selflessness and sincerity. Weekly newspapers never missed the occasion to point out "the debt of gratitude . . . due [to] these civic minded souls who give tirelessly and uncomplainingly of their time and effort on our behalf."[48] The common term civic worker also connoted honesty and uprightness. Alongside these praises of civic workers were descriptions of civic activity as pleasurable—as a leisurely, yet constructive, activity. "Every resident could well become a member of one or the other of our several local civic organizations with great benefit to the community and with no small amount of interesting pleasure to themselves," wrote the editor of the *Bayside Times* in 1936. "When one takes part in civic matters . . . a person gets that satisfying feeling of really being a part of the community. It's a grand feeling. It's quite a natural one, too. . . . Taking a real interest in community affairs . . . will fast become an enjoyable 'pastime.' "[49] The very language that was used to describe the purpose of community activism—service, benefits, improvements, betterment—conveyed this positive value.

This ethos of civic responsibility found further reinforcement in the disparagement of politics, a rhetorical device also central in Queens civic circles. Indeed, evoking the negative pole of "politics" reinforced the civic as a sphere worthy of involvement; it encouraged participation in civic activities and lent further legitimacy to the demands of civic leaders. For instance, the unselfish contribution of community volunteers was highlighted by an implicit (and sometimes explicit) contrast to those whose service stemmed from ulterior motives: corrupt and self-serving politicians. As noted in the eulogy of a well-known civic leader, "He was always willing to do anything to help others without any thought of politics or fanfare."[50] A 1942 editorial of the *Bayside Times* conveyed a similar message: "We wish to congratulate the members of the civic units for their fine display of community spirit and interest. Most, if not all, of the organizations, are sincere in their requests and demands; and we are sure that none have any special axe to grind or personal gain to achieve."[51]

As local newspapers praised community leaders for their good work and sincerity, they not only contrasted them to politicians but downplayed the fact that civic work was by definition political. Often heard in civic circles was the statement that "civics and politics don't mix"—even though the two were inextricably linked. Civic leaders constantly lobbied their government or ran for office in order to secure their "vital needs." Also, their demands were inevitably linked to a broader political field, one that involved struggles over the distribution of power and resources both within and beyond their own communities. These struggles were at times obscured by the distance that they put, rhetorically, between their civic work and politics.

This is seen, for instance, in the fact that community associations and weekly newspapers typically shied away from a critical evaluation of the various and potentially conflicting demands emerging from a large and diverse population. The 1942 *Bayside Times* editorial cited above is a case in point. Praising the work of the various civic groups in the area, it begins with the following disclaimer: "At present we are not going to discuss the merits or disadvantages of the various proposals which have been placed before City authorities." Such a discussion would have opened up difficult questions: Should the construction of new schools be given priority over a public library or improved public transportation? Should the further development of Queens be stopped, as those fighting rezoning proposals argued, or should public housing be encouraged, as other members of the community wanted? These were divisive questions that community leaders preferred to avoid whenever they could.[52]

In a similar fashion, the delicate problem of whether the needs of northeastern Queens were more or less urgent than those of other neighborhoods in the city was generally avoided. The efforts to solve the problem of double-session classrooms in their schools, for instance, was never discussed in light of the substandard conditions that beset schools in African American or Puerto Rican neighborhoods of Manhattan. That the satisfaction of their needs was directly linked to the distribution of resources among the diverse communities of Queens or New York City—an inescapable political reality—was ignored.

In a more immediate sense, the rhetorical rejection of politics that one finds in civic circles reflects a desire to avoid partisanship. Partisan neutrality had long been a policy devised to maintain a united front among community activists. At a time when the population of northeastern Queens was increasing and becoming more diverse, it was even more imperative. In order to rally residents of all persuasions into their ranks, community organizations usually shunned official affiliation with partisan organizations.[53]

The critical importance of nonpartisanship is illustrated by the controversy created by the United Civic Council's decision to support specific candidates for the 1950 election. The UCC was an umbrella organization that represented individual home owners' and civic associations in the area of South Flushing. Its departure from the rule of partisan neutrality caused great commotion within its ranks.

The UCC's "political swim" was reported with great fanfare in the *Meadow Lark*: "In a precedent-shattering move," wrote editor Leonard Kanter, delegates of the Council had decided to "offer direct recommendations of political candidates on a non-political basis." The Council's plan was to form a political action committee that would examine each candidate's record and make public recommendations. The "non-political" (i.e., nonpartisan) basis on which the candidates were to be evaluated would ostensibly be their willingness to support the Council's antitax crusade—for civic leaders were increasingly angered by the "maze of unfair assessments" thrust upon them. This area was then in the midst of the controversy over moderate-income public housing, which we discussed in Chapter 2. As explained by Kanter, "The combined weight of accumulated tax assessments on sewers and real estate, subway, bus and gas rate raises, and the threat of auto taxes and further tax-exempt housing developments finally incited the Council . . . to a do-or-die fight to elect men sympathetic to the taxpayers' cause." The *Lark*'s editor applauded the Council's fighting spirit and welcomed its determination "in shaping their future in the world of government." Here was "a well-placed body blow to government by crony."[54]

This dramatic "new departure in civic history" was far from unanimous. John J. O'Connor, president of the Harding Heights Civic Association and one of the founders of the Council, was one to raise questions publicly about the "controversial issue of mixing civics with politics." Although he agreed with the other members of the council that "single unit home-owners [should] not [assume] an unreasonable share of the tax burden," he feared that departing from its traditional position of partisan neutrality could only undermine the Council's unity of action and "discourage registered and loyal party members from becoming active with their civic groups." He bitterly protested, "Once civics play political favorites they lose their effectiveness." Joseph A. Corello shared O'Connor's reservations. "The action of the United Civic Council in endorsing certain politicians for public office," he wrote in a letter to the editor, "not only shatters a precedent, but shatters the very foundations of the true civic associations for which Queens is famous." He further explained, "The membership of a civic association is made up of all the political faiths [which] are bound to each other by a common interest in service to each other and not by political ties."[55]

No doubt lurking behind O'Connor's and Corello's protests was the fact that, although the area covered by the UCC comprised significant Democratic strongholds, the "friends" of the home owners endorsed by the UCC were Republicans. Civic leaders were divided on the wisdom of this "political swim" not so much because they disagreed on the substantive issue motivating the move but because they realized that, given the increased partisan diversity of northeastern Queens, stepping out of a position of neutrality bore the potential for divisiveness. The UCC's 1950 policy to support candidates was short-lived. In subsequent years, the organization returned to its original position of nonpartisan neutrality.

One last aspect of civic workers' rejection of politics and partisanship deserves mention. Politicians, in the eyes of civic leaders, were professional power brokers whose loyalty to a political establishment (often perceived as corrupt) kept them from a genuine devotion to the needs of grassroots communities. As we have seen in the previous chapter, this distrust was especially strong among liberal Democrats, who were alienated by the conservatism of the regular organization in Queens. It also manifested itself through support for numerous "independent" candidates who stemmed from civic ranks. In the rhetoric that surrounded these campaigns, a familiar figure emerges: the informed and critical citizen, the ideal citizen of Queens political discourse.

The independent political actor (especially the independent voter) was receiving a great deal of attention in the 1950s when political commentators and analysts started noticing a decline of partisan loyalty. This manifested itself through ticket splitting (mostly in the form of Democrats voting for moderate Republicans such as President Eisenhower). Popular movements such as the Citizens for Eisenhower and the Volunteers for Stevenson, groups formed to attract "soft partisans," were also part of this new phenomenon, which worried many. In classic analysis of voting behavior, for instance, the independent voter was portrayed as less attentive, interested, and informed than the partisan. But not all commentators on this question shared this negative assessment. Discussing the electoral independence of Jewish voters, for instance, Lawrence Fuchs noted in 1956 that the phenomenon "please[d] the leaders of civic betterment organizations" and that they "note[d] their acceptance of ticket splitting as a mark of intelligence and rationality." This certainly reflects the positive assessment of independent voting that one finds in Queens civic circles.[56]

A few examples can be used to illustrate the spirit of independence that characterized Queens voters and political actors. At the occasion of the 1953 mayoralty election, the Queens County Democratic Organization was split between the regulars, who supported incumbent Mayor Vincent Impellitteri, and a reform wing made of liberal Democrats who supported the candidacy of Robert F. Wagner Jr. The Kew Gardens Hills Regular Democratic Club was among those who supported Wagner. Many of its active members were political neophytes: "Quite a few of us are fairly new at the game of politics," they acknowledged. They asked for James Roe's resignation as Queens County leader, accusing him and the "old guard politicos" of being indifferent to "the pulse of the community." (The area which it represented had supported Wagner 7 to 1 in the primary.) In this attack against "boss rule," the reform Democrat—"a new type of voter"—was hailed as the ideal, engaged citizen: one that was not only making an informed and rational electoral decision but doing so with the interests of the community in mind. As one could read in the club's newsletter: "He will not be dictated to, he will read, he will demand the facts concerning a candidate, his platform, his past performances, his future intentions and his supporters." The truly representative Democratic Party leader would "personify and reflect the thinking of the community."[57]

A similar message was heard from the camp of Rudolph Halley, Liberal Party candidate who was then carrying a campaign for "clean" government and was winning support in Queens. Among those who formed the Queens Independent Party for Halley (also referred to as the Queens Voters for Good Government) were a cluster of civic leaders, including Joseph L. McKenna, UCC president at the time, and John F. Rapp, president of the East Queens Civic Organization. Many of the members of the group were former leaders of the Volunteers for Stevenson, a bipartisan group of volunteers who supported the election of the Democratic candidate Adlai Stevenson in 1952 and 1956. Halley's reputation as a fighter against corruption (built by his participation in the Senate's investigation of organized crime led by Estes Kefauver) appealed to civic leaders who saw him as the perfect anti-boss candidate. This "Independent, Unbossed, Unbossable" candidate spoke to the spirit of engaged and critical citizenship for which they wished to be known. As declared by the group's campaign managers:

It is our intention to show the rest of the City of New York the long forgotten voters of Queens will be among the most adamant fighters for a return to morality and efficiency in government. No man or woman can remain indifferent to politics today. The price we are paying for delegating the responsibilities of government to the political hacks can be measured every time we pay our subway fare and every time we pay our rents.[58]

Only the citizens' rigorous attention to politics could ensure morality and efficiency in government.

Although Halley was defeated in 1953, the Queens Voters for Good Government continued its "independent" anti-machine campaigns in 1954, when it supported the candidacy of Julius Feigenbaum in the Fourth Congressional District Democratic primary. The group then boasted of representing more than 300 civic leaders. According to Edward Costello, executive director of the group and member of the Flushing Hillcrest Civic Association, what inspired Feigenbaum's candidacy was the desire for "politically conscious civics to combat irresponsible politics." Feigenbaum claimed to be "closer to the core of the community problems of Queens" than his opponents; he carried what he called a " 'grassroots' campaign against boss rule and machine-picked candidates." His "philosophy of government," he explained, was one devised to "insure the maximum benefits to the entire populace, untrammelled by selfish interest blocks and cynical political bossism."[59]

A final example of the spirit of independence that was common in Queens is the case of the two registered Democrats who formed the Independent Voters for Better Politics in support of liberal Republican candidate Nat H. Hentel for the state asssembly in 1956. (Hentel was then running against the popular incumbent, Louis Wallach, who had a strong record of community services, as all local politicians did.) Described in the local press as "free-thinking . . . ladies," they drew public attention when they "descended" on the district's beauty parlors to promote their candidate. "Where better to spread the word of their candidate than in that female sanctuary at its busiest time," remarked the *Long Island Herald*. (The action won them the name "Petticoat Brigade.") Asked to comment on the fact that Hentel had already been nominated on the Republican Party ticket, Natalie A. Katz, one of the leaders of the group, explained the position of her group:

We want Mr. Hentel as our independent candidate because of his competence and community leadership. We are not interested in party labels. We wives and homemakers are the ones most aware of the needs of our community. And because of his outstanding record of community service, we are convinced that Mr. Hentel will put up the hardest fight to fill the needs of our community.

The Independent Voters for Better Politics made the local news again in October when the Board of Election refused their 2,100–name petition. Disqualifying the signatures of twenty-one-year-old voters who were ineligible to sign a nominating petition unless they had registered in a preceding election, the Board had "butchered" their petition, complained Katz. If necessary, she announced, they would fight to amend the election law itself "so that free-thinking people like ourselves who want to run an independent candidate for office won't be at the mercy of ruthless professional politicians."[60]

As illustrated in these examples, the corrupt professional politician was a common figure in Queens. The image stood for the elected representative or party official (the "boss") who was motivated by a selfish thirst for power rather than by service to his constituency. In contrast stood the selfless, devoted community leader, the engaged citizen, who best knew the needs of his or her community. The citizen's responsibility to monitor the action of elected representatives was defined in this juxtaposition.

In the 1950s, the residents of northeastern Queens represented a diverse community, yet they shared a common political culture. Although home owners boasted of being "better citizens" than their renting neighbors, the latter proved them wrong by taking an active role in their community's public life. This ethos of civic participation was celebrated in well-established, older neighborhoods and in the recently developed sections of the borough. Republicans and liberal Democrats, men and women, Christians and Jews shared the same commitment to securing the needs of their communities and, by doing so, fulfilling their duties as active citizens. In the pages of their community newspapers and associations' newsletters, and through local electoral campaigns, civic leaders encouraged their neighbors to act as independent, informed, and engaged citizens. As we will see in the next two chapters, this dedication to the community and to active citizenship was more than empty rhetoric—it manifested itself on a daily basis in the numerous struggles led by residents (mostly women, in fact) to secure basic community needs.

Chapter 5
The School Crisis and Citizens' View of Metropolitan Development

As we have just seen, Queens residents had a strong sense of their responsibility as citizens, which was defined by their willingness to work on behalf of the residential community. In the following pages, turning to the struggle to obtain adequate educational facilities, we will see that they held an equally strong sense of the state's reciprocal responsibility toward its "responsible" citizens. The state's responsibility was defined in terms similar to their own: by its ability to meet the concrete and immediate needs of its citizens. This belief in the concept of governmental responsibility brought middle-class Queens citizens fully within the fold of the New Deal liberal consensus.

To say that Queens citizens subscribed to New Deal liberalism requires clarification of what is meant by the term in American political culture. As is now widely acknowledged by scholars, a greater role on the part of the state in the nation's economy became increasingly accepted in the 1930s and 1940s. From the 1940s to the 1960s, liberalism was further defined by a belief that social inequalities (including racial and economic) would be eradicated by economic growth. Although this moderate support for racial and economic equality was more controversial than the acceptance of state intervention, these were the two central tenets of postwar liberalism.[1]

Identifying Queens citizens' position in this broader political landscape requires that we come back briefly to the housing controversy that we analyzed in Chapter 2, and that may have suggested an antiliberal stand. As we saw then, between 1948 and 1950, civic and home owners' associations joined builders and realtors in pressing the municipal and state government to interrupt innovative attempts to encourage the construction of middle-income housing. The projects that were opposed were sponsored by labor and veterans' organizations and, unlike other public housing projects, were aimed at the lower middle class: organized workers and veterans, most of them white, who at the peak of a severe housing shortage in the New York metropolitan area were unable to find affordable housing in the private market. Ultimately, the programs' foes were more effective than their supporters in shaping the terms of the debate. They succeeded in replacing the pressing question of access to affordable housing by the specter of an increased and unfairly distributed tax burden. The narrow definition of economic liberalism that was reasserted as a result of this campaign—an economic liberalism strictly defined not to interfere with the private industry's dominance of the market—left many families inadequately housed. (As we have also seen, race was absent from this controversy. I return to the position of Queens residents on racial liberalism in Chapter 8, when I examine the 1960s debates over racial integration.)

The participation of Queens home owners in the campaign to block the extension of state-assisted public housing can be explained through a complex set of factors. The influence of local realtors and builders in stirring community associations to action was significant, but so was the residents' own fears of the impact that new residential construction would have on already stretched public services. In this chapter we come back to the second part of their argument. As reflected in the residents' long-standing battles to obtain sufficient public schools, Queens citizens fully expected that the state would provide their communities what they considered basic needs. Rather than asking for a curbing of state intervention as had been done in the field of housing, Queens citizens unanimously and repeatedly demanded a consistent policy to assist families with young children. They wanted greater (or better-coordinated) state intervention to ensure the social goods that they expected as members of the middle class.

The argument that I present here, that Queens citizens were supportive of economic and social liberalism, is predicated on my understanding that some issues and debates are more revealing than others of grassroots opinion. I consider the struggles for schools a better indicator of the pulse of Queens citizens for many reasons. First, unlike the housing controversy, which was heavily influenced by forces external to the Queens population (namely, the national real estate lobby), the battle for schools was truly indigenous to middle-class communities. It originated from these communities and was carried by local residents. Second, it was shared by a cross-section of the population (conservatives and progressives, homeowners and renters) and rallied citizens who were divided on other issues. Third, its longevity speaks to its influence in shaping the residents' political outlook. While the housing controversy lasted approximately two years, the battle to obtain adequate educational facilities was ongoing. In northeastern Queens, it informed the residents' relationship with their municipal government from the 1930s to the mid-1960s.

Although scarcely noticed by scholars, the struggle of Queens parents to ensure their children adequate educational facilities was at the center of the daily struggles of New York middle-class communities throughout the 1940s and 1950s. Especially in the neighborhoods that had received a net increase of population with the post–World War II suburban migration, school seats were chronically deficient. At the height of the baby boom, the reality of overcrowded schools operating on split sessions confounded parents. The struggle to alleviate this condition generated masses of letters and telegrams to city officials, as well as numerous public demonstrations, and fed a growing distrust of policy makers among the residents of suburban Queens.[2]

The seriousness of the situation was noted in December 1945 by Rose Shapiro, president of United Parents Association (UPA). She called on the newly elected mayor, William O'Dwyer, to adopt a "constructive, progressive program designed to correct as rapidly as possible the evils of our school system." Half of the children in the grades below senior high school in New York City, she estimated, were in classes considered overcrowded by current educational standards. She also protested that more than 1,000 classes were teacherless, or doubled up with classes not their own, thereby affecting 35,000 pupils. "We realize that this whole situation is not a simple one, and that much of it springs from years of neglect," she acknowledged. In the name of UPA's 240 affiliated associations, she demanded an "energetic, well-directed and properly financed action" to alleviate the current situation.[3]

In the following months, the situation only got worse from the UPA's point of view. In another letter to the mayor in April 1946, Shapiro protested the changes in the 1947 Capital Outlay Budget recently recommended by city construction coordinator Robert C. Moses. Moses' recommendations was to reduce the six-year school construction plan by two-thirds, decreasing the number of new schools and school additions from 95 to 31, which "would result in making the City of New York, from the viewpoint of families with children, an undesirable place to live." While the initial proposal was not in itself sufficient to make up for the wartime moratorium on school building construction, this was "woefully inadequate," wrote Shapiro. She predicted that these cuts would be "tragic for the future of the City," forcing "families with small children to move to the suburbs to get away from the broken-down schools." This view was also expressed by Ella Streator, chair of the Local School Board, District 52 (Queens), as she conveyed the board's unanimous opposition to Moses' recommendations "to delay any longer the necessary action to replace or rehabilitate some of our schools." The school building program as originally approved for 1946–47, she stated, "represented a minimum or less. To curtail it further is unthinkable."[4]

Evoking an argument that would be repeated by countless associations of parents and teachers in the next fifteen years, Streator presented her case for quality schools as a civic responsibility. "The building of needed schools is a MUST in the city's program if the children of today are to get the kind of training that will fit them properly to be the citizens of tomorrow." Or as put by Helen Lateiner of the Tyholland Civic Association to Mayor Vincent R. Impellitteri, "Part-time education results in partly educated citizens. To be worthy of the responsibility of citizenship in our great democracy, our children need to be fully and well educated."[5]

Shapiro and Streator were right in pointing out the negative impact of the wartime building moratorium on New York public schools. Had the construction program continued during the war at the same pace as between 1918 and 1942 (when an annual average of eighteen new buildings and additions were constructed), seventy-two new schools and additions would have been added.[6] These were necessary to replace the sixty-five school buildings constructed between 1844 and 1889 that were still being used in 1947. (These were described by Rose Shapiro as "damp, odorous because of outmoded plumbing and the porous condition of floors and walls, drafty, incapable of proper heating, and unsightly").[7] Between 1946 and 1949, appropriations for education constituted the largest single item in New York City's expense budget (amounting to almost 24 percent). During that period, the O'Dwyer administration invested close to $120 million in the city's program of school construction and modernization. Of that amount, 31 percent was allocated to the borough of Queens for the construction of nineteen new schools and the modernization of six buildings. This was slightly more than was allocated to the borough of Brooklyn (29 percent for the construction of sixteen new schools and the modernization of sixteen others) and significantly more than the 18 and 17 percent spent in Manhattan and the Bronx, respectively.[8] But even though Queens residents received the largest share of the city's school construction budget, it was still insufficient for what they estimated their needs to be.

The shortage of schools was most acutely felt in areas where a steady population growth had occurred since the 1930s. Such was the case in South Bayside. When the Alley Pond school (P.S. 46) opened in

1951, it was the first public school to be built in Bayside since P.S. 31 in 1940. From the day its construction began, the parents of Oakland Gardens and Bell Park Gardens were already predicting overcrowding. The 800-pupil P.S. 46, they argued, would fast become insufficient to accommodate children of their two garden-apartment complexes, which respectively housed 716 and 800 families.[9] Indeed, as the parents had predicted, P.S. 46 was severely overcrowded when it opened in 1951 (1,600 children were registered). According to the Board of Education's own figures, the school was utilized at 179 percent of its seating capacity. Projections were for 1,800 children in September 1952 and 2,000 in 1953. By this time, parents of the area were demanding the immediate construction of a new school, P.S. 213. After two years of incessant requests, they obtained its inclusion in the 1953 budget.[10]

These tensions felt in rapidly expanding communities were exacerbated when the city granted privileges to developers of large-scale projects in decisions over the location of new schools. This had been the case with the building of Fresh Meadows and Parkway Village. Ever since a fire had destroyed their neighborhood school in the mid-1930s, residents of the Fresh Meadows–Hillcrest area had pressed for a replacement while their children attended a school in Queens Village, three miles away from their home.[11] When in 1946 the Board of Estimate finally voted an appropriation for the completion of P.S. 26, but announced that the school would be located closer to the New York Life's garden-apartment complex in order to serve its 3,000 tenants, the older residents felt cheated. "It would be regrettable if plans for the Cunningham Crest school, so long sought and so badly needed, were now to be altered simply because that seems to be the way school facilities for Fresh Meadow children can most easily and quickly be provided."[12] The decision to speed the construction of a public school to accommodate the Parkway Village families also frustrated parents who had long fought for additional schools in the area. (The case of P.S. 165 is interesting to note in light of the trials that the UN had encountered in trying to provide for its personnel's families. As noted by Moses, when he insisted on the prompt construction of the school: "We cannot afford to have the children of the United Nations representatives shoved around and sent to a half dozen schools located from one to three miles from Parkway Village. There already has been too much criticism of the accommodations provided for these people in New York City.") In October 1946, Daniel Russo, chair of the United Civic Council's Education Committee and of the Local School Board's Housing and Sites Committee, conveyed the sentiments of his neighbors: "Since the City Fathers saw fit to rush plans for P.S. 26 in the Fresh Meadow housing development and P.S. 165 for the UN housing development (Parkway Village) . . . perhaps concerted action on our part will convince them that the older and permanent residents of the area must be given the same consideration."[13]

In spite of occasional clashes between older and newer residents, however, the two usually fought side by side to obtain adequate educational facilities for their children. Indeed, the struggle to alleviate the shortage of school seats generated a widespread mobilization in the neighborhoods of Queens, involving representatives from parents', home owners', civic, tenants', and community associations. The Bayside Joint Council for Schools is a case in point. Organized in August 1950 at the initiative of the Oakland Area School Committee and the School Committee of the Bell Park Gardens Community Council, it soon counted fifteen affiliates—including eight civic or community associations representing home owners and the parents' associations of seven schools.[14] (Two years earlier, Bayside home owners and renters at Oakland Gardens had opposed granting a tax exemption to Bell Park Gardens, yet they united with the residents of Bell Park Gardens when confronted with a shortage of school seats that affected them all.) Such concerted action was typical. In 1952, seventy-seven civic and school organizations joined forces to demand the construction of a new high school in east and north Queens. Leading the struggle, in particular, was the former Bayside Joint Council, which had changed its name to the Northeast Queens Council for Schools and, in 1954, represented fourteen parents' organizations, six civic associations, and four community councils.[15]

The message that underlined the residents' struggle for additional schools was straightforward. New York City policy makers were allowing for, and in some cases were directly encouraging, the construction of thousands of new homes in their neighborhoods; the residents expected them to ensure that the number of school seats would correspond with the increase in the school-age population. School building had to match residential construction. As succinctly put by the PTA of P.S. 184 in Whitestone, city officials should guarantee the "parallel construction of both housing and school facilities."[16] Or as expressed by the parents of South Bayside who organized a motorcade in 1952, their advice to "prospective buyers of homes . . . [was] to check on school facilities before making their investment."[17] This message had been expressed in the residents' opposition to public housing, and it was reiterated over and over in their struggles for schools. It was, more specifically, in their correspondence with city officials that this expectation for a balanced policy of metropolitan development was most repeatedly, albeit implicitly, conveyed.

Among the strategies used by Queens residents to secure additional public services was the gathering of facts and figures, documenting their neighborhoods' needs. Based on these figures, tables and graphs were included in letters, memoranda, petitions, and briefs (some of them six to seven pages long) to the various municipal authorities involved in the planning and funding of school construction (this included the Board of Education, the City Planning Commission, the Board of Estimate, and the Mayor's Office).[18] Gathered through neighborhood surveys conducted by female volunteers, these data highlighted the discrepancy between the number of available school seats in neighborhood schools and the population of school-age children, both actual and anticipated.

An example of these surveys includes one conducted by the parents of the Oakland-Bell Park area in 1950. Under the direction of Simona Sheppard of the Oakland Area School Committee, "hordes and hordes" of volunteers polled the neighborhood, counting the current number of school-age children and contacting builders of planned or unoccupied homes in the area in order to predict future additions to the current child population.[19] Clearly the parents understood that long-term planning was necessary, as reflected by the Kew Meadows Schools Committee's demand that the municipal government appropriate rapidly vanishing vacant land for the construction of future schools. They insisted that "since available land is being built up so rapidly by private builders, suitable sites for schools are fast disappearing, more schools will have to be built and sites must be procured now!!!"[20] This demand, no doubt, would have raised eyebrows in the real estate industry.

Queens residents' views that a balanced metropolitan development demanded better planning is evident in their use of a social scientific approach that emphasized rationality and demonstrable facts. This can be seen, for instance, in the comment made by the chair of the Bell Park Gardens School Committee when she announced that the group, which was recently formed, would conduct a survey: "We must know our problem before we can attack it intelligently," explained its chair.[21] Or as described in the *Meadow Lark*, "A determined group of women from the Oakland Area School Committee met with top officials of the Board of Education and presented 'tell-all' statistics verifying the over-crowded school conditions of P.S. 46."[22]

Thus acting upon the conviction that their demands were objectively justified, and faithful to their populist sensibility, Queens citizens refused to be intimidated by politicians who disregarded the needs of the people or by bureaucrats who seemed to have only contempt for their demands. Even the relevance of the statistics gathered by public officials was challenged by the parents, as in this letter from the Tyholland Civic Association to the Board of Education vice president: "[Your letter] is filled with the gibberish that the Board of Education continually engages in when replying to the average person. It is intended to confuse, confound and perplex the average person with unrelated purported facts." This angry letter continues with a critique of political manipulation and an assertion of the parents' own mastering of bureaucratic jargon: "We believe that this policy of confusion is a calculated one. However, we are well aware of the facts, we know what the terms 'Cluster and Index of Utilization' mean and further, we know the capacities and areas which the schools you list are intended to serve."[23] In a similar way, in June 1955, a local parents' association addressed a letter to the superintendent of schools that included four appendices documenting the Board's oft-repeated promises for an addition to their school. The Board's report, they wrote, was "replete with errors of fact from which erroneous conclusions are drawn."[24]

Explicit in their time-consuming fact-gathering strategy was the belief that policy makers would—or, at least, should—give serious consideration to "responsible" citizens with thoroughly documented and rationally presented arguments. This can be seen in the memorandum, which included five pages of tables, submitted by the Northeast Queens Council for Schools to the Board of Education for its "conscientious and determined consideration."[25] After having been refused an appointment with the Board vice president in June 1952, another group of parents (the Joint Committee for Queens High Schools) also insisted that Board members "should always be available to responsible parents' groups wishing to present facts and figures in support of their request for additional schools."[26] As "responsible" citizens they had made the effort and taken the time to inform themselves about the situation at hand; they were presenting their "reasonable" claims in a rational, respectful manner; they expected reciprocity on the part of their government.

In contrast with what the parents considered self-evident truth was the city officials' rationale for allocating scarce resources. The gap between the parents' and city officials' priorities became clear in the fall of 1952, when the Mothers' Club of P.S. 41 and the Bayside Joint Council invited the Board of Education associate superintendent to explain to the residents the Board's decision to delay the construction of a new school to serve a large-scale garden-apartment development, Bay Terrace, soon to be built in northern Bayside.[27] Although the project promoter had donated four and a half acres of property to the city for the construction of a new elementary school and high school, the Board had decided that no school would be built until the construction of the development was well under way—in case it failed to materialize. At a mass public meeting in Bayside, the city official further explained that the Board was concerned with the possibility of long-term underutilization of schools. He then informed the parents that the Board of Education was using a ratio of one child per four families to estimate the future needs of projected public schools. While a safe way to limit the number of empty seats in the future, this information appeared ludicrous to parents at the height of the baby boom.[28] In short, the Board was concerned with ensuring long-term uses of expensive facilities; the parents' priority was to ensure one school seat per child while their children were still of school age. No matter how many facts and figures the parents gathered, the two rationales seemed irreconcilable.

As promised, the 3,700 family garden-apartment Bay Terrace was built between 1955 and 1957 and the 1,206-seat P.S. 169 opened in 1957. In 1962, the parents' association of P.S. 169, whose school was still overcrowded, was concerned with the effects of yet another round of apartment house construction. The result of their "door-to-door child population census of the whole community" predicted an estimated elementary school population of 1,938 by September 1967. In 1967–68, however, P.S. 169 had an enrollment of 1,044 and was underutilized.[29] Balancing the satisfaction of immediate needs and the serious possibility that expensive facilities would be underutilized in the long run was a delicate exercise.

In contrast with the debate over public housing, which divided the Queens citizenry and was influenced by elements external to it (namely, the national real estate lobby), the struggle for additional school seats in Queens was carried by a cross-section of the population and was truly indigenous. It presents, I believe, a clearer expression of the grassroots' opinion on public policy. The central message that citizens conveyed through their demands for additional schools was that the state (New York City officials, in this case) had a responsibility to provide educational facilities for their families through a sufficient number of schools. That their neighborhoods were undergoing a rapid demographic growth made the problem of inadequate public services especially acute but by no means unique to suburban Queens. Indeed, the neglect of neighborhood needs was criticized by citizens throughout the city in the 1950s and noted by many observers of New York City politics since. Finally, that this rapid growth in the number of school-age children was temporary (an argument suggested by city officials, concerned with future underutilization) was irrelevant to parents.[30]

Chapter 6
As Mothers or as Parents?

Public hearings were a familiar feature of New York City politics. The Board of Estimate and the City Planning Commission, two institutions crucial to the distribution of resources among the five boroughs and dozens of communities that formed New York City, were required by the City Charter to hold them. But this "sounding board for public opinion," editorialized the *Long Island Daily Press* in 1949, was outright impractical for the public.

> [T]here is a large sector of the home owning, taxpaying public that is never represented at a public hearing . . . for the very simple reason that they work for a living. . . .
> The man who works for an hourly wage cannot sacrifice a day's pay to attend a public hearing, no matter how important it may be.
> The average merchant cannot close his store and travel to City Hall. The doctor cannot drop a busy practice; the lawyer cannot pass up a court appearance.[1]

For all his legitimate suspicion about the effectiveness of such methods of opinion gathering, the editorialist had missed what was, perhaps, the most characteristic feature of public hearings in the 1950s: the presence of housewives. At the public hearings of important municipal decision-making bodies, as in other public sites, the "home owning, taxpaying public" was represented not by the working man, sometimes by the merchant or lawyer, but mostly by the full-time housewife. She who could attend public hearings during the daytime when children were away at school, or when a neighbor looked after the younger ones, was at the center of the dialogue that took place—or not—between policy makers and Queens communities in postwar New York.[2]

Women played a crucial role in various community struggles. And yet their presence is often difficult to ascertain. The fight of a 100 home owners of the Fresh Meadows Civic Association against a proposed gas rate increase, in 1949, is a case in point. Since the formation of the group, its presidency had been assumed by men, although, as was often the practice in civic associations, women had occupied the positions of treasurer and corresponding and recording secretaries.[3] However, as became apparent in the midst of the 1949 gas rate fight, not only was women's legwork crucial to the home owners' battle but the central role that they played in their community's struggles was often concealed behind the public celebration of male leadership.

This was reflected, for instance, in the *Meadow Lark* story on the launching of the petition campaign at a meeting of "more than 100 irate home owners . . . in the home of Mrs. Herbert Pomerance" (whose basement was understandably "crowded to capacity"). Two days later, community activists had gathered nearly 2,000 signatures; their petition would include 5,000 names by early April. The *Lark*'s initial report made the contribution of women clear, while asserting male leadership: "Leading the protest group, Irwin Appel, president of the Fresh Meadows Civic Association, credited the small 'parlor groups' of women . . . with the 'job they have done recruiting support of these petitions.' " In an editorial published the same day, the *Lark* further praised Appel's leadership and downplayed women's initiative: "We extend a hand of congratulations to Irwin Appel, President of the Fresh Meadows Civic Association, as well as these women for his initiation of action against the gas increase. His work along with [attorney] Isidore Levine['s], in drawing up and circulating the gas protest petitions deserves the thanks of all."[4] In subsequent articles, headlines remained silent as to the sex of the fighters, referring simply to "home owners," even as the seven-member working committee appointed to coordinate the petition drive was staffed by six women—and the meetings were still held at Mrs. Pomerance's home.[5]

In addition to this kind of reporting, another reason that women's role in community activism was so difficult to identify is the public persona that they themselves embraced: more specifically, their insistence on downplaying their feminine specificity and casting themselves as gender-neutral individuals. An example of this can be seen when the Oakland Hills Civic Association elected an all-woman slate of officers in 1948—an event dramatically reported in the *Long Island Star-Journal* as the end of "male dominance." The "four-woman cabinet" made clear, however, that the program of activities "will not be radically different from previous ones . . . and will be based on 'the welfare of the community.' " Myrtle Rogers insisted, "All of us [men and women] think pretty much alike out here."[6] Like many of their contemporaries, female community activists in Queens downplayed gender differences and their feminine identity, and privileged a communal form of group-identification when intervening on the public and political scene. It was as home owners, tenants, taxpayers, parents, or community members, not primarily as women, that they presented themselves.[7]

The attempt by female activists to downplay their feminine personae is most striking in the context of their struggle to improve educational and safety conditions for their communities. Since education and children's safety were generally acknowledged as women's responsibilities in the 1950s, and since mothers and housewives were the driving force in these battles, one would expect a more direct assertion of their gender roles. One would expect them to use the kind of maternalist strategy found, for instance, in the peace and anti–Civil Defense movement of the late 1950s and early 1960s. Community activists did organize events that featured their maternal personae, such as baby carriage blockades or parades. They did understand that street protests, and especially those that staged mothers and children, were key ingredients to a successful political strategy. However, maternalism (defined as the use of women's socially recognized status as mothers as a source of political authority) was not the preferred strategy of community activists.[8]

Queens community activists appealed to expertise and rationality in their struggle to obtain additional school seats for their children. This was especially evident in their written correspondence with city officials. By doing so, they embraced the middle-class model of the informed, rational, and objective citizen that was introduced during the Progressive Era and was, by the 1950s, fully integrated in American political culture. This model presumed a political actor who was gender neutral.[9] When "facts and figures" failed to sway their audience, community activists traded the posture of the disembodied, gender-neutral citizen for that of the aggrieved mother—and occasionally the caring father. When examined in the context of their overall political strategy, however, and when disentangled from sensationalistic media coverage, the use of motherly images appears to be the exception, rather than the norm. Thus, the strategy adopted by Queens housewives was both realistic and flexible: they recognized the importance of factual analysis in modern bureaucratic decisions, and rightly assumed that they had to engage with policy makers in those terms. Yet they refused to be limited by the gender-neutral social scientific argument. Their ability to switch from rational citizens to aggrieved mothers shows their astuteness as political strategists.

In the context of the tremendous demographic growth and rapid metropolitan development of the late 1940s and 1950s, the residents of northeastern Queens were confronted with what appeared to be a chronic lack of traffic regulations. While old-timers could remember when their environment was made up of golf courses, country clubs, and farms, Queens suburbanites now inhabited a land crisscrossed by parkways, expressways, and boulevards that had been widened to accommodate an increasingly heavy load of traffic. In 1948, it seemed that just crossing Horace Harding Boulevard was an adventure, if one is to believe the local residents who asked that lights be installed every four blocks along this main artery. "As it is," wrote the *Meadow Lark*'s editor, "unless you are at Utopia Parkway, 179th Street, or 188th Street, your chances of crossing the street without running are low. Try this sometime with a baby carriage and watch the cars charge at you."[10] That year more than 1,000 persons signed a petition requesting the installation of traffic lights on this busy boulevard adjacent to the Fresh Meadow Development.[11]

In 1949, the traffic problem in the metropolis had been deemed serious enough to warrant the formation of a permanent, full-time municipal agency.[12] Underfunded and understaffed, the Department of Traffic Engineering had more responsibilities than it could efficiently handle: It was in charge of establishing rules and regulations for the conduct of vehicular and pedestrian traffic, compiling traffic data and analyzing traffic conditions in the city, deciding upon the "design, type, size and location of all traffic signs and signals," and supervising such matters as parking and meters. All this was to be done in collaboration with the Traffic Commission, formed of representatives of various departments and agencies: the Police Department, Triborough Bridge and Tunnel, Board of Transportation, City Planning Commission, and Board of Estimate.[13] In June 1950, both the Department of Traffic Engineering and the Traffic Commission were replaced by a Department of Traffic, headed by Lloyd B. Reid. After Reid's resignation in June 1951, following "many sharp clashes" with city commissioner Robert Moses, the position remained vacant until August 20, 1952, when Deputy Commissioner T. T. Wiley, a resident of Douglaston, Queens, was appointed. At the time of his appointment, only seventeen engineers out of thirty-five allowed by the budget were on staff.[14] In the midst of this administrative chaos, getting a traffic light installed in New York City was no easy matter. As expressed by a newspaper editor, with "a small budget and a small staff to study and to act on traffic control needs in five huge boroughs, it should surprise no one that a neighborhood petition for a 'stop' sign or a traffic light gathers dust for months before it is acted on . . . if at all."[15]

As in the case of the struggle to obtain additional school seats, the residents of northeastern Queens used conventional channels to press their needs upon New York City bureaucrats. They formed coalitions of local civic and parents' associations to coordinate their efforts.[16] They sent letters and petitions to the city traffic commissioner pleading for traffic regulation. (In the first eight months of 1957, for instance, Wiley's office received 1,800 requests from individuals and groups, citywide, for remedies to traffic problems.)[17] They mobilized their elected representatives to speak on their behalf.[18] At times, they even installed their own traffic signs only to see them taken down by Wiley's men. (In 1953, for instance, the Tyholland Civic Association bought eighteen signs, reading "Slow—Children At Play," and posted them on light poles in the area. They were removed by the Traffic Department one month after their installation.)[19] In short, as the *Bayside Times* noted in 1960, "[a] traffic light is not approved as a matter of casual routine by the Traffic Department. Lots of hard work, writing, phoning, pressuring, and talking must precede any decision."[20]

As was also the case in the campaign for schools, local residents based their demands for additional traffic regulation on their own firsthand, "objective" knowledge of local conditions, only to realize that city officials were assessing the situation according to different criteria. On many occasions, Traffic Commissioner T. T. Wiley decried the "public's theory that signals solve the pedestrians' problem." Arguing that most traffic accidents involving children occurred between intersections and that of those which took place at intersections, over three-fourths happened where there were traffic signals in operation, he sustained that "traffic signals were not the answer to every traffic problem." As he acknowledged to a Brooklyn councilman, however, "This creates a very difficult public relations problem for public servants." Yet he insisted that "when the facts are appraised on the basis of experience and the resulting judgment concludes that signals will probably do more harm than good, then we must decide against the public demand."[21] Residents had little patience for Wiley's theory. Reflecting the exasperated sentiment of many of its readers, the *Times* offered its own local counterexpertise:

The Traffic Department will agree to send a statistical team to an intersection for a "scientific survey" of "traffic density." What results from a complex series of formulas and equations developed by these "traffic engineers" almost always results in a big no on requests for signs or lights. Who knows this area best? The residents, of course. The traffic engineers inspect an intersection for a couple of hours and make a report to headquarters. We live here, we see our children cross busy streets, we hear screeching brakes at midnight, we count the accidents and near-accidents at corners. . . . We aren't interested in a mathematical formula to tell us a stop sign is needed![22]

When exasperated with the Department of Traffic's red tape and unable to make their own expertise prevail, Queens residents resorted to a strategy that spoke louder than petitions or letters and did not fail to get them media attention: baby carriage parades. During such street protests, community activists seemed willing to trade their rationality for a much more disorderly and clearly gendered mode of political discourse. Examining how this particular form of political pressure fits in the community associations' strategy is revealing of the residents' political consciousness.

In June 1950, the community newspaper, the *Meadow Lark*, reported the following event: "Half a hundred mothers . . . formed a human blockade across Main Street at 72nd Avenue [off the Long Island then Horace Harding Expressway in Kew Gardens Hills]." It also specified that this action was taken as a last resort. "After more than a year of unsuccessful attempts to obtain a signal at the corner . . . the parents finally resorted to a mass demonstration and held up traffic for more than an hour."[23]

Although the community weeklies occasionally reported such events, it was in the daily newspapers, the *Long Island Daily Press* and the *Long Island Star-Journal* (both under the same ownership and running the same stories), that one can find the most detailed—and sensationalistic—coverage of what were alternatively called "human blockades," "baby carriage blockades," or "baby carriage parades." For instance, in contrast to the brief two-paragraph story printed in the *Lark* (and quoted above), both the *Daily* and the *Star* offered extensive coverage of the event over the three days that it lasted. "Kew Hills Mothers Block Road with Baby Buggies," read the headline on June 13. The article described in graphic terms a heated confrontation in which mothers "ANGRILY DEF[IED] police . . . even when a 'paddy wagon' rolled up to the scene." Although the *Star* informed its readers that the action was orchestrated by the Residents Association of Kew Gardens Hills after a year of conventional lobbying "through official channels," the drama featured predominantly individual mothers (and a lone father) confronting police officers in an effort to secure protection for their children. Gone was the rationality that community activists were claiming in other contexts.

The dailies' stories are worth quoting at length.

[Mothers] began assembling . . . at about 1:30 p.m., most of them pushing a baby carriage with one hand and leading children by the other.

Led by 30 women who formed the nucleus of the blockade, they wheeled their carriages into the street at 1:45 p.m.

Four members of the blockade carried large red signs on which was printed: "The cost of a light is the price of a life"; "Safety first, a dead child never"; "Stop injuring our children"; and "Give us a light and save a life."

Ten minutes into the demonstration, five patrol cars of the Flushing Precinct arrived at the scene, alerted by "the loudly honking horns of the hurried motorists."

The mothers explained to police that they wanted "to force city officials to give us a traffic light on this corner to protect our children."

Sergeant Joseph G. Whelan replied:

"I don't have a signal light in my pocket right now, ladies, but your demonstration is illegal.

"If you don't break it up right now, I'll have to arrest at least some of you."

Whelan's suggestion that they "use proper channels" to get their traffic light was met by derision.

"We used 'proper channels' for a year and a half without getting our traffic light," a spokesman for the mothers declared, "and now we'll use force to get it."

When Whelan's men, ordered to disperse the crowd, broke up the human chain and picked up a baby carriage and carried it to the curb, they were accused of using strong-arm tactics and roughhouse action. A woman "charged that her baby's head had been banged against the side of the carriage when a patrolman tried to push her and the carriage off the street." Another complained, "My child, who has always been taught to respect officers, won't stop crying because that strong armed cop yelled, 'Get that kid out of here.' " The *Daily*'s story was even more dramatic:

Ten policemen spent most of the time tugging and shoving to force the buggies back to the sidewalk, while the mothers clung firmly to the handles and were dragged along, scraping their shoe leather against the pavement. Many held on with only one hand, grasping a young child with the other.

As fast as one carriage was forced to the curb by police, another took its place.

The police did not actually touch any of the women, but when a man started to push a stroller across with a 4-year-old child in it, a patrolman seized him by the back of the neck and the seat of the pants and dragged him off the road with the stroller and child, announcing that he was "a prisoner."

Women rushed to the man's defense, jeering and booing. "You don't dare arrest a woman," they screamed. Babies and the young children began whimpering and crying.

By three o'clock, concluded the *Daily*, the mothers gave up, although they did threaten to "be out here for an hour and a half every day this week" if they didn't get their light. "If we get shunted off again, we'll be right back out there with our baby buggies and signs," warned a representative of the neighborhood residents' association. As recounted by the dailies, mothers were using the last available resources—their bodies and children—to obtain what they had tried in vain to get "through official channels." And it was effective: They were promised that a traffic light would be installed shortly and that a patrolman would be positioned at the busy intersection meanwhile.[24]

Other cases can be cited to illustrate the contrasting treatment of baby carriage parades by the weeklies and the dailies. Consider, for instance, the *Meadow Lark*'s account of the final obtaining of a traffic light in 1948: The victory "was hailed today by parents as the result of concentrated effort on the part of community civic factions. The light . . . has been the subject of continual demands by the school's Parent-Teacher Association, in cooperation with local civic organizations." The emphasis here was clearly on the communal and long-term lobbying effort. Nowhere in this article published on October 7 did the weekly mention the event which had made the *Long Island Daily Press*'s front page a week earlier. In "Marching Mothers Win School Crossing Fight," the daily had reported that fifty mothers "marched on Borough Hall . . . to demand action," then, "later in the day, 20 of the mothers with 50 children accompanying them, trooped into the Flushing police station" to win a promise that patrolmen would be stationed at the crossing. Just as the *Lark* had failed to mention the more dramatic part of the culminating struggle, the *Daily*'s article presented the event as a spontaneous one and did not mention that these mothers were acting as members of local civic and parents' associations.[25]

The media coverage of baby carriage parades raises interesting questions about the intention, or political consciousness, of community activists. On the one hand, it is clear that this dramatic display of maternal care was intended to draw media attention, as a means of forcing public officials to respond to long-sought demands. The use of baby carriage parades by grassroots groups was not unusual in the early 1950s, and as Robert Caro has noted, daily newspapers were sure to cover such events.[26] In this light, the dailies, which reported these events with great sensationalism, reflected the parents' desire for publicity. This being said, one must be careful not to equate the activists' desire for publicity and the staging of media events with their self-identification as political actors. For the latter, one must turn not to the dailies but to the weeklies.

Edited and published in various neighborhoods of Queens, by people directly involved in or closely associated with local associations, community weekly newspapers can be considered a fair barometer of the perception of community activists. Unsurprisingly, given their communal focus, the weeklies typically credited the staging of baby carriage parades to community associations rather than presenting it as the spontaneous initiative of individual "fed up" mothers. More significantly, however, is their emphasis that these were not isolated events but part of the community's long-term lobbying effort. In this light, maternalism was clearly a strategy of last resort, used when the language of reason, which was understood as the normal means of political communication, had failed to yield results. Many examples indeed point to the fact that baby carriage parades were considered by community activists as extreme measures to be used "only if other means fail."[27]

In 1955, for instance, the *Glen Oaks News* stressed that it was only after 400 residents of Glen Oaks had signed a petition that their representatives "threatened to blockade the street with baby carriages unless something was done."[28] As also illustrated in the case of the Horace Harding Civic and Improvement Association, the "threat" of a blockade was used deliberately to expedite a long-sought demand. Explained Alfred Glicker, the association's president, "the organization had decided to set up a baby carriage blockade at the controversial intersection, but had, on the request of Captain T. Ennis [of the local] Police Precinct, agreed to wait 30 days . . . before resorting to such an extreme measure."[29] In one case, a civic association went as far as denouncing such events as unbecoming of respectable citizens. "Women and other [*sic*] responsible for the series of baby carriage blockades in our borough acted unlawfully and showed an un-American spirit," declared Peter Belsito, president of the Flushing Manor Civic Association, in 1952. He further insisted that his members "believe in campaigning by other means. Yet sometimes we wonder if demonstrators don't get more attention from city department heads."[30] This strong denunciation, however, was not common in civic circles; civic leaders, while boasting of their rationality and moderation, fully acknowledged the effectiveness of street protests. The fact that they referred to it as an "extreme measure," or "threats" to be enacted when and "if other means fail," makes clear that such was not their preferred mode of political action. Lobbying through "official channels" was.

As was the case in the struggle for traffic regulations, the means used by parents to press their demands for additional schools covered the full range of strategies available to a grassroots movement. In addition to written correspondence with city officials, these included mass demonstrations in neighborhood streets and mass attendance at public hearings. These public forms of collective protests were more likely to lend themselves to the use of a gendered persona. And yet the image of "the mother" as the special defender of children's interests was notoriously absent from the struggle for schools or used only in very limited terms. In its stead stood "parents," an image which downplayed gender differences by including both women and men, mothers and fathers. By thus including men in their rhetoric, community activists stripped the struggle from its specific feminine character. As in the case of the struggle for traffic lights, the battle for school was presented as communal, that is, shared by men and women of the community, rather than gender specific.

Examples of mass rallies included the one organized in September 1952 by the Parents' Association of P.S. 46 (formerly the Oakland Area School Committee), which then counted more than 1,000 members representing several civic associations in the area. As announced in the *Long Island Herald* on September 25, 1952, "Irate Parents Call Mass Protest Rally." The rally featured a demonstration on Saturday of 500 parents and children who marched from P.S. 46 to the site which they wanted the city to purchase for the construction of P.S. 213. The *Bayside Times* also noted the familial nature of the event: "Mothers, dads and children, on foot, in baby carriages, on bicycles and in cars comprised the parade which marked the latest action by the Bayside parents to bring attention to the serious overcrowding of Public School 46." This rally was followed the next day by a motorcade through the neighborhood.[31]

A similar event took place in April 1953, when the Mothers' Club of P.S. 41 and the Bayside Joint Council for Schools staged a public rally at the Bayside High School to demand the immediate construction of an additional public school, P.S. 169. The additional school was requested for the children of the planned Bay Terrace apartments. As reported by the *Bayside Times*, "A motorcade directed by Mrs. H. A. Winterbottom of P.S. 41 will tour Bayside throughout the day of the rally urging parents to attend the meeting, the topic of which will be 'Crisis in Education.' " More than 1,000 people were at the meeting.[32]

In the case of the Bay Terrace school battle, more direct information from the organizers themselves allows us to confirm the impression of gender neutrality gathered through the community newspapers. In a communication sent to Mayor Impellitterri in April 1953 by Mrs. Winterbottom, a member of the Mothers' Club of P.S. 41 and organizer of the public rally, her intention was obviously to stress the participation of men. In this short invitation to the event, she wrote that the rally was "sponsored by the Bayside Joint Council for Schools, which is composed of *mothers, fathers* and *civic leaders* of this Bayside area. It is of *prime* importance to us as a mother and a father of school children that we have your *help!*" (Emphasis in the original.)[33] Although hand-written on letterhead bearing her name, she signed her letter "Mr. and Mrs. Arthur W. Winterbottom." She clearly wanted to emphasize that the struggle was conducted by parents and endorsed by the com-munity, that this was not strictly a maternal issue.

Another communication sent to the mayor by a Bayside resident is also interesting to consider. Less than a week after Winterbottom's let-ter, Don Sieverman (whose name did not appear elsewhere in the community newspapers' reporting of the event) wrote to Impellitteri, "The mothers and fathers of Queens are fighting mad—particularly the mothers—over the crowded public schools." While praising the particular determination of mothers to fight for their children, he also emphasized their ability to further their reasonable cause precisely be-cause of their expertise, thereby evoking a gender-neutral source of authority: "When American Mothers take up a cause on behalf of their children—a full-time seat for every child in his neighborhood school (a not unreasonable claim)—they are not dissuaded by double talk, buck passing, nor misstatements of facts and figures."[34] Even in this exceptional case where the maternal identity of the protesters was highlighted, their factual knowledge, not their maternal instinct, was emphasized.

This emphasis on the gender-neutral aspect of the struggle—a "parental" and "communal" one—was typical of the community week-lies' reporting of mass attendance at public hearings, which were orga-nized on a regular basis by community associations. As in the case of the baby carriage parades, the weeklies' coverage differed from that of the dailies that played up the maternal card. When delegations from throughout Queens attended the City Planning Commission hearings in October 1950, for instance, the *Long Island Daily Press* headline read, "300 Mothers Storm City Hall to Demand Schools in East Queens." The text also refers to "mothers" in contrast to the community newspapers' reference to "parents."[35] A month later, the day before several busloads of delegates were planned to leave north-eastern Queens for a mass delegation to the Board of Estimate, the *Meadow Lark* announced the event under the headline, "Hundreds of Parents Set for School 'Zero Hour.' " The caption accompanying the picture of local PTA representatives assembled to prepare for the event—several women and one man—also emphasized the "maternal and paternal concern for the future of the community's children." The text of the article also made clear that the protesters' intention was to impress city fathers not with a mere display of motherly care but with irrefutable statistical data. As the *Lark* insisted, "The strongest weapon at their command will be cold, hard statistics."[36]

In a way that is reminiscent of Sieverman's letter, the community press sometimes referred to the activists as mothers, but even when they did, they emphasized the factual analysis on which their demands were based. "Irate Oakland Mothers Confront Boro President on School," read a *Long Island Herald* headline in November 1951; the article explained that their criticism of triple session "was based on a door to door survey conducted by the Oakland Area School Committee."[37] Also revealing is the article that reported in February 1952 that "a group of Bayside Hills mothers have warned the Board of Education that they will march on its Brooklyn headquarters next week to renew their demands for quick construction of a wing for P.S. 162." It also described their intended strategy: "Pointing to a recent census conducted by the Bayside Joint Council for Schools, the mothers feel that they must bring the facts of increasing school population to the personal attention of Associate Superintendent George F. Piggott Jr. They believe that, on hearing that there are 910 students in a school built to accommodate 616, he will move to remedy the situation."[38] Examples such as these abound. They all point to the protesters' assumption that irrefutable facts, rather than emotional appeals, would sway city officials to their view. Or, as Edith Hack, president of the Bayside Joint Council for Schools, said in 1953 of the group that she represented, it "was organized four years ago by a group of mothers who have since become statisticians, brief writers and conferees, for the soul [*sic*] purpose of gaining a full school program for each pupil as required by the state."[39] The struggle for schools transformed mothers into statisticians. It was to the authority of social scientific arguments approached from their own grassroots perspective that they turned in their search for political legitimacy.

Community activists, the majority of whom were mothers, deliberately refused to play up the maternal card in their dealings with public authorities. Clearly gendered forms of actions, such as baby carriage parades, were part of their repertoire, but they were neither the preferred nor the usual form of intervention. The reason they were used is evident: They attracted media attention. The same was true of mass attendance to public hearings. As can be clearly seen in the following scene, described by the *Kew Hills News*, the presence of mothers and young children had publicity value. "Parents thronged the Board of Estimate hearing. . . . The overflow spilled out into the corridors at City Hall. Photographers snapped pictures of delegations which included mothers with toddlers who could not be left at home."[40] (Were the children there to attract media attention, or were their mothers simply unable to find baby-sitting?) Community activists were fully cognizant of the power that these images had. Wrote a representative of the Oakland Area School Committee to the mayor in December 1951:

We haven't had parents march up and down City Hall with placards advertising our problem; pictures of our children crying for a seat in school have not been printed in newspapers . . . but we have made it a point to have two or three well-informed, intelligent parents visit interested persons who should know about our situation and who are in a position to do something to alleviate it.[41]

Their preferred strategy was to present their case personally to decision makers and, above all, to address the problem rationally, hoping that city officials would respond likewise.

This chapter concludes our analysis of 1950s community activism in suburban Queens. In this section, we have seen that the local political culture was dominated by a dual emphasis on active civic participation and attention to local needs. These two main features reinforced each other. We have also seen that although women played a central role in local struggles, and although many of the issues relevant to the residential community could be defined as "feminine," public life was not an arena where gender differences were emphasized.[42] The language of politics in the views of Queens suburban citizens was based on reason and facts, and such traits were shared by both men and women. As Myrtle Rogers had stated in 1948, "All of us, men and women, think alike." This is not to say, of course, that Queens suburban residents were not thoroughly aware of their differences as men and women; when necessary, they did appeal to their gender identity to win their political battles.

Part III
Turning Points

Gender and the Middle Class in the Postwar Era

Chapter 7
Betty Friedan, the Volunteers for Stevenson, and 1950s Housewives

In *The Feminine Mystique*, Betty Friedan rejected "the endless whirl of worthwhile community activities" as little more than a device to "fill the time available." But this was 1963. More interesting for our purposes are the drafts of articles that she wrote in the early days of her career as a freelance author, while living in northeastern Queens in the early 1950s. As we will see in this chapter, they tell the story of how housewives grew to assert themselves as individuals and to challenge the authority of male professionals through their community involvement. Also revealing of the public image of 1950s housewives is the little-known case of the Volunteers for Stevenson, to which we turn first. In its appeal to female voters, this national movement crafted a strategy that appealed to the intelligence and rationality of women—it portrayed housewives not only as political actors but as informed citizens able to exercise critical judgment. More accurately than Friedan's 1963 best-seller, these examples reflect the experience of 1950s housewives.[1]

As we well know, popular and political culture in the postwar period was thoroughly gendered. Women's traditional roles, centered on their domestic and maternal functions, permeated the culture of Queens, as reflected in the community newspapers of the area. The weekly column published in the *Meadow Lark* in 1948, "Baby Talk," written by a local pediatrician, is one example. Another is the weekly regular feature on "Personalities at Fresh Meadows," which introduced the readers to "Pearl . . . lovely in her chic pastel blue maternity dress" or "Eleanor . . . charming in her navy blue housegown and matching slippers."[2] Yet, as Joanne Meyerowitz's rereading of the contemporary popular press has shown, models of assertive and publicly active women coexisted quite well with the glorification of their more traditional roles.[3] Again, for local examples of this mixed message, one can turn to the *Pomonok News*, which announced in 1952 that it was "planning to be as old-fashioned as the hoop skirt or the bustle" and conducted "sidewalk chats" with housewives to gather their views on community affairs.[4] In 1955, the *Long Island Herald* published an "exclusive interview" with Lucille Friedman, president of a local parents' association, stressing her perseverance and success in the fight for the Northeastern Queens High School.[5] Similarly, in 1960, Vivian Potemkin of the *Glen Oaks News* introduced to her readers Adeline Rubin, active in both her local PTA and League of Women Voters. A typically well-rounded 1950s housewife, Adeline was married, a mother of two, employed part time, and leading an active "community career."[6] The central role played by women in their community was even used as a model of civic responsibility for men to emulate. As the male editor of the *Glen Oaks News* noted in 1956, men were "fulfilling a less vigorous role in community affairs than the female contingent." He called for them to "no longer delegate our civic responsibilities to the women in the houses."[7]

No example, however, is more telling of the coexistence of different models for women than the launching of an annual beauty contest for a "Civic Queen of Queens" in 1958. Here a powerful symbol of women's objectification was juxtaposed with the acknowledgment of women's active role in civic circles. As explained in the *Home Town News* in 1958, the annual event was endorsed by the Federation of Civic Councils (an umbrella organization then counting many civic associations as members) and held in conjunction with "Civic Week." It was meant to boast the "social aspect" of civic activities and enhance "the awakening of civic consciousness."[8] In 1960, the organizing committee of the Civic Queen Contest, cochaired by Julia Jerry (also the first woman to be elected president of the United Civic Council the same year), pushed the irony as far as changing the qualifications required from the contestants that they be not only "a wife or daughter of a member" but "also a paid up member of their respective civic association." Hence, in this rendition of 1950s feminine/civic roles, women were required to be active participants in the public life of their community in order to qualify as sexual objects of civic pride.[9]

That women had an important role to play in the public life of their community was readily acknowledged in the local community newspapers. But this message, far from being limited to local communities, was heard in national forum during the 1950s as well. Meyerowitz's analysis of national magazines is one example. Another example is to be found in the experience of groups such as the Volunteers for Stevenson, or even the immensely popular Citizens for Eisenhower, who played an important role in the 1950s presidential campaigns. While historians have paid little attention to these national associations of political "amateurs," the efforts that these groups deployed to recruit female volunteers and to court the vote of housewives speak volumes about the recognition of women's public and political role in the decade.[10] This national example shows that the dynamics at work in northeastern Queens were not exceptional.

The Volunteers for Stevenson and the Citizens for Eisenhower were formed by supporters of the two presidential candidates to win the support of independents and weak partisans (or "switchers," as they were also known) in the 1952 and 1956 elections. Although these organizations coordinated their activities with, respectively, the Democratic and Republican National Committees, structurally they remained distinct and autonomous. Both nationally and locally, they had a separate staff and headquarters and conducted their own fund-raising and public relations activities. As Jane Dick, cochair of the Volunteers for Stevenson, explained to a correspondent in 1952, "We try to work closely with the [regular] organization, but [also] to maintain our separate identity in order to be more effective in attracting the independent voters."[11] Their contributions to the campaigns were significant. After the 1952 election, for instance, Citizens' national chairman Walter Williams claimed that the group had about 16,000 clubs and 2 million members at its peak strength, many of them political neophytes.[12] The same year, the Volunteers had raised $749,000 in campaign contributions, more than half of which was spent on radio and television broadcasts.[13]

In their effort to attract independent voters, the national staff of the Volunteers for Stevenson explicitly acknowledged the importance of enlisting female volunteers. For the national party, the fact that women and young people "lack or shun contact with party organizations" was sufficient reason to delegate the task of seeking the support of female voters to the Volunteers.[14] This was no doubt a self-serving strategy, meant not only to attract "the women's vote" but to tap into the strength of women's support work and their ties to women's associations.[15] As illustrated in a set of instructions sent to local groups, "Women are good campaigners, and most have more time to give than men. They generally have many contacts through women's organizations which they can reach far better than men. Arousing the interest of the women in your community should be of prime importance and will pay off when door-bell ringing and poll-watching time comes."[16] Judging from the letters that Volunteers national chairman Herman Dunlap Smith sent to numerous women after the 1952 election, thanking them for their contribution to the "endless routine of filing and copying, stamping and sealing," it is clear that not only door-to-door canvassing but also clerical work was performed by female volunteers.[17]

In addition to this reliance on women's traditional roles in political movements, the Volunteers also appealed to their traditional domestic responsibilities. More specifically, the group targeted housewives with a message centered on inflation, an issue considered one of special interest to the homemaker. Yet this was combined with an explicit assertion of women's critical and independent political judgment. As reflected most clearly in the campaign blitz orchestrated by the Volunteers in 1956, courting the "independent" female voter produced a peculiar fusion of domesticity with political acumen. In contrast with Adlai Stevenson's oft-cited commencement address at Smith College in 1955, in which he told the seniors that "they were destined for 'the humble role of the housewife,' whether they liked the idea or not," the housewife publicized in the Volunteers' campaign was one capable of political responsibility and discernment.[18]

The emphasis on women's special knowledge of matters such as the cost of living that the Volunteers embraced was at odds with the position taken by female strategists of both parties who, in their desire to emphasize women's humanity, opposed targeting women as a special group. This was revealed, for instance, in an article published in the *New York Post* by journalist Sylvia F. Porter in September 1956. As she reported, according to Mrs. S. Gutwillig, chairwoman of the Campaign Committee of the Women's National Republican Party, "Women today are mature human beings and want to be treated as such. Basically, their problems are the same as those of men and they face them squarely and sensibly." "There are no women's issues and no woman's vote, as such," concurred Mrs. Katie Louchheim, director of Women's Activities for the Democratic National Committee. But Porter presented a contrasting view, one that combined women's maturity and intelligence with their specific interests. "As a woman and a reporter concentrating on the bread-and-butter aspects of the news, I'm not so sure their judgment about our interests and attitudes is accurate. And I strongly believe there is a great issue in which women take a deeply personal interest—far more so than men. That issue is the cost of living." That inflation had risen by only 2 percent during Eisenhower's first term no doubt fared well in comparison with the 12 percent increase under the Truman administration, but—"and it's a big but," noted the Democratic partisan—the Stevenson campaign could capitalize on the increase in the cost of living that had taken place since January. Porter concluded by stressing the immediate relevance of the issue to women—housewives, in fact:

It is the woman who manages most of the family budget in our land. It is the woman who goes to market and who—without a single statistic to back up her statements—can tell a man exactly what is happening to the cost of living.

With dignity, I accept the politicians' recognition of us as equal to men in maturity, intelligence and interest. But because we are equals doesn't mean there are no differences in our attitudes or in our emphasis on issues. There are differences, I submit, and there always will be.[19]

Porter's article was one of the main documents used in the preparation of a special pamphlet addressed to housewives and published in the last month of the 1956 campaign. Produced and distributed by the national staff of the Volunteers for Stevenson to thousands of women nationwide, this pamphlet offered an alternative to the image of the passive, apolitical, or unthinking housewife. While emphasizing her feminine identity, it attributed to her a positive political role and portrayed her as a knowledgeable, intelligent, and rational citizen.

For the most part, the pamphlet focused on the increase in the cost of living—the price of food, the price of a house (fuel, interest rates on home mortgage, lack of an appropriate federal housing policy), that of doctors' fees—and on the problem of education, including the shortage and overcrowding of classrooms and the lack of teachers. Although the threat of nuclear escalation was discussed in one of the drafts, the printed version resolutely focused on inflation. The issues relevant to their homes and families were defined as matters of national political concern:

The housewife does not need to be told her problems. She is surrounded by them. Her home, her family, the cost of obtaining the one, the cost of maintaining the other, these have day-to-day urgency for her. . . .
These costs are domestic prices for the housewife but they must be policy prices for the national parties.

In the various drafts that were written prior to the publication of the pamphlet, one finds a constant appeal to housewives' political judgment. One of them, for instance, was modeled on the motif of "The brain has no sex," explicitly referring to Porter's article:

Some seers to the contrary. Vital issues in the Presidential campaign *are* women's issues.
Independent voters among housewives are gravely concerned about lagging public schools, about the soaring cost of living, about the dragging effort to beat the annihilating Atom into a productive plow-share. . . .
A noted feminine columnist says: "The brain has no sex." The real issues are addressed to the brain.
Take the schools . . . Consider living costs . . . And the fateful Atom! . . .
These issues are addressed to the mind.
These are women's concerns!

The last page repeated the same theme, insisting on defining serious political matters as women's issues and vice versa: "Here again the Eisenhower Administration gives Housewives much food for serious thought. *These are 'brain' matters! These are women's concerns!*" Other notes for the pamphlet included an emphasis on the housewife's special knowledge of cost-of-living matters: "Nobody knows better than the American housewife the practical price of politics. Nobody knows better than the American housewife that she's paying the highest price for beef in three years. . . . Nobody knows better than the American housewife that she is paying more for less." Two other drafts, titled "Adlai Stevenson Talks Sense to the American Housewife" and "Mrs. Joe Smith Talks Cents with Adlai Stevenson," clearly conveyed the image of an interested and articulate female constituency participating in a national political dialogue.[20] Hence, while focusing on inflation—an issue deemed of special interest to women as women—this appeal to housewives also stressed women's rationality as citizens.

That the Volunteers insisted on the critical judgment and rationality of women voters is not surprising given the way that they understood the nature of the "independent" or "switch" vote, a new phenomenon on the 1950s political landscape. While political scientists have traditionally cast the decline of partisan loyalty in negative terms, both parties tried to take advantage of the new trend by attracting these volatile voters to their camps.[21] Naturally, this was best done by emphasizing their positive qualities. Most interestingly, the Volunteers combined their appeal to housewives with their courting of the independent-rational voter, equating the two in the process. This is most clearly evident in the major public relations blitz undertaken by the Volunteers for Stevenson, in collaboration with the national campaign staff, in the last three weeks of the 1956 campaign.[22]

As described in a "Message to the Independent Voter," signed by the Democratic presidential candidate and published in the Volunteers newsletter, *The Bandwagon*, the undecided voter was offered positive reinforcement:

The so-called independent voter is, as we all know, the most talked-about man in American politics today. He is sometimes pictured as an indecisive fellow easily misled by slogans and beguiled by promises. . . . On the whole, it seems to me, he is quite misunderstood and in my mind's eye I have quite a different image of him.

The independent who has not signed up with either major party is, I believe, deeply aware of his political responsibilities in this world of rapid change. He recognizes, however, that there is not necessarily a conflict between practical politics and the use of the human mind.[23]

Volunteers developed various strategies to popularize this view of the independent as a responsible and intelligent voter. The national staff encouraged local clubs to organize broadcasts featuring preferably well known switchers, to purchase advertisements in local newspapers, and to display banners and placards saying, "I'm Proud to be Switching to Stevenson." As explained by Stanley Karson, a Volunteers field organizer, "Many of these 1952 Ike voters still hesitate to admit they made a mistake then. Many still want to make the socially proper decision but feel that the switcher is unpopular and a member of a tiny minority." Or as elaborated by Lemoine Skinner Jr., public relations expert for the Volunteers, the campaign launched both nationally and locally was intended to inform the public of this nationwide trend and to give it a positive aura: "to encourage the waverer who may feel it not quite loyal to switch parties, or quite respectable."[24]

As illustrated by the script for a five-minute radio broadcast prepared by the Volunteers national headquarters, housewives were central figures in this campaign to court the "honest, intelligent, middle-of-the-road" voter. The program, which focused on the wave of inflation that had plagued the national economy in the first months of 1956, argued that the economic performance of the first Eisenhower administration was nothing but "paper prosperity": "It looks good in print but very bad in our pocketbooks." It staged three "local townspeople"—a grocer, a teacher, and a housewife—two of them had voted Republican in 1952 and were considering a switch to the Democrats. As described in the instructions provided to the local committees, the switchers were to be portrayed not as "undecided" voters acting on the impulsion of the moment, but as informed citizens exercising critical judgment: "These people are challenging the local committeeman, and through him the whole [Democratic] party on the issue of prosperity." The program, centered on a dialogue between these three voters and the party representative, culminated with the reaching of a rational decision: "I voted for Eisenhower in '52. And when you come right down to it I guess I made a mistake," one of the participants was to conclude. Or, as illustrated in the text of the teacher's repartee: "From what we've discussed and the facts that you've presented—this November I'm voting for Stevenson and Kefauver."[25]

As indicated in the staging of a housewife in this radio program, the Volunteers explicitly put women at the forefront of the "Switching" campaign. Giving instructions regarding local radio programs, Skinner insisted, "Get as many participants as possible—*including the very maximum number of women*. . . . Try and get as many people as you can who voted for Eisenhower in 1952 and are switching to Stevenson, particularly women who have switched" (emphasis in original). For instance, Mrs. Fiorello LaGuardia, widow of the former New York mayor and national vice chairman of the Volunteers, publicly declared, "I am an independent voter, not—as I tell my friends—a Party girl. In 1952 I voted for Mr. Eisenhower. This year I have switched; . . . There are many independent voters like myself; we are a growing group."[26] Skinner further specified that "spot announcements by women should be scheduled heavily during the daytime to reach the women's audience."[27] Other ways to reach the "undecided women in the final crucial days" of the campaign included the distribution of cost-of-living fliers "at all points where substantial crowds gather," namely, shopping centers. As described in a document distributed by the national headquarters, "We put the facts on 'prosperity' into the hands of every woman shopper who goes to the grocery store between now and election day. . . . Organize a corps of women who will distribute the . . . fliers to shoppers during peak shopping hours on every shopping day from now until election." A last item on the national headquarters' directive to local groups included "Getting to Women on the Telephone." (It also specified to "call at a reasonable time—avoid dinner and pre-dinner hours and those times when popular TV programs are being shown.") It was in the midst of this campaign to encourage the "switch" vote that the pamphlet directed to housewives was published and that a special program—entitled "For Women Only"—was broadcast on national television.[28]

For the Volunteers national staff, which planned the October 29 broadcast, the event was to be more than a televised speech. In this short address to the nation's housewives, Stevenson would talk about issues likely to capture their vote: inflation, schools, the nuclear threat. In addition, housewives themselves were asked to play an active role by hosting a "Coffee Listening Party" to accompany the morning broadcast. Already in 1952, Volunteers had encouraged its local clubs to organize "home meetings" to discuss campaign issues, preferably at a time when Stevenson appeared on television and radio.[29] In 1956, they turned the suggestion into a systematically organized campaign event. "Invite your neighbors to join you in your home," pressed the national headquarter to the prospective hostess. "Invite as many friends and neighbors as your home will hold. Aim at reaching every woman in your neighborhood—particularly the undecided voters. Urge all your friends to do likewise." Or, as casually put by the New York Committee for Stevenson, Kefauver, and Wagner, "It is easy and fun to organize a Stevenson Get-Together. You need only a living room, a TV or Radio set, simple refreshments, friends, neighbors and relatives."

All housewives certainly had that—and Adlai would provide the rest: "A great man is your attraction." With Stevenson "talking sense" to the women of America via their television sets and radios, the guests, prompted by their hostess, were to be not only politically informed but also energized. In sample kits prepared for the TV parties, the New York Committee explained that "these Get-Togethers become a POLITICAL POTENTIAL. People are inspired to act." The kit, prepared by Alice M. Kaplan of the "Home Parties Division," even offered prospective hostesses a small pitch, complete with emphasis and intonation, to serve along with the coffee and cookies after Stevenson's speech. ("Adapt it to your needs. Use all or part of it," the organizers specified.) As envisioned by the professionals in public relations who devised the strategy, the housewife-hostess in her living room would shut off the television set and tell her friends, neighbors, and relatives:

I think the speech we have just heard is brilliant proof of why it is important to hear Adlai Stevenson as often as possible. But we need your support *to insure* that he will continue to talk on TV and Radio. This costs money. We know the Republicans have a lot of money for a lot of TV time. We can match their budget ONLY by getting many, many small contributions. A LOT OF DEMOCRATS GIVING A LITTLE CAN EQUAL A FEW REPUBLICANS GIVING A LOT. It's more democratic, too.

Ideally, the guests would open their purses and make a contribution to the campaign.[30]

The example of the 1956 "Coffee Listening Parties," and more generally that of the Volunteers for Stevenson's efforts to win the housewives' vote, raises important questions about women's relationship to party politics in the postwar period. First, the decision by the Stevenson's staff to target housewives, rather than women workers, or focus on inflation, rather than sexual discrimination on the labor market, was by no means the only option that they had available to reach the female voter. As James A. Finnegan, Stevenson's campaign manager, wrote to Harvard historian Arthur Schlesinger Jr., one of Stevenson's campaign strategists, "A number of women have pointed out that they are being completely overlooked by the candidate in respect to equal rights. I had no idea that so many of them were anxious to gain an equal footing with men but apparently there are several million who are." Finnegan's bewildered remarks might have been inspired by the letter he received from a female civil servant, complaining about the discrimination in promotion that women faced on the labor market.[31] The fact that the proportion of married women in the labor force doubled between 1940 and 1960 should have been enough to justify treating women's work as an issue.[32] Still, most women were full-time housewives, and perhaps in order to stay on familiar and safe grounds, it is that group that was chosen as most representative of 1950s women.

Another point of contention that the Volunteers' strategy raised was the role reserved to female volunteers in the campaign itself. As revealed by a three-page memorandum written by Mrs. Elizabeth Taylor, a resident of Lexington, Kentucky, and formerly national director of the League of Women Voters, to Barry Bingham, cochair of the Volunteers, at least some female volunteers were dissatisfied with the support role to which they were confined. In her memorandum she suggested an ambitious plan to make better use of women's contribution. She envisioned thousands of volunteers to be trained to discuss Stevenson's candidacy with fellow citizens and then relay the content of their conversations to the national headquarters. In Taylor's views, women constituted the perfect candidate for fulfilling this intermediary role between the citizenry and the presidential campaign staff: "The average woman in the average day talks to 21 people," she estimated. She also emphasized the intrinsic democratic and electoral value of her plan: "This poll of public opinion done BY people WITH people casually and constantly should be rewarding to party policy makers and strategists. . . . This technique gives the interviewer and the interviewee a sense of personal worth and hopefully raises the level of political discussion." For Taylor, such a contribution to the campaign would ostensibly be more rewarding than the work conventionally expected of female volunteers: "It is very frustrating to have the yen and be told that you may stuff envelopes and give money. These suggestions fortunately satisfy some but unfortunately waste much, much talent and energy." Bingham did take Taylor's proposal seriously enough to send it for consideration to several state chairmen of the Volunteers. But he ultimately rejected it, explaining that although each of the chairmen expressed interest in the proposal, it seemed to them impractical. Among the specific reasons, he mentioned that only very careful training of the volunteers could prevent "confusion and misinterpretation" in the reporting; some state chairmen had also felt that "most women . . . would be inclined to argue rather than to listen, and might therefore do more harm than good."[33]

One may suspect that the distrust that party officials (mostly male) had for "amateurs" in general, and for female volunteers in particular, also lurked behind their rejection of the plan. Indeed, as Jane Dick, herself a veteran "amateur politician" and cochair of the Volunteers, has noted, an ambiguous and tensed relationship existed between volunteers and professional politicians. Reviewing in retrospect the role that amateurs played in presidential elections since 1940, Dick discussed the resistance that they encountered in both the Democratic and the Republican Parties. "Politicians . . . regarded amateurs as a bore and a nuisance," she wrote in *Volunteers and the Making of Presidents*. Similarly, in a memorandum drafted after a meeting of the Democratic National Committee in June 1956, Bingham summarized the ambiguous nature of their relationship: "There was definite, though not enthusiastic admission that there will be a role for volunteers to play in the campaign."[34]

It is beyond the scope of this study to examine further the potential and limits for women's participation that parallel channels such as the Volunteers for Stevenson offered. Similarly, the tensions between female volunteers and male professionals at work in this particular organization have yet to be analyzed systematically. This being said, while placing limits on the role that women could play in the campaign, the Volunteers' efforts to attract independent voters and, more specifically the housewives' vote, did present a positive political model for women. By defining them as independent political thinkers, able to make connections between their day-to-day homemaking activities and the world of national politics, it presented an alternative to the strictly domestic and private role long thought to be dominant in the 1950s. Moreover, campaign events such as the "Coffee Listening Parties" politicized the home by presenting it as a site of electoral and collective discussion. But most important in the context of this study was the Volunteers' focus on rationality. In the script of the radio broadcast discussed above, for instance, although the Democratic Party representative finally gets his point across and brings the "switchers" to pledge their support for the Stevenson ticket, the decision was made after a consideration of "the facts" by voters who were ready to "challenge" the party official. This model of the informed and critical citizen parallels that prevalent in the political culture of suburban Queens.

This theme is also one that finds echoes in some of Betty Friedan's pre–*Feminine Mystique* writings. The early 1950s was a period of professional transition for Friedan. After leaving her job as a reporter for the labor press, she began writing for popular magazines.[35] Some of the early articles she wrote in the mid-1950s, while living at Parkway Village, are especially revealing of the political environment she then inhabited. One of these was "They Found Out 'Americans Aren't So Awful, After All!' " In this unpublished article, the author not only celebrates Parkway Village's multiculturalism, but describes a process by which politically timid housewives were gaining assurance through their involvement in community politics. Such is the gist of her discussion of the internal dynamics of the Village's numerous committees:

Parkway Village abounds with committees. . . . (At first these committees consisted only of American and Canadian women, and men from the other countries—they considered committees not only men's business, and our men left it to the women.) The women, of course, did most of the work—getting playgrounds built, starting a nursery school, running international potluck suppers. So pretty soon the Dutch and Indian men were getting their wives to run in their place. My Dutch friend . . . had never been on a committee before. She didn't say a word the first few meetings. At the end of the year she was running the whole show. "In my country everything is done by officials, we would not think of organizing ourselves to improve matters," she told me. "But with a committee you can do anything, are they not wonderful, committees?"[36]

American and Canadian women, in this case, had shown their neighbors—first the men, then their wives—the virtues of a female-led participatory democracy.

The women's initiative in community affairs that Friedan described above, and the assertiveness that they gained through their experience of volunteer work, figure prominently in "More than a Nose-wiper," the original draft of an article published in *Parents' Magazine* in 1957 under the title "Day Camp in the Driveways."[37] In this article, which relates the experience of housewives who organized a backyard camp for their kids, Friedan focused her investigation on Bell Park Manor and Terrace. This garden apartment, built in Hollis Hills in 1951, represented a suburban haven for lower-middle-class families. As the author described in her original draft, the residents had "paid $1,200 down to move out here, 20 minutes beyond the end of the subway line, so their kids could play in fresh air and sunshine and green grass." They were "ex-GI salesmen and postal clerks and $100–a-week accountants who'd played in the streets of Brooklyn and the Bronx themselves."[38] Unfortunately, the pastoral life promised had turned sour:

The trouble was—they had a thousand kids under eight among them—and no place out here for kids to play at all! . . . All the rest of Bell Park's fifty, long, low, red-brick and white-shuttered buildings had the same grassy lawns—chained to keep the kids off. The cement drying yards were always full of wash. The black asphalt driveways just led to garages most tenants couldn't afford to rent. And so many kids had already cracked their heads in the pintsize [*sic*] playgrounds, the swings had to be taken down. There wasn't even a Y or a library or a candy store out here at the end of Queens—just miles and miles of new little houses and raw developments as crowded with kids as theirs.[39]

Friedan's story, based on interviews with Alice Barsky, a thirty-two-year-old housewife and mother, describes how a group of energetic young housewives had "masterminded" the " 'Bell Park Manor-Terrace

Summer Day Camp'—a fabulous operation which she [Barsky] and other housing project mothers have created out of the bare asphalt driveways of their own backyard." In contrast with the published "Day Camp in the Driveways"—which was printed under the rubric "Child Rearing" in *Parents' Magazine* and which presented the case as a "parental do-it-yourself story"—the original version stresses women's accomplishment and assertiveness.[40] It is the story of how the process of dealing with the various experts involved in this project—from city officials to the young, college-educated, male directors who were hired to supervise the summer activities—led to a growing politicization.

At the outset it is clear that Alice Barsky and her neighbors were eager to defer to the authority of experts. As related by Friedan, extensively quoting Barsky,

It was "simply to get out of the house for a change" that she went to her first meeting of Bell Park mothers on "the summer problem" back four years ago [1951]. She certainly didn't expect "a bunch of ignorant housewives" (which was the way she thought of herself then) could figure it out. Like all the rest, she "ran to Spock every time the kid cried, and checked with Gesell before saying yes or no."

In spite of the class differences between herself and Barsky, Friedan described the young housewife in terms similar to her own experience. Like Friedan, Barsky was a college graduate—albeit from Hunter, not Smith—and "once . . . [had] been a bright girl." Like Friedan, she had worked during the war, although not as a reporter, but "designing bombsights" in the war industry. Five years after the end of the war, she had felt in a most immediate way the weight of the feminine mystique: "Brains! Alice Barsky didn't even feel 'like a person anymore—all that counts is how strong my back for lugging kids and groceries, and how thick my skin before my hands start bleeding from detergent.' "[41]

Eight women were present at the first committee meeting called by Pat Berkowitz to discuss the "summer problem." Against the best advice of "various experts [who] told her it would be 'impossible' " to organize a summer day camp run by volunteers, eight women "talking at once" decided to take up the challenge:

"Private day camps charge $200 or $300 a child," reported 30–year-old Mrs. Berkowitz, an optometrist's wife, "or they're run by big agencies with thousands of dollars from charities. You rent an estate with a fence around it, and indoor facilities for hot lunches, and rests, and toilets, and all kinds of equipment. You have to get a license from the Health Department, and the lady there said it would cost us $20,000 just to hire a staff. Anyhow, she said you can't run a decent day camp with 800 children."

The first task was to persuade the management of Bell Park Manor and Terrace to let them use the ground: after being told to stay off the grass, they were granted use of the driveways! They then went from door to door registering each child and collecting registration fees, and bought badminton sets and wading pools by the dozen. For Barsky, related Friedan, "It wasn't too different from comparing cans of tomatoes at the supermarket, but she felt 'absolutely liberated.' " Once the basic structure was in place, it was time to hire what Barsky called "outside experts" to handle the kids. Explained Friedan,

They themselves didn't have the time, didn't know enough, and, as Alice Barsky put it, "it'd be hard to fire each other." But it seemed even harder for nine "ignorant housewives" to hire an expert. The few who answered their ads just shook their heads when they heard "800 kids . . . driveways." A tweedy, pipe-smoking Ph.D. looked around the apartment living room at the nine women in slacks and cotton skirts, knitting, and politely inquired for whom would he be working. "Us," said Pat Berkowitz timidly. He gulped, and left. They decided a man would be more impressive, interviewing, drafted Henry Robinson [whom they had already officially put on their committee, "in case they needed a man 'to impress people' "] and gratefully hired the first man with degrees willing to take the job—promising not to "interfere" at all in the running of the camp.

In the course of that first summer of 1952, though, it became clear to the committee members that the "outside expertise" would have to be kept in check. The counselors did not know what to do with these kids; the director patronized his bosses; mothers watching from behind the venetian blinds complained that their children "[weren't] doing anything at camp." In September, Barsky called an "open meeting" for the complaining mothers and enlisted fifty of them to canvass all "850 supervisors behind the venetian blinds" and find out what they wanted. The story that Barsky told, through Friedan, is one of gradual self-assertion: "This is our chance to be something more than nosewipers and diaper changers. Work on our committee, you're an individual, you're a person, you're you. . . . If our husbands say they'll divorce us—at least, let's share the risk."[42]

Throughout the fall, winter, and spring of 1952–53, the committee members continued to work on the various technical problems involved in running a backyard summer camp. As women were "standing in front of Food Fair (the forum where most housing project decisions [were] made) with their shopping carts and baby carriages full of groceries and the kids pulling at their skirts," they decided to hire buses for the coming summer to take the kids off to nearby parks and beaches. Once more, related Friedan, after "the idea came to five female brains simultaneously," they had to deal with official authorities. With "precious baby-sitting services . . . freely offered" by their neighbors as their "contribution to camp," Pat and Alice went down to City Hall to get a license from "the day camp expert who'd made them so mad at first," Miss Lillian Margolin, chief of the Health Department's Day Camp unit. They obtained it.

The second summer, they encountered more problems with the director and counselors they hired: "They hired a director with all the progressive ideals they'd read about for 'developing the whole child.' But the counsellors he hired tended to know more about psychoanalysis than baseball. 'For warmth and affection we don't have to pay,' complained the supervisors behind the venetian blinds." The next winter, they continued to improve the camp, deciding that the children would have to learn to swim. To that effect, they had to lobby yet another city official: "Gentle Mrs. Robinson . . . spent the winter besieging the Board of Education for a high school swimming pool. A call every other day for three months, a wait in the outer office—'he'll have to get back from lunch sometime.' No self-respecting Bell Park mother would take 'unprecedented' for an answer. She got the pool, in writing."[43]

Gaining experience in dealing with "outside experts," when the time came in the spring of 1955 to hire their director for the next summer, the once self-effacing housewives adopted a different strategy:

"We've got to be more businesslike," said ex-chairman Pat, an elder statesman now on the committee. "Maybe we should stop serving coffee."
Before the applicant came in, the team would pass around his letter, noting degrees, experience—but now that was just the beginning. Mrs. Sari Berns, ex-Powers model sitting in slacks on the couch, Mrs. Dornee Robinson, ex-secretary, taking notes at the dining table, 8–months pregnant Mrs. Pat Berkowitz on the easy chair, Mrs. Alice Barsky who had just taken up knitting—would pounce on the 6–foot tweedy Ph.D. with questions that left him gasping. And if he was too suave, and didn't start asking them questions—they'd signal with their eyebrows to each other, cut the interview short, and rush to the next apartment where another team was interviewing. A man who passed the first team, had to come back and be interviewed by the full 21 camp top brass.
"Never went through such a trial in my life," said Harry Janoson, a livewire New York public school principal. . . .
He asked: "Whom will I be working for?" "Us," said the women calmly.
He's an up-and-coming big city educator, and his colleagues thought he was crazy. Despite his misgivings, he took the job—because "I was impressed, I couldn't believe such women existed." He still finds it hard to believe, working now for the second summer for his housewife bosses.[44]

In its third summer, the Bell Park Manor–Terrace Day Camp was a success. Registration was no longer done "from door to door, on foot,

but in a basement room 'like registration to vote.' " The budget committee was now handling a $40,000 budget; 870 children were taking
the bus every day to Alley Pond Park or to other outdoor activities,
leaving "not a child in the community at loose ends, only women going about their business." Even Miss Margolin, "the once dubious
social worker," was impressed by the work accomplished: " 'A true pio-
neer,' she said when she introduced this not a bit nervous housewife
from Bell Park [Alice Barsky] to speak to a national conference on
children's problems. . . . Now housewives from housing projects miles
away, and many experts too, follow Alice on a 'guided tour' through
Bell Park's 'backyard.' " Friedan concluded her twenty-page article on
a triumphant tone:

> [As the local] PTA . . . recently put on its own original musical comedy
> about "this new breed of Jill," Alice Barsky, and at least 200 others on Bell
> Park committees, recognized themselves as the heroine[,] dumped a bag of
> frozen food in her husband's arms as he came in the door from work, and ran
> out herself to "the nominating meeting."
> "Where's mommy going?" asks the little girl in the play. "She's going to be
> president," says daddy. "Of the United States?" asks her little girl. "Could be,"
> says daddy, "could be."[45]

In this account of the Bell Park mothers' accomplishment, Friedan
portrayed volunteerism as pregnant with possibilities, not only for
women who use this outlet to grow personally, but for their communities as well.

> There never was a camp like it before. But there may be many in the decade
> to come. For Alice Barsky and the other Bell Park mothers, sociologists say,
> are a new kind of pioneer—out of the social frontiers of the new suburbia
> where the birthrate is multiplying problems so fast only a parental 'do it your-
> self' can solve them. The Bell Park mothers had to solve theirs without train-
> ing and experience, without funds or facilities, without ever having been to a
> 'real camp' themselves. And if Alice Barsky isn't quite the same frustrated
> housewife she used to be—well, they say our great-great-great-grandmothers
> thrived on pioneering, too.[46]

True pioneers they were.

More accurately than her later published work, "More than a Nosewiper" reflects the dynamics at work in community politics. Women at
Food Fair making decisions about their future endeavors while kids
pulled at their skirts, or "gentle" Mrs. Robinson "besieging" the Board
of Education for a permission to use the high school pool were familiar images for the observer of grassroots politics. Equally illuminating
of her neighbors' experience as community activists was Friedan's

characterization of the defiant relationship that these "ignorant," yet resourceful, housewives entertained with experts of all kinds. Although having encountered the incredulity of social workers at the Health Department, then the condescension of the pipe-smoking Ph.D. whom they interviewed for the position of director, they succeeded in asserting their own authority—with the help of a man at first, but eventually on their own. Significantly, the success of the Bell Park "pioneers" was marked not only by the creation of the day camp but by the metamorphosis of once-ignorant housewives into experts. In brief, in this account, Friedan draws a picture of mothers who, concerned for the well-being of their children, did not hesitate to confront bureaucratic and professional expertise head on and emerged transformed in the process.

Friedan's mid-1950s writings raise interesting questions about the political consciousness of housewives at the height of "the feminine mystique." It sheds a new light on the conclusion that the author herself reached in her 1963 influential best-seller. In *The Feminine Mystique*, Friedan was concerned with exposing the oppressive nature of the domestic ideology of the time "which defined woman only as husband's wife, children's mother, . . . and never as person defining herself by her own actions in society." A housewife's personal and individual fulfillment in that context—her cure to the "terrible feeling of emptiness" that haunted her—had to be sought outside the bounds of family and home, although this by no means required the breaking of domestic bonds: "She does not have to choose between marriage and career; that was the mistaken choice of the feminine mystique." Access to the status and social respectability conferred by paid work, however, was crucial: "But even if a woman does not have to work to eat, she can find identity only in work that is of real value to society—work for which, usually, our society pays." But if being "just a housewife" was not enough, neither could "a job, any job" allow women "to grow up to their full human capacities." The "endless whirl of worthwhile community activities" was also inadequate in providing the type of long-term personal commitment and societal respect that was necessary to women's actualization as individuals. The "new life plan for women" that she prescribed was indeed very specific: only if women were to "let themselves develop the lifetime interests and goals which require serious education and training," dispose of their " 'guilty feelings' about being ambitious," and "learn to compete" could they achieve self-realization. In brief, not a job, not voluntary activities, but a career was the path toward liberation. As reflected in her call for "a national educational program, similar to the GI Bill, for women who seriously want to continue or resume their education," Friedan was not totally blind to the structural constraints that made such a solution illusory for the majority of women. But she did uncompromisingly embrace the professional ethos as not only the best but the only way for women to escape the traps of the feminine mystique.[47]

Friedan was certainly not unique in her dismissal of volunteerism or in her celebration of professionalism. But what set her aside from both critics of suburbia and twentieth-century feminists was her combination of these elements. In the 1950s, critics of postwar culture had noticed a remarkable level of volunteer activities in the new suburbs: William Whyte described Park Forest, Illinois, as "a hotbed of Participation"; Harry Henderson observed that "Nearly everyone belongs to organizations and, generally speaking, tries to be actively involved." They interpreted this active civic involvement on the part of suburbanites, however, as a sign of the moral and existential emptiness of the times—marked by the rootlessness of the organization man, the decline of individuality, and the pressures of conformity—rather than as symptomatic of a vibrant political culture.[48] Their critique of volunteerism, of course, fell short of leading to a glorification of professionalism. The latter, after all, had accompanied the rise of the modern, bureaucratic society which they identified as the source of the problem.

Friedan's project of women's liberation through professionalism was also reminiscent of generations of feminists before her who had considered access to higher education and the professions crucial to women's struggle for individual and collective advancement.[49] But unlike her feminist predecessors, whose commitment to getting fair and equal access to the professions had been accompanied by an active involvement in volunteer activities of all kinds, Friedan's celebration of professionalism was based on a rejection of volunteerism.[50] This repudiation of volunteerism that 1970s feminists also embraced was a sharp departure from the modern feminist tradition.[51]

Because of Friedan's forceful rhetoric, it is easy to forget that her indictment of female volunteerism in *The Feminine Mystique* was time-specific. In 1954, neo-Turnerian historian Stanley Elkins and political scientist Eric McKitrick had argued that the "new suburban frontier" constituted fertile ground for meaningful civic participation. As they explained, the "time of troubles" that new settlers in a community necessarily encountered gave rise to a breed of politically competent citizens.[52] Friedan suggested a similar pattern when she noted that, in the beginning of the postwar suburban migration, community involvement was both necessary and rewarding for those women who were strong, independent, and intelligent enough to seize the opportunity. But all this changed, she surmised, when the feminine mystique "hit" and community work was relegated to little more than a device to "fill time." In her words:

Like the empty plains of Kansas that tempted the restless immigrant, the suburbs in their very newness and lack of structured service, offered, at least at first, a limitless challenge to the energy of educated American women. The women who were strong enough, independent enough, seized the opportunity and were leaders and innovators in these new communities. But, in most cases, these were women educated before the era of feminine fulfillment. . . . Such a commitment in the suburbs, in the beginning at least, was likely to be on a volunteer basis, but it was challenging, and necessary.

When the mystique took over, however, a new breed of women came to the suburbs. . . . Women of this kind, and most of those that I interviewed were of the post-1950 college generation, refuse to take policy-making positions in community organizations; . . . The kind of community work they choose does not challenge their intelligence—or even, sometimes, fill a real function. Nor do they derive much personal satisfaction from it—but it does fill time.[53]

As suggested in this excerpt, central to Friedan's argument was her conception of a historical process by which women's voluntary involvement had become less rewarding and less respected. This is to be understood as part of the larger theory of declension that framed her narrative. As Joanne Meyerowitz reminded us, Friedan believed that the portrayal of women's roles in mass culture had narrowed in the late 1940s and 1950s compared with the 1930s when "women's magazines encouraged women to participate in the wider world outside the home."[54] By the late 1950s, when she researched and wrote her book, she was convinced that the era of women's fulfilling and meaningful volunteerism was past: "In some suburbs and communities there is now little work left for the nonprofessional that requires intelligence—except for the few positions of leadership which most women, these days, lack the independence, the strength, the self-confidence to take." Her conviction that "professionals have taken over most of the posts in the community requiring intelligence" drove her negative evaluation of women's ability to fulfill themselves through volunteerism as well as her call for women's entry in the professions.[55]

Whether or not this transition from meaningful to meaningless voluntary community work occurred and, if it occurred, when and why remains to be demonstrated (rather than assumed as has been the case following Friedan). As this study shows, no evidence suggests that in the latter part of the 1950s women were any less innovative and assertive than an earlier generation had been. Why then did Friedan present the experience of her generation as she did in *The Feminine Mystique*? According to Daniel Horowitz, her experience in the Rockland County

Intellectual Resources Pool, which she created in 1958 (the Friedans had left Parkway Village and moved to Rockland County in 1956), seems to have been influential in shaping her criticism of volunteerism. (The pool's main focus was to bring together public school students with professionals in the area to enrich their education.) Although the leadership of this complex organization was challenging and formative for Friedan, she apparently grew frustrated with other women involved in the group who "did not really understand the importance of the work they were doing." Horowitz identifies this moment as crucial in terms of Friedan's personal association with professional women, as well as for her own self-identification as a professional woman. As he wrote in conclusion to this section, "She had developed an antipathy to volunteer activities that were limited in scope, preferring instead women's professional efforts that sought to change society."[56]

Regardless of Friedan's personal experience and her later criticism of female volunteerism, the experience of women in the 1950s was critically and, I believe, positively shaped by their participation in such activities. As she described in her 1950s writings, this was a way for housewives to gain experience as well as self-confidence. As we have also seen in this chapter through the example of the Volunteers for Stevenson's courting of the female vote, images of women as intelligent and rational political actors were prevalent in 1950s political culture. This is not to say that men and women acted as equals in the political field: The frustrations expressed by Jane Dick, for instance, as well as those suggested by Friedan, were no doubt real. But it was from within the political arena, not from outside, that women worked to yield a measure of power and respect.

Chapter 8
Middle-Class Antiliberalism Revisited

In spite of the unitary connotations implied by the phrase the middle class, no single (or simple) definition of the term exists. One's access to property, one's position in the occupational ladder, even one's political sensibility (or lack thereof) are all criteria that have been used in reference to this quite elusive social category. For instance, in his 1951 study of the American middle classes, *White Collar*, C. Wright Mills traced a profound transformation from the "old" middle class of the nineteenth century, defined by its access to a small business or a farm, to the "new" middle class of the twentieth century, identified by both its white-collar occupational patterns and its political insignificance. Having lost the independence that property ownership conferred, and being subjected to the whims of the modern corporate bureaucracy, the white-collar man, or the "Little Man" as Mills put it, was completely devoid of political awareness and interest. They were "strangers to politics"—"idiots."

While derided in the 1950s sociological literature for its political apathy, the middle class (more specifically, its white and northern members) has been associated with an insurgent popular and populist conservatism since the 1970s. Indeed, occupational distinctions have become less relevant to discussions of the middle class, and politics more prominent. Hence the "lower middle class," as the term was coined in the early 1970s, included both blue-collar and low-echelon white-collar workers. No longer politically insignificant as Mills had deemed them, "Middle Americans" were now "politically reactionary." Both antiliberal and racist politics have thus been intimately connected with the northern, white middle class in both popular and academic representations.

Images of the middle-class produced in the 1970s are familiar. The popular television character Archie Bunker, the "average American," was racist and suspicious of political and economic elites. Construction workers who "reached their boiling point" and attacked antiwar protesters in 1970, making the *New York Times* headlines, or the main characters in films such as *Joe* or *The Deer Hunter*, were "white ethnics" prone to violence. According to sociologist Seymour Martin Lipset, they had authoritarian, antidemocratic personalities. Irrationally prejudiced and intolerant, antiliberal and populist, "the lower middle class" was at the center of what became known as the "white backlash."[1]

Since the 1970s, scholarly analysis has added both contextual and historical depth to this rejection of liberalism by white middle-class folks. Ronald Formisano and Jonathan Rieder have revealed the intricate combination of factors that led to explosions of racial hatred among the Italian and Irish Catholics who violently opposed school integration in Boston, or New York Jews who turned against racial minorities and the "liberal establishment" in Canarsie, Brooklyn. These include a strong ethnic and neighborhood identity and an acute sense of economic entrapment. Along similar lines, David Halle has argued that the middle-class status embraced by industrial workers in the 1970s was closely associated with a sharp populist resentment of those with political and economic power and a defense of racially exclusive neighborhoods and schools. (The middle-class identity that he describes is shaped by their lives away from the workplace, a relative access to material possessions, and a residence and neighborhood of quality.) This combination of racist defense of residential communities and populism can also be found in the strong opposition to racial integration that Thomas Sugrue and Arnold Hirsch have documented in Detroit and Chicago in the 1940s and 1950s. Finally, this scholarship is congruent with Michael Kazin's contention that, in the postwar period, populism has been appropriated by antiliberal groups and politicians. Taken together, this body of work reinforces the image of a reactionary middle class already well established in the 1970s; it also directly links its reactionary politics to the populist defense of home and neighborhood. The white middle class, in other words, has become synonymous with reactionary populist politics.[2]

The case of northeastern Queens allows us to reconsider this accepted paradigm. In this rapidly developing area, we find many of the dynamics that have been noted by observers of middle-class life and politics. As in Sugrue's and Halle's works, concerns for the interests of the residential community were central to local politics and middle-class consciousness in Queens. The citizens' sense of obligation toward their residential community was one of the key elements of Queens political culture. If we follow Halle's definition of middle-class consciousness as centered on issues related to the family and the residential community, it was a political manifestation of their middle-class identity. Also, an unmistakable populist sensibility—reminiscent of that described by Kazin—permeated the area's political culture. Yet, unlike many other metropolitan areas at the time, northeastern Queens remained untouched by overt racial conflicts in the 1950s. For most of the period under study, community politics cannot be reduced to racism and antiliberalism.

Racial integration, however, did become an issue in these neighborhoods when the Board of Education enacted integration plans in the early 1960s and when Mayor John Lindsay initiated his scattered-site housing program in 1966 (a program devised to promote racially and economically integrated communities). In one sense, the residents' reaction did not differ from what we've come to expect of northern, white middle-class communities. While some supported integration, the majority fiercely opposed it. But most interesting was that their response also revealed a theme expressed in community politics for two decades.

Queens citizens assessed the New York City government's policies to speed residential and racial integration with the same criteria they had used to evaluate their elected representatives throughout the late 1940s and 1950s: they considered not only the issues at stake (integration, busing, or the quality of schools and neighborhoods) but also the process involved in decision making. The local government's lack of consultation with and responsiveness to the local community was a major part of their opposition to the integration plans of the 1960s. That New York City officials were acting without appropriate knowledge of their neighborhoods, or without consulting them, was central to their criticism. This was more than a facade behind which racist animosity was hidden; it was a sore point in the state-citizens relationship that was years in the making.

As we have seen most pointedly in Chapter 3, ideological diversity rather than homogeneity characterized the citizenry of northeastern Queens. Some neighborhoods, especially those where a large Jewish population resided, had been outspoken in their support for progressive causes (including racial justice) and continued to be in the late 1950s and early 1960s. The support for school integration expressed in 1957 by parents in the Glen Oaks area is a case in point. At the time the Board of Education was accepting, albeit with reservations, the recommendations of its Commission on Integration, created in 1955, to take measures to integrate its schools.[3] The Parent-Teacher Association of P.S. 186 supported the initiative "heartily and enthusiastically." It expressed its hope "that the widest possible support be insured for a workable and realizable plan to root out segregation in the New York City public schools in the quickest possible time, and assign monies for this purpose." Their position contrasted with that taken by the Queen Chamber of Commerce, which protested "the appropriation of tax-payers' money for a program of questionable merit."[4] It also contrasted with their neighbors' reaction when it was announced that a local junior high school would be part of the integration program in the fall of 1963.

The first implementation of the Board's integration policy had taken place in 1959. It involved the voluntary transfer of almost 400 black elementary pupils from the black community of Bedford-Stuyvesant, Brooklyn, where schools were overcrowded, to underutilized schools in the all-white neighborhoods of Ridgewood and Glendale, in the southwestern part of Queens. Although the school superintendent, John Theobald, downplayed the racial motivation behind the Board's decision, emphasizing instead the need to rationalize utilization across the city, his disclaimer fooled no one. White parents organized a massive resistance against the transfer of minority pupils to their neighborhood schools, including a boycott on the first day of school that kept almost half of the white pupils home. The Parents and Taxpayers Association (PAT) was formed in the midst of this battle to "defend the principles of the neighborhood school concepts."[5]

The reaction of these white parents anticipated that of their neighbors in northeastern Queens, when a decision was announced that one of their schools would be part of the integration program. The plan, announced in the early fall of 1963, was to rezone and pair the all-white Queens Village Junior High School (J.H.S. 109) with Linden Junior High School (J.H.S. 192), a new school located in the racially mixed neighborhood of St. Albans.[6] At the September meeting of the Local School Board for Districts 51 and 52 (covering almost all of northeastern Queens), the chairman announced that "since this District does not have schools of over 50% non-white population," it would work with another district to correct the situation. The issue was further discussed at the October meeting, which already drew a crowd so large that the meeting was adjourned early by order of the New York City Fire Department. Before adjourning, however, Chairman Bernard Helfat made clear the Local School Board's intention to further the goals of integration as he stated "that in accordance with our responsibility as good Americans we will implement a policy of integration in the best possible manner; that hopefully there will be cooperation; and that many hearings and careful consideration and thought will be involved." Unfortunately, Helfat was soon to realize that neither the cooperation of local residents that he had hoped for, nor the process of meaningful public consultation that he alluded to, were forthcoming.[7]

The opposition of northeastern Queens citizens to the integration of J.H.S. 109 was loud and clear. The first extensive discussion of the plan with parents took place at the Local School Board meeting in November. In spite of the reassurance that both junior high schools offered the same programs and services (from French and Spanish classes to orchestras and experimental science programs), all the representatives of parents' and civic associations present spoke against the plan citing polls they had carried with their constituents. Although some spoke in favor of the plan, including a representative of the Jamaica branch of the NAACP, these were marginal voices. The supporters of the plan continued to speak out at subsequent meetings, but the overwhelming sentiment was clearly against it. At the December meeting, for instance, one who spoke in favor of the plan was reportedly "harangued by opponents in the audience who became noisy and emotional."[8] Two months later, Helfat recalled that "extensive police protection" was required to hold the December meeting "so violent was the opposition of the community thereto."[9]

The reasons cited by the opponents of the integration plan are familiar to students and observers of similar battles. They ranged from the practical (added busing would interfere with cultural and religious after-school instructions, maintaining parent-school relationship with a school out of the neighborhood would be difficult) to the principled ("the area is very community minded and believes in neighborhood schools"). But throughout the debate one could also hear a complaint familiar in Queens civic circles: It related to the lack of appropriate communication between the Board and parents. In this case it was articulated most clearly by Bernard Helfat, a liberal Democrat from the upper-class neighborhood of Douglaston, who, as chair of the Local School Board, had clearly supported integration and continued to do so throughout the controversy.[10]

The Local School Boards had been reorganized only recently (in 1962) in response to a major scandal involving the misappropriation and mismanagement of the city's school-construction funds. At that time, their purpose had been reasserted: They were to provide an opportunity "for effective participation by the people of the city in the government of their schools."[11] The citizens of northeastern Queens welcomed the reorganized local school boards as "an effective link between the local community and the Board of Education."[12] But in 1964, both Helfat and the local residents already seemed disillusioned. They were skeptical that the Board would make room for effective participation by the people.

In a letter to the chair of the Board of Education, dated February 4, 1964, Helfat made clear his concerns that the Local Board was ignored by the central Board—the Local Board's central function, as a consultative body, was at risk, and with it meaningful consultation between the parents and the central Board. This lack of communication with the community, argued Helfat, was manifest on a number of issues, from the assignment of full-time librarians or secretarial staff, to the paving of school yards and availability of portables. It also marred the Board of Education's integration plan.[13]

Helfat's main grievance had to do with the "repeated failures of the professional staff to co-ordinate with our Local Board. Our recommendations have often gone unheeded." Not only were the Local Board's reports "gathering dust in a file" and not being answered, but Helfat also complained that the Local Board was asked to explain the central Board's decisions to residents without appropriate information or power to affect these decisions. Regarding the request for a full-time librarian, for instance, Helfat expressed in no uncertain terms his frustration:

If past practice of the professional staff were followed, we will then either hear nothing, or we will receive a letter telling us that there are no funds for such a librarian. In either case, we will have to report to the parents at some later date that there is nothing we can do. We will not receive the courtesy of an explanation of where a librarian is justified and where not, nor is it conceivable that we will be given any discretion as to which schools should have a librarian or which should not. This problem is aggravated by the fact that the Board last year publicly announced that it had placed money in the budget for increased librarian service.

On the Local Board's request for additional secretarial help, Helfat noted that "our letter on this point, which will be sent detailing our reasoning, will normally be acknowledged and filed. No action is likely to result." On the paving of a school yard deemed necessary by parents for their children's outdoor activities: "Worst of all, we are not even consulted as to the decision. We find ourselves hard-put to maintain face before the community." On the decision to deny a portable for an overcrowded schools, "We were not advised of the reason for the denial, and normally will not be so advised. This leaves us [the Local Board] looking foolish as well as futile." Decisions of the "professional staff," repeatedly protested Helfat, were uninformed by the Local Board's opinion, and left unexplained to the Local Board's chair and members. As such, they could hardly be satisfactory to the local parents.

Helfat's questioning of the role that the central Board was expecting its local counterparts to play inevitably led him to the integration controversy. "Finally, we are distressed to find ourselves in the midst of the integration program, again with a poorly defined role." After recalling the strong opposition to the program in his district, he called for the Board "to recognize that the people of North-East Queens must be approached differently on the subject of integration than those in Manhattan." Above all, he called for the central Board to give the Local Board some latitude in responding to the situation and "bringing integration to the community." As this last statement suggests, Helfat and the other members of the Local Board in Districts 51 and 52 had openly endorsed integration, and they were committed to it still, but they also recognized that without a meaningful process of consultation they were doomed to lose the respect of local parents. On this point he noted:

> While this Local Board is willing to continue, as it has in the past, to act as the community spear-head and educational agency in the field of integration, we are distressed by your latest report on integration which again casts us in the role of buffer between the community and your Board and again gives us no authority whatsoever to adjust individual situations or even to recommend deviations from the criteria you have established. We assure you that we can serve no useful purpose in bringing integration to the community unless the community believes that there is some purpose in talking to us. If our hearings are to be merely educational, our status on this issue and on all future issues will be gravely diminished.

The fact that the central Board had reported that Queens supported the rezoning of Junior High Schools 109 and 192 in spite of the violent opposition that local residents had expressed was further mentioned by Helfat as yet another example of the Board's disregard for local communities. "This opposition was evident from the first meeting to the last, and we cannot conceive how the professional staff made the statement in its report without even consulting this Local Board."

The much debated rezoning and integration of the two junior high schools actually took place in September 1964. As reported by Helfat in March 1965, the decision to go ahead with the plan was "recommended by our [local] Board after long and bitter public hearings . . . [and] the rezoning appears to have been effected with a minimum of difficulty."[14] In September 1964, a short-lived boycott to protest forced busing organized by the citywide PAT and a newly created Bayside branch was indeed supported by some Bayside parents, but it was far from widespread. Local newspapers reported that the rate of absenteeism in local high schools was only slightly higher than usual and well below the city average. Also, the influential Northeast Queens Council for Schools, representing forty-two parent and civic organizations, openly spoke against the PAT's boycott and supported "the Board of Education's efforts to improve quality education for all children—both white and non-white—integrate the schools, and increase educational opportunities and facilities."[15] But in spite of the compliance of parents to the limited desegregation plan, and in spite of the vocal support of some for integration, the community had voiced its opinion clearly. Local community activists had a long history of conflicts with city officials over their schools. Integration carried its own racially explosive baggage. But Queens residents continued to be skeptical of the Board of Education's plans for their schools.

Although Helfat had disagreed with the position on integration taken by the parents of northeastern Queens, he continued to be sympathetic to their position as well as vocal in his criticism of the process involved in the Board's integration strategy. This can be seen in a long letter he wrote to the Board's officials, conveying his district's reaction to a massive reorganization of the public school system proposed in the wake of the Allen report. Released in May 1964, the Allen report, named for state commissioner of education James Allen Jr., criticized the Board of Education for its timid attempts at integrating schools and proposed a complex, expensive, and ultimately unrealistic plan for integrating the New York City school system. (The plan included a reorganization of the grades from six years in elementary, three years in junior high school, and three years in high school to four years at each level.) Elementary schools would remain "in the neighborhood and as close as possible to the homes of the children," therefore segregated; integration would take place in middle schools and high schools. The report also recommended a massive investment of $250 million for the construction of new high schools. The Board of Education's response to the Allen report, which was spelled out in its "Blueprint for Further Action toward Quality, Integrated Education," called for the transfer of 40,000 students starting in 1965. As Diane Ravitch explains, "It endorsed the four-year comprehensive high school and authorized large-scale shifts of sixth graders into junior high schools and ninth graders into high schools."[16] The Board's blueprint was discussed in northeastern Queens at a public forum organized by the Local School Board in March 1965 (attended by close to 1,000 people), and, as Helfat reported, the community's reaction was, once more, skeptical.

In his March 25 letter, Helfat reasserted his conviction that the Local School Boards had a crucial role to play as channels of communication between the central office and the local population. "In an effort to fulfill our role as intermediary between the Board of Education and the residents of our district, we will first report to you the sentiments of the community, from which you would otherwise be completely insulated," he wrote. His tone was clearly protective of the local residents who, once more, were reacting negatively to what he called "another untried and possibly ill-prepared program." "The public representatives who have written and spoken to us, incidentally, are for the most part responsible persons who should not be classified as illiberal or inflexible." They are "fair-minded people," he added later in the letter. The parents were concerned about the impact the plan would have on the already overcrowded high schools. No detail had been provided on the high school rezoning necessitated by the reorganization. (To further complicate the matter, the opening of the new Northeast Queens High School was scheduled for September 1966, for which yet another rezoning would be required.) But mostly the residents opposed the Board's choice to target J.H.S. 109, which had already been included in the rezoning and pairing plan of 1964. The implementation of the Blueprint for September 1965 seemed hasty to parents who were still recovering from the rezoning controversy. (As Helfat put it, the latter "has left the community exceptional[ly] sensitive to further change.") Moreover, "the change would merely accelerate by one year an integration pattern already fixed by last year's rezoning." Above all, both the parents and the Local Board felt that the program was implemented in haste, without adequate assessment of the impact it would have on the schools involved and without sufficient information communicated to the parents. The Local Board voted against the proposed Blueprint, while reasserting its support for a feasible and acceptable plan for integration: "This Local Board has consistently demonstrated its dedication to the principle of integrated education to the extent that a token gesture in that direction, which would be educationally unsound at this time, is not only unnecessary but also ill-advised."[17]

Dynamics similar to those noted in northeastern Queens were found in the western part of the borough, specifically in Local School Board Districts 47 and 48, an area including communities such as Forest Hills, Elmhurst, Corona, and Jackson Heights. There the Local Board, also chaired by a liberal Democrat who supported the goal of integration, Murry Bergtraum, tried to lead the community to accept the Board's integration plan but, as was the case in Districts 51 and 52, faced fierce opposition from parents. A strong resistance to the 1964 pairing plan had already shaken the community when the Blueprint was discussed the year after.[18] The Local Board's report on the community's views of the Blueprint, gathered at a public hearing on

March 22, echoed themes elaborated by Helfat. As reported in the minutes:

We feel that before attempting to evaluate all the comments it is only honest reporting to state that on one subject there was complete unanimity: lack of time allowed for proper study. If the New York Board of Education desires public consensus of opinion before making decisions they must distribute concrete material, not vague "plans[,]" sufficiently in advance to allow for comprehensive study prior to intelligent evaluation.

The most often mentioned single factor was time-table: the majority of the speakers both for and undecided about the general plan, felt that putting it into effect in September, 1965, did not allow sufficient time for implementation, except in the most haphazard fashion. There are so many factors involved from top administration down to the physicial [*sic*] body of the child that great care must be exerted or the program will be a chaotic failure.

That the local communities expected a well-informed approach to issues as important as integration and education, rather than "experimentation for the sake of experimentation," was further emphasized in the minutes' closing statement:

One conclusion was obvious—all, for, against, or undecided, groups have done as much study and research as time permitted, sent out questionnaires to their memberships, held study meetings, and did all they could to make dignified and intelligent reports. Most speakers presented briefs, many with additional research material attached, all of which will be kept on file by this Board.[19]

This not only echoed a theme heard for years in the dealing of Queens parents with city officials but reflected the comments of Reverend Burton Davison of Elmhurst Methodist Church, quoting from the Book of Isaiah, during the 1964 pairing debate: "Come now, let us reason together."[20]

Both Local School Boards, in northeastern and western Queens, were supportive of the goal to provide quality, integrated education for all children. Both were faced with forceful resistance by the parents in their districts to the Board's plans for integration. Both understood and conveyed to the Board that more than racial fears were involved in the parents' resistance. In Bergtraum's words in 1965, the crisis New York City then faced "demands hard work, logical, well thought out solutions to difficult problems." Queens parents did not feel that this was what city officials were offering.[21]

The attempts to promote school integration in 1964 and 1965 had given Queens citizens the impression that New York City bureaucrats were acting hastily to address social problems and imposing half-baked programs without consulting them. The debate over residential integration reinforced that view. In 1966, shortly after his election as mayor of New York City, John Lindsay announced his "scattered-site" public housing program, which promised to build low-income projects, whose beneficiaries would be African Americans, on vacant lots within stable, white middle-income communities. As explained by Jewel Bellush, this was "a deliberate policy aimed at producing a community integrated along racial, as well as economic, lines."[22]

The program is perhaps best known for the opposition that it encountered in the Italian and Jewish neighborhoods of Corona and Forest Hills, in western Queens, where one of the proposed sites was located.[23] But the residents of Kew Gardens Hills, in northeastern Queens, also rallied against Lindsay's initiative when a site located near the racially integrated neighborhood of Flushing Suburban was announced. The Flushing Suburban Civic Association (FSCA), a group representing white and black home owners in the area and chaired at the time by an African American, Aldean Moore, led the neighborhood fight against the city. The vacant lot targeted by the city, a wooded five-acre plot at 71st Avenue and 160th Street, was chosen for the construction of the six ten-story buildings to house 360 families.

The area had long been a bastion of progressive politics and continued to be so. But the choice of their community for a low-income project, argued Moore, threatened the existence of their already integrated community. Leading a delegation of 250 residents to City Hall in May 1966, Moore explained the residents' position. As reported in the *Kew Hills News*:

Leaders of the group expressed the community's strong desire to keep the excellent racial balance of the area, and of the schools serving it, as it now stands. A low income project, with its high proportion of minority groups would result in changing the area into a ghetto, they feel. "White families would begin moving out and the process would be completed by the usual block-busting techniques," Mr. Moore fears. Residents stressed the problem[s] that further congestion of this already highly populated area would bring, particularly mentioning school seating and transportation.

Maintaining the viability of their lower-middle-class, racially mixed community and avoiding further overburdening of their public services were the residents' main concerns. They were fully aware that they were stepping into a mined terrain and that their position would be unpopular with some, yet from their neighborhood-based point of view, neither racial nor economic integration would be well served by this initiative. As further explained in the community newspaper, "Mr. Moore stated that he anticipated opposition from various civil rights groups at next month's hearing. 'Unfortunately, although those who support the plan for this new housing may have the best of intentions, they do not really know the facts about this particular neighborhood that they are hoping to integrate. Our neighborhood already is integrated. Let's not ruin it.' "[24]

"They do not really know the facts," and they failed to consult those who do. This was also the position taken by Queens borough president Mario Cariello at the City Planning Commission's public hearings on this and two other proposed sites. The "Lindsay administration's government-by-guesswork," he charged, its failure "to gather the grass-root opinions he professes to seek but really shuns," was leading to ill-advised decisions. Moreover, as Moore himself had emphasized, Cariello insisted that investment in public services had to accompany demographic growth. For the residents of northeastern Queens, the city had failed to maintain that delicate balance ever since the 1940s. In Cariello's words, "In addition to all these factors, I must repeat, and repeat over and over as often as is necessary, that new housing in Queens—public or private—cannot be considered until Mayor Lindsay recognizes the injustices done to our borough over the years and the crying need for TOTAL PLANNING." The tone and emphasis (the capitalization was his) are revealing of a long-standing frustration.[25] Finally, the borough president spoke a language familiar to his constituents when he "call[ed] upon Mayor Lindsay to sit down immediately with me and other chosen representatives of the people of Queens, to discuss our problems factually. Only then can progress be made in new housing, or any other field."[26]

As Jewel Bellush has noted in his study of the scattered-site controversy, many sites identified by Lindsay's staff were indeed poorly chosen, including the Flushing one.[27] The twelve-site package presented shortly after the mayor's election in 1966 had been put together hastily and with no prior consultation with the borough presidents. The attempt to bypass these powerful players in New York City politics was deliberate on the part of Lindsay's aides. They were young Manhattan reformers who saw themselves as defenders of a citywide "public interest"; the borough presidents, in their view, were much too sensitive to the pressures of specific communities interested only in their own particular interests. In Bellush's words, "From the view point of reformers, the borough president represented only a segment of the city; he was therefore more parochial in outlook, easy prey to the narrower, more selfish interests opposed to public housing."[28] The attempt to push for social reforms by ignoring the realities of local neighborhoods, where ironically many reformers and progressive citizens themselves resided, was bound to backfire.[29]

A complex set of interrelated factors were at play in the residents' resistance to Lindsay's programs. Low-income housing was associated with poverty, ghettos, crime, and delinquency. Racial (and racist) fears were often related to these anxieties about economic and social status (but not always, as in the case of Flushing Suburban, where the residents wanted to preserve their racially integrated community). But overarching this already explosive situation was the decision on the part of Lindsay's reformers, and the Board of Education in the case of school integration, not to involve local communities or their representatives in the decision-making process. In light of what we have seen in the previous chapters, we know that the residents had felt, for almost two decades by then, that the reality of their particular neighborhoods was ignored by city bureaucrats. Not only was their opinion often disregarded but the structural needs of their residential communities were ignored. Had the Lindsay administration and the Board approached the integration policy in a truly democratic fashion the outcome would probably not have been different. Perhaps the fate of the 1960s' integration crisis was already sealed by two decades of frustrating encounters between suburban citizens and their government.

Conclusion

After World War II, social critics and commentators deplored the impact that the rapid expansion of suburbia had on their fellow Americans. The burgeoning of mass-produced suburbs was symptomatic of a larger malaise: The development of mass society, with its homogenizing effect, was creating a new breed of Americans. David Riesman categorized them as other-directed individuals who abdicated self-direction for the sake of social conformity; C. Wright Mills compared them to the Greek idiots, private individuals uninterested in the collective life of their communities; Betty Friedan, drawing inspiration from Riesman and a host of other suburban critics, urged housewives to escape the trap of domestic, consumerist mass society. To be sure, some authors (Mills and Friedan especially) were critical of the society that produced such automatons; nevertheless, their analyses posit ordinary Americans as victims, devoid of agency and incapable of resisting the forces at work in postwar America.[1]

Until recently, the historical scholarship on the post–World War II era reproduced the analysis suggested by contemporary critics. For instance, an older set of studies in the history of popular culture and mass consumption attributed hegemonic power to the corporate-advertiser nexus, leaving little room for the historical agency of ordinary people.[2] The work of most feminist historians until the 1990s reinforced the image of apolitical domesticity publicized by Friedan.[3] Finally, developments such as the rise of professional expertise and the bureaucratization of political institutions (related phenomena which started in the late nineteenth century but accelerated after World War II) have also been interpreted as marking the end of meaningful democratic participation. As Harry C. Boyte explained in his analysis of the decline of grassroots democracy, a transfer of power from ordinary citizens to a managerial-political elite occurred in the last century: "In the twentieth century Americans handed over to experts, technicians, and professionals the power to make the key decisions about our 'commonwealth.' "[4] In this narrative, the majority of Americans, especially those of middle-class status and women, are portrayed as retreating to the private sphere of consumption and domesticity and abdicating to experts their responsibilities as citizens.

The experience of the residents of suburban Queens in the immediate postwar era forces us to reject this accepted paradigm, as do a number of newer studies in the broad and rich field of twentieth-century history. The works of the contributors to Joanne Meyerowitz's anthology, *Not June Cleaver,* show the diversity and complexity of women's experience in the 1950s. The myth of apolitical domesticity is shattered by evidence of a variety of public and political involvement. Rosalyn Baxandall and Elizabeth Ewen's *Picture Windows* debunks the myth of the homogenized and conformist postwar suburbs. Thomas Sugrue's study of racial relations in Detroit shows the importance of ordinary Americans' collective action in shaping their social and political environment immediately after the war, as does Andrew Hurley's documentation of grassroots environmentalist activism in Gary, Indiana. The contributors to Burton Bledstein and Robert Johnston's anthology on the American middle class document the complexity and the political importance of this vast, diverse, and grossly misunderstood social formation. All these, and more, form a provocative and exciting body of material which historians now have to weave into a revised paradigm. How did the experience of Queens suburbanites resemble or depart from that of their contemporaries, as historians are now reconstructing it? How does it reflect broader trends in the politics of the postwar middle class? Examining these questions, and more generally discussing the representativity of this case study for our renewed understanding of postwar history, is our task now.[5]

In the preceding pages I have presented a number of observations about the political consciousness of Queens suburbanites and the political environment in which they operated. First, I identified them as political actors and citizens, that is, individuals who showed an interest and took part in the collective life of their communities. Both community newspapers and documents found in municipal archives (for instance, letters from Queens residents to city officials) provide ample evidence of a dynamic network of citizens' groups in northeastern Queens. The organizations in which Queens active residents participated ranged from PTAs to home owners' and tenants' associations, to religious, fraternal, political, and veterans' organizations. Whether these organizations were indigenous to the local community itself (as

most PTAs and civic associations were, albeit with connections to a
larger structure) or local branches of citywide, state, or national organizations (as was the case for the Democratic Party or veterans' organizations), they shared a clear understanding that their viability was
directly tied to their relevance to issues affecting the residential community. The issues that galvanized the political energy of Queens suburbanites were those affecting their homes and neighborhoods. This is
not to say, of course, that other political issues were of no interest to
Queens residents; many were also active, for instance, in union politics or civil rights groups. But it was through community politics that
they acted on their political consciousness and interests as *suburbanites*.

The first set of questions then becomes: How representative of postwar suburbanites were Queens active citizens? Were there elements in
the location or development of northeastern Queens as a suburb, or in
the demographic composition of its population, that may have created
an unusually high level of political activity among its residents? Reviewing briefly the elements that distinguish this area from other suburban areas, as well as the points of similarities, is helpful in assessing
its representativity.

As I mentioned in the introduction, northeastern Queens is located
within the legal and administrative limits of New York City. This fact
in itself distinguishes the area from a more typical suburb which most
authors define as an independent administrative entity. What made
this area of New York City suburban, I argue, following a loose (and
resident-centered) meaning of the term, were its pastoral and family
environment and its proximity to the city center. Northeastern Queens
in the 1940s and 1950s (less so in the 1960s and after, when density increased) offered suburban living within the limits of New York City.
Morever, many of its neighborhoods were new—large sections of
northeastern Queens represented what some authors called "the new
suburban frontier." What impact did the particular nature of northeastern Queens as a "suburb within the city" and its relatively young
character have on the political involvement of its residents?

Few studies of suburbia provide a systematic analysis of the factors
that hindered or encouraged the political participation of suburbanites. In 1954, Stanley Elkins and Eric McKitrick pointed to the early
stage of suburban development (a "time of trouble") as especially favorable to residents' political participation: urgent material needs required their public involvement. This analysis partly applies to the
case of northeastern Queens, where residents were sorely concerned
with securing basic needs for their communities. In our case, however,
the "time of trouble" was not limited to the early stage of suburban de-

velopment, but became endemic. It was a structural problem rather than one that quickly got resolved as these communities matured.[6]

The fact that the residents of northeastern Queens competed for resources in the large administrative entity of New York City no doubt explained the difficulty they encountered in securing many of their immediate needs. Indeed, long and sustained struggles were necessary before a request was granted, and sometimes it was left unfulfilled. This was due to a number of factors. The distribution of resources in the large metropolis from the 1930s to the 1960s was geared toward large infrastructural projects (such as highway construction), often at the expense of neighborhood needs.[7] This was compounded by a snobbish attitude, bordering on contempt, held in key circles of the city's bureaucracy and political elite toward "local" and "parochial" interests. As Roger Sanjek has noted in a similar context, this "cosmopolitan" disdain of "local" and "parochial" values, which sociologist Robert Merton articulated in 1949, was especially acute toward the neighborhoods of the "outer boroughs" where the majority of working-class and lower-middle-class New Yorkers lived (as opposed to the city's center in downtown and midtown Manhattan).[8]

That housewives were often those to lead delegations of citizens (especially at daytime hearings) and more generally to present the neighborhoods' concerns to policy makers might have hampered the effectiveness of their struggles. As Robert Caro suggested in his thorough analysis of political struggles in New York City in the age of Robert Moses, the credibility of housewives as serious political players was probably minimal in the eyes of bureaucrats and politicians. For instance, his description of a protest led by "New York's most prestigious and influential private citizens," by "men [who had] influence on New York's affairs," was introduced thus: "This was no protest that was going to go unheard. This was no circulating of petitions by a group of housewives out in Flushing." One can only imagine the reception such groups received when approaching policy makers armed with statistics gathered by, "counting little noses." The dismissal of neighborhood-based concerns and local expertise that we have seen expressed by the Board of Education representatives, or by the traffic commissioner, were not explicitly framed in gendered terms, but it is likely that the gender and status (as housewives) of the community main spokespersons played a role. Female community activists who insisted on downplaying their femininity when addressing policy makers (by emphasizing their rational arguments rather than maternal instinct, for instance) probably understood too well the dynamics at work and acted accordingly. In other cases, such as the struggle against the civil defense campaign documented by Dee Garrison, or that of Women Strike for Peace against nuclear escalation analyzed by Amy Swerdlow, similar groups of white middle-class women emphasized their feminine and their maternal identity and did so effectively. But the day-to-day lobbying involved in securing basic community needs was a different kind of struggle, one that included, but that could not be limited to, sensationalist public demonstrations.[9]

Finally, although the borough president who represented their interests had power, it was mostly a veto power used to block rather than to shape policy. Hence, devoid of a direct and influential role in the shaping of policies, Queens residents and their political representatives adopted a defensive position, reacting to decisions affecting their lives rather than actively shaping these decisions.[10]

That Queens suburbanites had to deal with the large and unsympathetic New York City bureaucracy directly affected the effectiveness of their political involvement, but not their level of civic and political commitment. The point needs emphasis given the common belief that the bureaucratization of politics led to a general depoliticization of ordinary citizens. As decision-making centers become more complex and staffed by professional experts, this narrative goes, popular participation declines. This paradigm was applied indirectly to the analysis of suburban politics by Robert Wood in 1958. The small scale of administratively independent suburban towns facilitated direct participation in local affairs, he argued, further linking this tradition of "localism" (or participation in local political institutions) to the older Jeffersonian ideal of self-government.[11] Our case suggests in contrast that the direct participation of ordinary citizens in local affairs was by no means discouraged by the size or apparent inaccessibility of political institutions, even though effectiveness probably was. The New York City bureaucracy was imposing and often difficult to move. Yet it did not silence or disempower Queens citizens.

In addition to the administrative and political context, the built environment and population of northeastern Queens must be considered in assessing the representativity of this case. The type of housing available in the area was more diverse than in other well-known suburbs. Few single-family houses, attached or detached, were available in Queens below $8,000, as could be found in Levittown between 1947 and 1949.[12] However, the willingness on the part of New York State and New York City officials to assist the cooperative housing experiments of the late 1940s and early 1950s allowed many families of blue-collar workers and low-echelon white-collar workers to afford a slice of the "suburban dream." That they were doing so in an attached two-story and cooperatively owned building, rather than a single-family detached house, mattered less to these families with young children than the ability to live in a relatively pastoral environment. Also, an important number of migrants to northeastern Queens in the late 1940s were families of professionals and managers who moved to newly built middle- to high-end garden apartments. These two groups joined the larger number of families who owned the more typical single-family dwelling. As a whole, Queens was neither the "typical" Levittown suburb, nor the well-known Park Forest immortalized by William Whyte, nor the alternative cooperative communities imagined by housing reformers. It was a combination of all of these.

In turn, this diversity in the built environment contributed to the socioeconomic diversity of the population. Northeastern Queens was home to a cross-section of the vast middle class, ranging from blue-collar workers to professionals. If David Halle is correct in emphasizing occupational diversity as the hallmark of the postwar suburb, then Queens was not unique but a representative case.[13]

Along with this socioeconomic diversity came a significant cultural and religious diversification. While the racial composition of the population remained fairly stable (with the exception of the Flushing Suburban area), the migration of Jews to the area was noticeable. As we have seen, the neighborhoods where a significant number of Jewish families lived (large enough to create institutions such as Jewish Centers, for instance) tended to embrace ideologically progressive causes such as racial integration, civil liberty, and international peace.

Taken together as a combination of diverse neighborhoods, northeastern Queens offers a rich opportunity for comparative analysis. The fact that this case combines different groups of people operating in more or less the same environment adds to its richness. Were neighborhoods of small home owners more or less politically active than upper-class tenants or lower-middle-class residents of cooperative housing? Were Jewish families carrying the torch of civic involvement while their Gentile neighbors remained politically apathetic? No such conclusions can be drawn from this analysis of suburban Queens. Regardless of differences in their status as home owners, tenants, or cooperative owners; regardless of differences in their occupation or religious and cultural identification; regardless of their position on the controversial issues of racial justice or McCarthyism; Queens residents were all faced with a similar lack of public services. And, most strikingly, they all reacted in a similar fashion by organizing collectively as neighbors, building coalitions among different groups (for instance, when home owners' associations worked together with tenants' groups) to secure what they all considered essential needs. The high level of civic activity as well as the type of arguments and strategies that community activists used in their struggle against city hall was common to all.

In only one case during the period of twenty years that we examined were the residents of northeastern Queens confronted with choosing between seemingly competing needs. As examined in Chapter 2, the controversy surrounding the construction of publicly assisted housing for moderate-income families in the late 1940s involved those faced with an acute housing shortage and those confronted with overcrowded schools and increased density. Central to shaping this acrimonious debate was the local and national network of realtors and builders who had a vested interest in keeping the state out of the housing industry. Many Queens citizens who jumped on the anti-public housing bandwagon were probably manipulated by the real estate lobby's campaign, which was widely publicized through the daily newspapers. Yet an important reason why citizens opposed the controversial projects was their concern for the lack of public services. They felt that in the absence of concerted planning further residential development would exacerbate the shortage of adequate public services. The concerns of this last group were, I believe, most representative of the history and political culture of suburban Queens. Residents of northeastern Queens had fought for improved public services from the very beginning of the area's residential development (in the 1930s) and they continued to do so into the 1960s. As in the late 1940s, when the politics of residential needs became embroiled in the sensitive debate over public housing, in the 1960s it was imbricated in the explosive debate over racial integration. Community needs, which had remained a constant preoccupation during the 1950s, were now enmeshed with racial politics.

This brings us to the second set of questions that this analysis of suburban Queens raises. How should one assess the defense of residential needs in the broader context of New Deal liberalism? Does the case of Queens confirm or qualify the dominant scholarly interpretation, which associates community politics with an antiliberal stance?

The type of community politics that I examine in this study has been given a bad press—and for good reasons. From the older work of Charles Abrams to a flurry of recent studies on grassroots opposition to residential integration—Mike Davis in Los Angeles, Thomas Sugrue in Detroit, Theresa Mah in San Francisco, Arnold Hirsch in Chicago, Jonathan Rieder in Canarsie, Brooklyn, or Ronald Formisano in Boston—the defense of neighborhood interests has revealed racist and antiliberal sentiments.[14] In his study of Detroit, for instance, Sugrue noted that community organizations which were historically concerned with a variety of issues aimed at securing services for the neighborhood—issues very similar to those that concerned Queens residents—became, in the 1940s, single-issue organizations aimed at opposing racial integration: "Increasingly, they existed solely to wage battles against proposed public housing sites and against Blacks moving into their neighborhoods." A politics of "defensive localism," or "reactionary grassroots populism" as he puts it, mobilized the energy of Detroit's whites as they fought to protect their neighborhoods from blacks and their liberal allies. The story that Sugrue tells here is of an explosive combination of neighborhood politics, racism, antiliberalism, and populism. In the name of "protecting" their residential communities, white Detroiters acted upon their fears of racial integration and attacked liberal politicians for disregarding the rights of "all the people" to defend those of a "minority" of black residents.[15]

The sentiment expressed by white Detroiters is reminiscent of the populist sensibility described by David Halle and Michael Kazin. Analyzing the political consciousness of white workers in the 1970s, Halle uncovered a strong conviction that those with political and economic power—and especially politicians, who are considered "dishonest and corrupt"—act against the interests of "the people."[16] In his work on populism and grassroots conservatism in the twentieth century, Kazin also argues that, since the late 1940s, populist rhetoric has been appropriated by the antiliberal right.[17] In these studies, white middle-class neighborhood politics and the rhetorical appeal to "the people" and "the community" have become synonymous with the defense of racial exclusion.

The fact that many of the most visible, and best documented, instances of political intervention on the part of ordinary Americans have been related to racial issues has led to the impression that the sole purpose of community politics on the part of the white working class and middle class in the postwar era was to defend an antiliberal agenda. (An exception to this is the work of Andrew Hurley on environmentalism in Gary, Indiana, where we see a liberal middle-class citizenry lobbying for governmental regulation of industrial polluters.) But as Robert Johnston reminds us in his conclusion to *The Middling Sorts*, middle-class politics is neither intrinsically reactionary nor progressive. The same is true of the concern for residential needs and the populist language of grassroots democracy. The middle-class citizenry in suburban Queens was a broad, diverse, and internally divided constituency. Some harbored racist and antiliberal sentiments (and would no doubt have acted on them if racial integration had "threatened" their neighborhoods, for instance), but others aligned themselves with a progressive agenda.

What position then did Queens suburban residents occupy on the spectrum of postwar liberalism? Turning from racial to economic liberalism, one could argue that these suburban citizens were to the left of the postwar consensus. This is reflected, most centrally, by their demands for better metropolitan planning to ensure that public services match the pace of residential development. This was at the core of their definition of economic liberalism. For these citizens, the success of the postwar economy was measured not only in terms of income and conditions of employment but in terms of access to a residence and neighborhood of quality. A decent home at a reasonable cost, well-maintained apartments at a stable rent, and adequate public services were all ingredients that they considered essential to a real economic democracy. At a time when the private enterprise and its well-organized national lobbies (including the real estate industry) were actively working to limit the scope of state intervention in the nation's economy and society, Queens citizens were pressing New York policy makers to devote greater attention and funds to neighborhood needs. These two forces were working at cross purposes.

As deeply grounded in New Deal liberalism as they were (both on the issue of the state responsibility for its citizens and on the assumption that economic growth was such that their needs should be provided for), Queens citizens came to reject their government's attempt to redress racial injustice. In 1964 and again in 1967, most residents rejected the Board of Education and the mayor's plans for school and residential integration. But in the midst of this racially charged debate, an old refrain could be heard—even from those who actually supported the goal of integration: Policy makers were ignorant of the reality of specific neighborhoods and disrespectful of grassroots opinion. It was, indeed, the elitist and bureaucratic model of political decision making which was crucial to the modern redefinition of the role of the state that eventually turned them away from New Deal liberalism. In the late 1940s and early 1950s, when young families embarked on their suburban journey, they were optimistic not only that the state would support them in their effort to build a residential environment of quality, but that policy makers would listen to what informed and public-minded citizens had to say on the matter. By the 1960s, they knew that this was a naive assumption. Years of struggles to secure what they felt were basic, socially recognized needs shaped a growing disillusionment with the political process itself.

Appendix:
Queens Community Newspapers

The *Bayside Times* started publication on July 2, 1935. It was owned by the Bayside Times Publishing Corporation, which also published the *Broadway-Flushing Times*, starting in 1936, the *Little Neck-Douglaston Times*, which was combined with the *Bayside Times* in 1946, and the *Glen Oaks News*, starting in July 1954. Of all the weeklies consulted for this study, the *Times* was the only one owned by a chain. In November 1950, it was sold for five cents a copy (two dollars for a yearly subscription) and distributed in Bayside, Bayside West, Auburndale, Flushing Manor, Broadway-Flushing, Bayside Hills, Oakland Gardens, Bell Park Gardens, Alley Pond Park, Little Neck, Douglas Manor, Douglaston, and Fresh Meadows. Its motto was "More than a newspaper—a community service."[1]

When first published in January 1948, the *Meadow Lark* was freely distributed to the 3,500 families living in the area including and immediately surrounding the New York Life's Fresh Meadows Development, where editor-publisher Leonard H. Kanter resided. Six months later, the *Lark* was sold for five cents a copy. In November 1949, 15,000 copies were printed. A year later, with seven members on its staff, it served the following communities of home owners: Fresh Meadows, Cunningham Crest, North Cunningham Crest, Jamaica Estates, Jamaica North, Flushing-Hillcrest, Hollis Hills, Surrey Estates, Bayside Hills. At the same time, it served the following garden apartments in addition to the Fresh Meadows Development: Northcrest Gardens, Oakland Gardens, Bell Park Gardens, and Alley Pond Park. On February 1, when it extended its readership to tenants and home owners of Glen Oaks, Bellerose, and Floral Park, the "largest circulated weekly in Queens" (its motto) then had twenty-four pages. It was renamed the *Long Island Herald* in October 1951. Harold J. Feldman was publisher in 1953.[2]

The *Glen Oaks News* was first published in June 1948, shortly after Glen Oaks Village, Gross-Morton's garden-apartment development, opened. Its editor was Sylvia Corliss, a Village resident. It was only in

January 1952 that the editor-publisher, then Abner Kohn, stopped the free distribution of the *News* to every Village family. (The January 1952 issue is also the first issue available at the Queens Borough Public Library.) In March 1953, the eight-page *News* was sold for five cents at the newsstand or for a yearly subscription of two dollars. It was distributed in Glen Oaks, Bellerose, Floral Park, New Hyde Park, Beech Hills, and Deepdale. Its motto was then "the suburban weekly with the urban approach." Robert and Sue Barasch bought the *News* in October 1953, and then sold it to the Bayside Times Publishing Corporation in July 1954.[3]

The *Home Town News*, first published in May 1949, had a circulation of 15,000 in January 1956 at a time when it was still distributed freely. (It is available at the Queens Borough Public Library from November 10, 1954 only.) Two years later, it was sold at a nominal cost of five cents per copy and served College Point, Malba, Whitestone, Beechhurst, Clearview, Robinwood, Flushing Manor, Flushing, Bay Terrace, Bayside, and Little Neck. Louis G. Condit was publisher, Edward Lonergan was managing editor, and Marion A. Condit was business manager.[4]

The first issue of *Pomonok News* was published in September 1952, serving Pomonok Houses, Electchester, and Campus Hall. The circulation rapidly grew from 6,000 copies in September to 7,000 in October, when Dara Gardens was added to its area of distribution, and 8,000 in December, when its readership extended to the whole Kew Gardens Hills area. For the first few months, until May 1953, Irving Rosenblatt was publisher, Samuel Schleifer was editor and advertising manager, and Muriel Kenton was associate editor. In September 1953, when Robert J. Kenton became publisher, the newspaper changed its name to *Kew Hills News*. It then had a circulation of 10,000. In October 1966, 13,700 copies were published.[5]

Notes

Introduction

1. The public role played by women at a time when they were defined, culturally, as domestic creatures is well documented for the Victorian period. This vast literature and its implications for our understanding of politics has been reviewed, for instance, by Paula Baker in "The Domestication of Politics: Women and American Political Society, 1780–1920," *American Historical Review* 89 (June 1984): 620–47.

2. Burton J. Bledstein reviews the shortcomings of some of the "objective" indices traditionally used to define the middle class as well as the lack of an adequate theoretical framework for identifying and interpreting this historically changing category in his contribution to *The Middling Sorts: Explorations in the History of the American Middle Class* (New York: Routledge, 2001), which he edited with Robert D. Johnston. In the same volume, Sven Beckert notes a great deal of confusion surrounding the term *middle class*, which has been used in reference to a range of socioeconomic groups (286). The work of David Halle documents especially well the connection that ordinary Americans (in this case, blue-collar workers in New Jersey in the 1970s) have established between one's status as a member of the middle class and one's place of residence. See *America's Working Man: Work, Home, and Politics among Blue-Collar Property Owners* (Chicago: University of Chicago Press, 1984).

3. T. H. Marshall and Tom Bottomore, *Citizenship and Social Class* (1950; London: Pluto Press, 1992), 8. This economic right was in addition to the more conventional civil and political rights, which were taken for granted by white Americans in the 1950s (as was not the case for African Americans); hence they were not salient in the residents' articulation of their citizenship (the population of northeastern Queens was predominantly white in the 1950s).

4. Judith N. Shklar, *American Citizenship: The Quest for Inclusion* (Cambridge: Harvard University Press, 1991), 5.

5. Many students of suburbia have noted the extent of suburbanites' civic involvement. William H. Whyte Jr. described Park Forest, Illinois, as "a hotbed of Participation" in his classic, *The Organization Man* (New York: Simon and Schuster, 1956), 317. Harry Henderson observed that in the new massproduced suburbs such as Levittown, Long Island, "Nearly everyone belongs to organizations and, generally speaking, tries to be actively involved" ("Rugged American Collectivism," *Harper's Magazine*, December 1953, 81). In *Suburbia: Its People and Their Politics*, Robert C. Wood also emphasized the active participation

of suburbanites in local civic and political life (Boston: Houghton Mifflin, 1959), 115. Except for the latter, however, this heightened civic activism was interpreted as a symptom of larger social ills (such as the pressures of conformity and the decline of individuality), rather than as a sign of a vibrant and healthy political community. A recent historical analysis of suburbia, Rosalyn Baxandall and Elizabeth Ewen's *Picture Windows: How the Suburbs Happened* (New York: Basic Books, 2000), also provides evidence of suburbanites' political activities (144, 152–57).

6. Daniel Horowitz provides a helpful analysis of the producer ethic in *Vance Packard and American Social Criticism* (Chapel Hill: University of North Carolina Press, 1994). See also Catherine McNicol Stock, *Main Street in Crisis: The Great Depression and the Old Middle Class on the Northern Plains* (Chapel Hill: University of North Carolina Press, 1992); Lizabeth Cohen, "Citizens and Consumers in the Century of Mass Consumption," in Harvard Sitkoff, ed., *Perspectives on Modern America: Making Sense of the Twentieth Century* (New York: Oxford University Press, 2001), 145–61.

7. C. Wright Mills, *White Collar: The American Middle Classes* (New York: Oxford University Press, 1951), esp. introduction and chap. 15, "The Politics of the Rearguard." "They are strangers . . ." is from 328. See also his essays "The Middle Classes in Middle-Sized Cities" and "Mass Media and Public Opinion," in *Power, Politics, and People* (New York: Oxford University Press, 1963), 274–91, 577–99; *The Power Elite* (New York: Oxford University Press, 1956); and "On Reason and Freedom," in *The Sociological Imagination* (New York: Oxford University Press, 1959). On the Frankfurt School, see Martin Jay, *Permanent Exiles: Essays on the Intellectual Migration from Germany to America* (New York: Columbia University Press, 1985). For good reviews of the literature on the 1950s, see Joanne Meyerowitz, ed., *Not June Cleaver: Women and Gender in Postwar America, 1945–1960* (Philadelphia: Temple University Press, 1994), 2–5, and Thomas J. Sugrue, "Reassessing the History of Postwar America," *Prospects* 20 (1995): 493–509.

8. See David Riesman with Nathan Glazer and Reuel Denney, *The Lonely Crowd: A Study of the Changing American Character* (New Haven, Conn.: Yale University Press, 1950), and Whyte, *The Organization Man*. See also Sloan Wilson's popular novel, *The Man in the Grey Flannel Suit* (New York: Simon and Schuster, 1955). For a useful historical analysis of this generation of social critics, see Richard H. Pells, *The Liberal Mind in a Conservative Age: American Intellectuals in the 1940s and 1950s* (New York: Harper & Row, 1985), 180–261.

9. As she explained in an application for funding for what would later become *The Feminine Mystique*, "I'm working on a book . . . about feminine conformity," thereby placing her work in the context of contemporary critics of suburban culture. See "Application for Funding for FM, 1959," box 20a, folder 707, Betty Friedan Papers, Schlesinger Library, Radcliffe Institute, Harvard University, Cambridge, Mass. Daniel Horowitz noted the influence that critics of suburbia, especially David Riesman, had on the author. See his "Rethinking Betty Friedan and *The Feminine Mystique*: Labor Union Radicalism and Feminism in Cold War America," *American Quarterly* 48 (March 1996): 23–24.

10. *The Feminine Mystique* (1963; New York: Dell, 1983) and "The Way We Were—1949," in *It Changed My Life: Writings on the Women's Movement* (New York: Dell, 1976). The quotations are from 18 and 14, respectively.

11. Meyerowitz, ed., *Not June Cleaver*; Daniel Horowitz, *Betty Friedan and the*

Making of The Feminine Mystique*: The American Left, the Cold War, and Modern Feminism* (Amherst: University of Massachusetts Press, 1998); Baxandall and Ewen, *Picture Windows.*

12. Administrative and political separation from the city is often cited as a defining element of a suburb. However, as J. John Palen noted, not all areas "suburban in appearance and lifestyle" match this definition. See *The Suburbs* (New York: McGraw-Hill, 1995), 9–11, and John Kramer, ed., *North American Suburbs: Politics, Diversity, and Change* (Berkeley: Glendessary Press, 1972), xv. Levittown, with its single-family detached houses, is the model most often associated with American postwar suburbs. See, e.g., Kenneth T. Jackson, *Crabgrass Frontier* (New York: Oxford University Press, 1985), chap. 13.

13. As Thomas Sugrue has argued in "Reassessing the History of Postwar America," it "was a period of intense cultural contestation, not of homogeneity or consensus" (494–95).

14. As explained by Judith Shklar in *American Citizenship*, "Active citizens keep informed and speak out against public measures that they regard as unjust, unwise, or just too expensive. They also openly support policies that they regard as just and prudent" (5). Along similar lines, historians and political theorists influenced by the work of Jürgen Habermas have presented the sphere of citizens' activity—"the public"—as "a sphere of criticism of public authority." See Craig Calhoun, "Introduction: Habermas and the Public Sphere," in Calhoun, ed., *Habermas and the Public Sphere* (Cambridge: MIT Press, 1992), 13.

15. Michael Kazin, *The Populist Persuasion: An American History* (New York: Basic Books, 1995).

16. A maternalist strategy was used by 1950s women involved in the pacifist, or antinuclear, movement. See Amy Swerdlow, *Women Strike for Peace: Traditional Motherhood and Radical Politics in the 1960s* (Chicago: University of Chicago Press, 1993), and Dee Garrison, " 'Our Skirts Gave Them Courage': The Civil Defense Protest Movement in New York City, 1955–1961," in Meyerowitz, ed., *Not June Cleaver*, 201–26. On the use of a maternalist politics in earlier generations, see Linda K. Kerber's work on Republican motherhood, *Women of the Republic: Intellect and Ideology in Revolutionary America* (New York: Norton, 1980).

17. On the various and overlapping forms that women's consciousness can take, see Nancy F. Cott, "What's in a Name? The Limits of 'Social Feminism'; or, Expanding the Vocabulary of Women's History," *Journal of American History* 76 (December 1989): 809–29.

18. There is an abundant literature on the racist and antiliberal sentiments associated with the defense of neighborhood interests in the postwar period. See Thomas J. Sugrue, *The Origins of the Urban Crisis: Race and Inequality in Postwar Detroit* (Princeton, N.J.: Princeton University Press, 1996) and "Crabgrass-Roots Politics: Race, Rights, and the Reaction against Liberalism in the Urban North, 1940–1964," *Journal of American History* 82 (September 1995): 551–78; Arnold Hirsch, *Making the Second Ghetto: Race and Housing in Chicago, 1940–1960* (New York: Cambridge University Press, 1983) and "Massive Resistance in the Urban North: Trumbull Park, Chicago, 1953–1966," *Journal of American History* 82 (September 1995): 522–50; Mike Davis, *City of Quartz: Excavating the Future in Los Angeles* (New York: Vintage, 1990); Jonathan Rieder, *Canarsie: The Jews and Italians of Brooklyn against Liberalism* (Cambridge: Harvard University Press, 1985); Ronald P. Formisano, *Boston against*

Busing: Race, Class, and Ethnicity in the 1960s and 1970s (Chapel Hill: University of North Carolina Press, 1991); and Theresa Mah, "The Limits of Democracy in the Suburbs: Constructing the Middle Class through Residential Exclusion," in Bledstein and Johnston, eds., *The Middling Sorts*, 256–66.

Chapter 1. "Queens Has a Street Named Utopia"

1. Barbara Lee, "Your Neighborhood—Study in Contrasts," *Meadow Lark*, March 9, 1950, 1. The term pioneers and the related term frontier have been used for that generation of suburbanites by both contemporaries and historians. See, e.g., Stanley Elkins and Eric McKitrick, "A Meaning for Turner's Frontier," *Political Science Quarterly* 69 (September and December 1954): 321–53, 565–602. Betty Friedan compared new suburbs to "the empty plains of Kansas" in *The Feminine Mystique* (1963; New York: Laurel, 1983), 244. See also Rosalyn Baxandall and Elizabeth Ewen, *Picture Windows: How the Suburbs Happened* (New York: Basic Books, 2000), 153.

2. "Facts to Help Us Face the Future," keynote address at the 1955 fall conference of the Queensboro Council for Social Welfare, Queens College, October 11, 1955, by Henry Cohen, senior management consultant, Division of Administration, Office of the Mayor. See folder "Queens Borough (General) 1950s and Pre-50s," Vertical Files, Municipal Reference and Research Center, New York City (hereafter MRRC-VF).

3. Jeffrey A. Kroessler, "Suburban Growth, Urban Style: Patterns of Growth in the Borough of Queens," in Barbara Mae Kelly, ed., *Long Island: The Suburban Experience* (Interlaken, N.Y.: Heart of the Lakes, 1990). See also his "Building Queens: The Urbanization of New York's Largest Borough" (Ph.D. diss., City University of New York, 1991). Local histories of many of these older communities of Queens County are available at the Long Island Division of the Queens Borough Public Library, New York City (hereafter LID-QBPL). For the history of Elmhurst-Corona, in western Queens, see Roger Sanjek, *The Future of Us All: Race and Neighborhood Politics in New York City* (Ithaca, N.Y.: Cornell University Press, 1998), chap. 1.

4. "Bayside Hills," *Bayside Times*, August 27, 1936, 4.

5. Chamber of Commerce, Borough of Queens, "Data about Queens," 1961, "Queens Borough (General) 1950s and Pre-50s," MRRC-VF.

6. For a detailed account of the construction of the New York metropolitan area's infrastructure, see Robert A. Caro, *The Power Broker: Robert Moses and the Fall of New York* (New York: Vintage, 1975) and Leonard Wallock, "The Myth of the Master Builder: Robert Moses, New York, and the Dynamics of Metropolitan Development since World War II," *Journal of Urban History* 17 (August 1991): 339–62. For a more general discussion of the governmental policies in matters of housing and transportation that encouraged suburbanization, see Kenneth T. Jackson, "Race, Ethnicity, and Real Estate Appraisal: The Home Owners Loan Corporation and the Federal Housing Administration," *Journal of Urban History* 6 (August 1980): 419–52; *Crabgrass Frontier: The Suburbanization of the United States* (New York: Oxford University Press, 1985); Mark H. Rose, *Interstate: Express Highway Politics, 1939–1989*, rev. ed. (Knoxville: University of Tennessee Press, 1990).

7. Statistics compiled by the United States Bureau of the Census, *U.S. Census*

of Population: 1950, part 7 (Washington, D.C.: Government Printing Office, 1952), table 3, "Characteristics of Dwelling Units, by Census Tracts."

8. This figure is from a survey compiled by the Consolidated Edison Company from the records of gas and electricity consumption. Letter to Maurice Fitzgerald, Queens borough president, from Robert W. Dasey, Gladstone-Dasey Associates, Realtors, May 4, 1950, folder "Parking #1313," box 125, Subject Files, Mayor William O'Dwyer Papers, New York City Municipal Archives, New York City (hereafter O'Dwyer Papers).

9. The proportion of adults in the age group 30–44 was higher in northeastern Queens (ranging between 26 and 28 percent) than in the rest of the borough (23.5 percent). This analysis of the demographic growth of Queens communities is based on Queens Community Council of Greater New York, *Queens Communities: Population Characteristics and Neighborhood Social Resources* (New York: Bureau of Community Statistical Services, Research Department, 1958), vii–ix, and the *U.S. Census of Population: 1950*, table 3, "Characteristics of Dwelling Units, by Census Tracts." For figures about specific neighborhoods, see my "Suburban Citizens: Domesticity and Community Politics in Queens, New York, 1945–1960" (Ph.D. diss., Yale University, 1994), chap. 1.

10. Edith J. Cahill and Thomas Furey, "The Move Is to the Suburbia within the City—Queens," *World Tribune and Sun*, July 11, 1963; "Queens Borough, General, 1961–1969," MRRC-VF.

11. "Queens Has a Street Named Utopia," *World Telegram*, October 14, 1948; "Bayside 1960s and Earlier," MRRC-VF. For similar descriptions of the pastoral quality of the borough before a building boom of apartment houses increased its urban character in the 1960s, see John Scullin Jr., "Bigtown Living Replaces Suburbia in Queens," *Long Island Advance*, April 21, 1968; "Queens Borough, General, 1961–1969," MRRC-VF.

12. The statistics on the types of dwellings and their value have been compiled from the *U.S. Census of Population: 1950*, table 3, "Characteristics of Dwelling Units, by Census Tracts." The specific information about the Tyholland Homes is from "Survey Shows Numerous Vets Living in Housing Projects Here," *Bayside Times*, July 24, 1947, 12. For Levittown, see Barbara Mae Kelly, "The Politics of House and Home: Implications in the Built Environment of Levittown, Long Island" (Ph.D. diss., State University of New York-Stony Brook, 1988), 7, and Baxandall and Ewen, *Picture Windows*, 131.

13. The figures for Queens are taken from Bureau of the Census, *U.S. Census of Housing: 1950*, table 1, "Characteristics of Housing for New York City, by Boroughs" and United States Bureau of the Census, *U.S. Census of Housing: 1960* (Washington, D.C.: U.S. Government Printing Office, 1961), table 1, "Characteristics of Housing Units for New York City, by Boroughs." The statistics for northeastern Queens have been compiled from *U.S. Census of Population: 1950*, table 3, "Characteristics of Dwelling Units, by Census Tracts." No comparable data for northeastern Queens is available for 1960. As reported by Jackson in *Crabgrass Frontier*, "between 1934 and 1972, the percentage of American families living in owner-occupied dwellings rose from 44 percent to 63 percent" (205).

14. The term suburban apartments was used, for instance, to describe Glen Oaks Village. See *Journal of Housing*, February 1948, 26, and *New York Times*, November 14, 1948, Section 8, 1.

15. "The Sky Line," *New Yorker*, October 22, 1949, 102–6.

16. *Architecture Record*, December 1949, 87.

17. *Architecture Record*, December 1949, 87–89. For a discussion of the philosophy behind the construction of garden apartments, see Stanley Buder, *Visionaries and Planners: The Garden City Movement and the Modern Community* (New York: Oxford University Press, 1990).

18. "The Inquiring Photographer," *Long Island Star-Journal*, February 22, 1949, in vertical file "Fresh Meadows," LID-QBPL.

19. Betty Friedan, "The Way We Were—1949," *It Changed My Life: Writings on the Women's Movement* (New York: Dell, 1976), 13–14. As described in the *New York Times* in 1948, "Ten basic designs with fifty-seven different facades are used on the 110 buildings in the development, which is in the form of a colonial village with landscaped areas" ("Last Unit Filled at U.N. 'Village,' " August 1, 1948, Section 8, 1). On the suburban character of Parkway Village, see also Daniel Horowitz, *Betty Friedan and the Making of* The Feminine Mystique: *The American Left, the Cold War, and Modern Feminism* (Amherst: University of Massachusetts Press, 1998), 155. Horowitz discussed the Friedans' career changes on 143–44.

20. Gwendolyn Wright, *Building the Dream: A Social History of Housing in America* (New York: Pantheon Books, 1981), 246–47.

21. The Gross-Morton Corporation built more than 7,000 single-family houses in Queens between 1921 and 1946 ("Home Building on Long Island . . . 1926–1946," *American Builder*, October 1946, 86–87). In 1947 and 1948, Alfred Gross was leading workshops at the annual meeting of the National Association of Home Builders on "How to make your 608 acceptable" (*American Builder*, May 1947, 38; March 1948, 60). On the profits made on Glen Oaks Village, see *New York Times*, April 14, 1954.

22. Advertisement, *Long Island Daily Press*, March 6, 1949, Q29.

23. "Spring Comes to Glen Oaks! New Queens Residents Like Open Spaces," *Long Island Daily Press*, April 3, 1949, 7.

24. "A Quick Look at Windsor Park," *Bayside Times*, September 7, 1950, 18, and "George Gross Announces Windsor Completion," *Long Island Herald*, December 6, 1951, 21.

25. I discuss the details of this program and the controversy that it generated in Queens in the next chapter.

26. Stichman, "New York State Gives Housing Aid to Lower Middle Class," *Journal of Housing*, May 1951, 165.

27. New York City Planning Commission, "Queens Land Use Policy," *Plan for New York City: A Proposal. 5: Queens* (1969), 7, MRRC. Also available at the New York Public Library, Map Division.

28. Although Levittown, with its detached, single-family, and privately owned dwellings, is the model most often associated with American postwar suburbs, the community at the center of Whyte's classic suburban analysis, Park Forest, was similar to Fresh Meadows. See Jackson, *Crabgrass Frontier*, esp. chap. 13.

29. Interview with Beatrice and Sidney Ifshin, Bayside, N.Y., May 13, 1992.

30. See *America's Working Man: Work, Home, and Politics among Blue-Collar Property Owners* (Chicago: University of Chicago Press, 1984), esp. 16–22. He takes issue here with scholars like Benneth Berger and Richard Hamilton, who have argued that postwar residential developments were strictly separated by occupation into working-class and middle-class suburbs. See Berger, *Working-Class Suburb: A Study of Auto Workers in Suburbia* (Berkeley: University

of California Press, 1960), and Hamilton, *Class and Politics in the United States* (New York: Wiley, 1972).

31. Cahill and Furey, "The Move Is to Suburbia within the City—Queens."

32. The rest were professionals (15 percent), operatives (11 percent), sales workers (7 percent), service workers (6 percent), private service workers (5 percent), and managers (5 percent). These figures are compiled from *U.S. Census of Population: 1950*, table 2, "Age, Marital Status, and Economic Characteristics, by Sex, by Census Tracts" and *U.S. Census of Population: 1960*, table P-3, "Labor Force Characteristics of the Population, by Census Tracts" (Washington, D.C.: Government Printing Office, 1961).

33. Some of the older neighborhoods, like Jamaica Estates and Bayside Hills, built in the 1920s and 1930s, had racially restrictive covenants. I do not have evidence of any other covenants, although they may have existed. During the period covered, these covenants were not challenged and the issue of racial integration remained dormant. For Bayside Hills and Jamaica Estates, see "Restrictions," *Beacon*, October 1940, Bayside Hills Civic Association Papers (Bayside Hills Civic Association, Queens, N.Y.) and Thomas J. Lovely, *The History of Jamaica Estates, 1929–1969* (Jamaica, N.Y.: Jamaica Estates Association, 1969), 20. The latter is available at the LID-QBPL. For a discussion of covenants in Jamaica and St. Albans, in southwestern Queens, see Leslie Wilson, "Dark Spaces: An Account of Afro-American Sub-urbanization, 1890–1950" (Ph.D. diss., City University of New York, 1992), 284. The enforcement of these covenants was invalidated by the Supreme Court in 1948. See Clement E. Vose, *Caucasians Only: The Supreme Court, the NAACP, and the Restrictive Covenant Cases* (1959; Berkeley: University of California Press, 1967), 205.

34. Blacks composed 28 and 32 percent of the population in census tracts 867 and 871 (Flushing) and 17 and 13 percent in tracts 1447 and 1451 (Bayside). Compiled from *U.S. Census of Population: 1950*, table 1, "Characteristics of the Population, by Census Tracts." The proportion of African American families in tracts 867 and 871 did not change significantly during the 1950s (it was, respectively, 18 and 37 percent in 1960); the black population in tract 1447 increased to 41 percent. Compiled from *U.S. Census of Population: 1960*, table P-1, "General Characteristics of the Population, by Census Tracts." For an account of the Bayside black community, based on oral history, see Bayside Historical Society, *Bayside Was a Wilderness Then . . . : Voices from Bayside's Black Community* (Bayside, N.Y.: Bayside Historical Society, 1988).

35. See Commission on Intergroup Relations, *Trends in the Racial Distribution in New York City between 1950 and 1957: An Ecological Analysis*, prepared by Harold Goldblatt, February 1961, 1.

36. "Tabulation of Tenant Data—Statistical Sheets," c. 1952, New York City Housing Authority Papers, folder 8, box 63E1, series 03, LaGuardia and Wagner Archives, LaGuardia Community College. In 1969, approximately 20 percent of the families in Pomonok Houses were African Americans. *Plan for New York City*, 82.

37. Flushing Suburban is represented mostly by tract 1257. Eighty percent of the housing stock was built in the 1920s (compiled from *U.S. Census of Population: 1950*, table 3, "Characteristics of Dwelling Units, by Census Tracts").

38. According to Marilyn Mossop, a black professional who moved to the area in 1950 from Harlem (she was a bacteriologist, and her husband was a self-employed accountant), a number of white families (whom she described as "low-class") moved out of the neighborhood when blacks started moving in.

Nevertheless, the neighborhood and civic life that she described was racially mixed. Interview with M. Mossop, Flushing, N.Y., March 13, 1992.

39. Among the male workers living in Flushing Suburban in 1960, 21 percent were operatives, 17 percent craftsmen, 16 percent service workers, 13 percent clerical workers, 10 percent professionals, 8 percent managers, and 7 percent laborers. Among female workers, 38 percent were clerical workers, 19 percent operatives, 15 percent service, 10 percent professionals, 5 percent sales workers, and 3 percent managers. Only the African American and Puerto Rican communities of western Flushing (853, 855, 863, 867) had a larger proportion of women in the labor force (about 50 percent) than Flushing Suburban (46 percent) (compiled from *U.S. Census of Population: 1960*, table P-3, "Labor Force Characteristics of the Population, by Census Tracts").

40. See Deborah Dash Moore, *To the Golden Cities: Pursuing the American Jewish Dream in Miami and L.A.* (New York: Free Press, 1994).

41. From C. Morris Horowitz and Lawrence J. Kaplan, *The Jewish Population of the New York Area, 1900–1975* (New York: Federation of Jewish Philanthropies of New York, 1959), table 9, cited in Sidney Goldstein, "American Jewry, 1970: A Demographic Profile," in Marshall Sklare, ed., *The Jew in American Society* (New York: Behrman House, 1974), 128–29. Based on impressionistic observations and on the substantial increase in the number of whites of German and East European origin recorded in the 1960 census, David Rogers noted in 1968 that most of the whites who moved to Queens in the 1950s were Jews. See *110 Livingston Street: Politics and Bureaucracy in the New York City Schools* (New York: Random House, 1968), 42 and n. 14, 549.

42. In 1970, the population of Pomonok, Electchester, and Flushing Suburban, in South Flushing, was 40–45 percent Jewish (see "Neighborhood Analysis, 1970," in "Flushing, 1970–79," MRRC-VF). In 1957, it had six synagogues or Jewish Centers, compared with three Roman Catholic and five Protestant churches. The area of South Bayside where Bell Park Gardens and Oakland Gardens were located also had a sizable Jewish population, as indicated by its one synagogue and four Jewish Centers compared with six Catholic churches and fourteen Protestant churches; so did Douglaston–Little Neck–Bellerose, on the Nassau boundary, which had five Jewish Centers or temples, three Catholic churches, and ten Protestant churches. College Point–Whitestone, bordering the East River and Little Neck Bay, had two synagogues, four Catholic churches, and nine Protestant churches. Finally Flushing, just north of Central Queens, had four synagogues or Jewish Centers, three Catholic churches, and twenty-one Protestant churches (see *Queens Communities*, 1958). On the residential concentration of Jews in specific neighborhoods of northeastern Queens, see Nathan Glazer and Daniel Patrick Moynihan, *Beyond the Melting Pot: The Negroes, Puerto Ricans, Jews, Italians, and Irish of New York City* (Cambridge: MIT Press and Harvard University Press, 1964), 162.

43. Compiled from *U.S. Census of Population: 1950*, table 1, "Characteristics of the Population, by Census Tracts," and *U.S. Census of Population: 1960*, table P-1, "General Characteristics of the Population, by Census Tracts."

Chapter 2. Housing and Access to Middle-Class Status

1. See Herman P. Miller, *Income of the American People* (New York: Wiley, 1955), 100.

2. See Nelson Lichtenstein, "The Making of the Postwar Working Class: Cultural Pluralism and Social Structure in World War II," *Historian,* November 1988, 50.

3. Michael Kazin, "A People Not a Class: Rethinking the Political Language of the Modern U.S. Labor Movement," in Mike Davis and Michael Sprinkler, eds., *Reshaping the American Left: Popular Struggles in the 1980s* (New York: Verso, 1988), 274–75.

4. Stuart M. Blumin, *The Emergence of the Middle Class: Social Experience in the American City, 1760–1900* (Cambridge: Cambridge University Press, 1989), 296; David Halle, *America's Working Man: Work, Home, and Politics among Blue-Collar Property Owners* (Chicago: University of Chicago Press, 1984). For the post-World War II period, see also Ely Chinoy, *Automobile Workers and the American Dream* (Boston: Beacon Press, 1955).

5. "The Great Housing Shortage," *Life,* December 17, 1945, 27–36; Gwendolyn Wright, *Building the Dream: A Social History of Housing in America* (New York: Pantheon Books, 1981), 242. See also Paul F. Wendt, *Housing Policy—The Search for Solutions* (Berkeley: University of California Press, 1962), 163–64 and table VI-1, 149, and Richard O. Davies, *Housing Reform during the Truman Administration* (Columbia: University of Missouri Press, 1966), 40–41.

6. See "Queens in Drive for More Homes," *New York Times* (hereafter *NYT*), February 1, 1947, 25; "To Convert 133 Homes," *NYT,* April 1, 1947, 56.

7. Nathaniel S. Keith, *Politics and the Housing Crisis since 1930* (New York: Universe Books, 1973), 104.

8. Nathan Straus, *Two-thirds of a Nation: A Housing Program* (New York: Alfred A. Knopf, 1951), 72.

9. For contemporary criticisms of the risks of home ownership, see Stuart Chase, "The Case against Home Ownership," *Survey Graphic,* May 1938, 260–67; John P. Dean, *Home Ownership: Is It Sound?* (New York: Harper & Brothers, 1945), 7. See also Nathan Straus's reconstitution of the experience of a typical factory or office worker in *Two-thirds of a Nation,* 74–97. Eric Hodgins's popular novel, *Mr. Blandings Builds His Dream House,* offers a fictional account of the unanticipated risks and costs of home ownership for a white-collar family (New York: Simon and Schuster, 1946).

10. For the 2:1 ratio between the cost of a house and a family's annual income, see Dorothy Rosenman, *A Million Homes a Year* (New York: Harcourt, Brace, 1945), 17; Rosalyn Baxandall and Elizabeth Ewen, *Picture Windows: How the Suburbs Happened* (New York: Basic Books, 2000), 139 and 165; *Long Island Daily Press,* February 21, 1949, Q27. The property value of northeastern Queens houses was compiled from *U.S. Census of Population: 1950,* table 3, "Characteristics of Dwelling Units, by Census Tracts." The figure reported by the *Wall Street Journal* (July 16, 1951) was cited in Straus, *Two-thirds of a Nation,* 15. These FHA figures are cited in *American Builder,* October 1954, 40. The average cited here is for a white male worker in 1951, as cited in Miller, *Income of the American People.*

11. The construction of rental housing decreased from 41 percent of the new dwelling units built for the period 1922–28 to 17 percent for the period 1946–50 (cited in Straus, *Two-thirds of a Nation,* 96). The fact that "the great housing shortage has long been recognized as primarily a shortage of rental housing" was acknowledged in *Architectural Forum,* August 1947, 67. Still in the early 1950s, critics argued that the new rental projects financed through the FHA did not meet the needs of families of moderate income. The majority of

apartments available were either too expensive or too small for families with children (*U.S. News & World Report*, May 5, 1950, 36–37, cited in Straus, *Two-thirds of a Nation*, 78). See also Wright, *Building the Dream*, 246–47.

12. Citizens' Housing Council of New York, *News*, July 7, 1947, folder 5, box 72E4, series 6, New York City Housing Authority Papers, LaGuardia and Wagner Archives, LaGuardia Community College, New York City (hereafter NYCHA Papers).

13. See Dean, *Home Ownership*, 1, and "The Ghosts of Home Ownership," *Journal of Social Issues* 7, nos. 1 & 2 (1951): 66–67.

14. United States Congress, *Congressional Record*, 81st Cong., 2nd sess. (Washington, D.C.: Government Printing Office, 1950), 3358.

15. See Timothy McDonnell, *The Wagner Housing Act: A Case Study of the Legislative Process* (Chicago: Loyola University Press, 1957); Mark I. Gelfand, *A Nation of Cities: The Federal Government and Urban America, 1933–1945* (New York: Oxford University Press, 1975); and Chester W. Hartman, *Housing and Social Policy* (Englewood Cliffs, N.J.: Prentice-Hall, 1975).

16. On the formation of a racially segregated housing market, see Herbert J. Gans, "The Failure of Urban Renewal: A Critique and Some Proposals," *Commentary* 39 (April 1965): 29–37; Kenneth T. Jackson, "Race, Ethnicity, and Real Estate Appraisal: The Home Owners Loan Corporation and the Federal Housing Administration," *Journal of Urban History* 6 (August 1980): 419–52; Michael N. Danielson, *The Politics of Exclusion* (New York: Columbia University Press, 1976); Clement E. Vose, *Caucasians Only: The Supreme Court, the NAACP, and the Restrictive Covenant Cases* (1959; Berkeley: University of California Press, 1967); Charles Abrams, *Forbidden Neighbors: A Study of Prejudice in Housing* (New York: Harper & Brothers, 1955); and "The Ghetto Makers," *Nation*, October 7, 1961, 222–25, reprinted in Jon Pynoos et al., *Housing Urban America* (Chicago: Aldine, 1973), 274–78.

17. Warren J. Vinton, "What Is a Low-Income Family Today?" folder 2, box 62D3, series 4, NYCHA Papers; and Hartman, *Housing and Social Policy*, 126–27.

18. Catherine Bauer, "The Middle Class Needs Houses, Too," *New Republic*, August 29, 1949, 17–20.

19. Gail Radford, *Modern Housing for America: Policy Struggles in the New Deal Era* (Chicago: University of Chicago Press, 1996), 184–91.

20. For a description of the bills and summary of the debates in 1949–50, see *Journal of Housing*, August 1949, 253–54; February 1950, 44; April 1950, 122, 126; Davies, *Housing Reform*, 116–21. For the fate of middle-income housing programs after 1950, see Keith, *Politics and the Housing Crisis since 1930*, 117, 142; *Congress and the Nation, 1945–1964* (Washington, D.C.: Congressional Quarterly Service, 1965), 482.

21. The image of the home in American culture has a long history. For an overview, see Clifford E. Clark Jr., *The American Family Home, 1800–1960* (Chapel Hill: University of North Carolina Press, 1986); for the postwar period, see Clark, "Ranch-House Suburbia: Ideals and Realities," in Lary May, ed., *Recasting America: Culture and Politics in the Age of Cold War* (Chicago: University of Chicago Press, 1989), 171–91, and Loren Baritz, *The Good Life: The Meaning of Success for the American Middle Class* (New York: Alfred A. Knopf, 1989).

22. John P. Dean, "The Ghosts of Home Ownership," 59. See also his *Home Ownership*.

23. *Congressional Record*, 81st Cong., 2nd sess., 3296, 3298.

24. Ibid., 3813–4, 3269–70, 3365.

25. Ibid., 3297.

26. See Boris Shishkin, "Homes for the Brave," *American Federationist,* March 1946, 11.

27. "Housing for the Nation," *American Federationist,* February 1945. See also "The Challenge of Housing," September 1945; "The Swedish Way," November 1953; "America Needs More Housing," May 1956; "Let's Provide Good Homes for All Americans" (by George Meany), May-June 1959.

28. "Housing for *Whom?*" *American Federationist,* December 1946, 32.

29. Butler's proposal was described in the *New York Times,* June 4, 1946, 1:5; September 9, 1946, 1:4. See also Maxwell H. Tretter, executive director of the NYCHA, in "Public Housing without Cash Subsidy," *CHC Housing News,* June 1947, folder 5, box 72E4, series 6, NYCHA Papers.

30. Letter to NYCHA, September 17, 1946, folder 3, box 69E3, series 6, NYCHA Papers. See also Michey Levine, Riverside chapter of the AVC, to Mayor O'Dwyer, September 11, 1946, folder "Housing General #642," box 64, Subject Files (hereafter SF), Mayor William O'Dwyer Papers, New York City Municipal Archives (hereafter O'Dwyer Papers) and "Asks City Act on Housing," *NYT,* March 19, 1947, 27.

31. Straus, *Two-thirds of a Nation,* 102. The opposition of city construction coordinator Robert Moses probably explains the rejection of the plan. For Moses' opinion of both Straus, "an impossible fellow . . . discredited in the public housing field," and his plan, a "quaint scheme to build housing on vacant land," see folder "Housing General #648," box 64, SF, O'Dwyer Papers. Straus had criticized Moses' "systematic efforts to destroy the public housing movement in New York City," *NYT,* May 22, 1947, 2. Moses had also opposed Butler's program. See memorandum from James Wm. Gaynor to T. F. Farrell, January 20, 1948, and from Gerald J. Carey to Farrell, March 11, 1948, folder 2, box 60D7, series 6, NYCHA Papers. For telegrams from chapters of the AVC and other organizations demanding action on the Straus plan, see folder "Housing General #637–40," box 63, SF, O'Dwyer Papers. For descriptions of the Straus plan, see *NYT,* April 20, 1946, 1; May 17, 1946, 23; May 19, 1946, 1; May 21, 1946, 1; June 15, 1946, 23; June 18, 1946, 38; July 20, 1946, 15.

32. "City Legion Calls for 50,000 Homes," *NYT,* May 2, 1946, 23.

33. For descriptions of the program, see *Journal of Housing,* April 1948, 99–100; press release from the Office of the Mayor, March 12, 1948, and Resolution of the Board of Estimate Cal. no. 212, folder 2, box 60D7, series 6, NYCHA Papers; *NYT,* March 13, 1948, 1. For letters of New Yorkers expressing their support for the city's "unsubsidized public housing program" in early 1948, see folder 2, box 60D7, series 6, NYCHA Papers.

34. *Long Island Daily Press* (hereafter *LIDP*), May 3, 1948, 1; "Public Housing," 1949, folder "Mayor's Departmental Reports—M-P #1002," box 95, SF, O'Dwyer Papers. See also memorandum from Farrell to O'Dwyer, January 10, 1950, folder 6, box 68B6, series 6, NYCHA Papers.

35. "Applications Received and Processed," folder 7, box 66A4, series 8, NYCHA Papers. The first three projects to be built under the No-Cash-Subsidy program were even more "swamped with applications": 35,000 for 1,357 apartments at Woodside Houses; 35,000 for the 1,266 units at Pelham Parkway; and 28,000 for the 874 units at Eastchester (Moses to O'Dwyer, February 15, 1950, folder "Housing #701," box 71, SF, O'Dwyer Papers).

36. *Building Homes for Those with Lower Middle Incomes* (State of New York, Division of Housing, 1949).

37. Governor Alfred Smith, "Annual Message" (January 6, 1926) and "Special Message" (April 1, 1926), Senate, *Journal, 1926*, vol. 2, "Executive Journal," 31, 98–100; see also *Message from the Governor Transmitting Report of the Commission of Housing and Regional Planning for Permanent Housing Relief*, legislative document, 1926, no. 66. The Amalgamated Houses built by the Amalgamated Clothing Workers of America in the Bronx in 1927 was the first development built under this program. See Evelyn Seeley, "The House: A Success Story," *Survey Graphic*, February 1948, 70–74, 85.

38. *NYT*, March 15, 1947, 15.

39. These cooperatives were built with the help of an FHA-guaranteed mortgage. (In 1950, the National Housing Act added its section 213, which authorized FHA to insure mortgages on cooperative developments.) See *Directory of Large-Scale Rental*, 9. The monthly charges at Clearview were $23, higher than the $15 at Bell Park Gardens, but lower than the $28 at Fresh Meadows.

40. Memorandum from Harry Taylor to George E. Spargo, March 2, 1948, folder "Housing Projects—Veterans Mutual Housing Project #819," box 77, SF, O'Dwyer Papers.

41. The policy shift from slum clearance to the use of vacant land was also one which had been advocated by Edmond Butler, chairman of the NYCHA until July 1, 1947. The relocation of low-income families was practically impossible given the current shortage. See *NYT*, April 16, 1947, 14; May 27, 1947, 28; June 6, 1947, 25. See also Rosalie Genevro, "Site Selection and the New York City Housing Authority, 1934–1939," *Journal of Urban History* 12 (August 1986): 334–52.

42. *NYT*, April 25, 1948, 1; *Long Island Star-Journal* (hereafter *Star*), March 4, 1948, 1; March 30, 1948, 1. Neufeld was a veteran in taxpayers' protests. In 1938, he initiated the formation of "an Organization of Taxpayer and Civic Groups to combat crushing tax burdens" (circular letter, June 2, 1938, Bayside Taxpayers and Improvement Association Papers, Bayside Historical Society, Queens, N.Y.).

43. See *NYT*, May 13, 1949, 41; *NYT*, May 14, 1949, 12; *LIDP*, May 18, 1949, 2.

44. The quote is from a memo from Bill Donoghue, executive secretary to the mayor, to Mayor O'Dwyer, May 19, 1948, folder 2, box 60D7, series 6, NYCHA Papers. On Newhouse's pressures, Donoghue wrote, "Norman Newhouse, of the Newhouse Papers . . . called today and said that they probably will not be able to divert from City Hall the criticism that has been developing against the unsubsidized housing program. . . . Norman says that they are so completely committed to the campaign that they will be unable to avoid directing the criticism at the Administration and no longer at the Housing Authority, which, up to now, has been the target of the criticism" (ibid.). See also memo from Jack Tiernay to O'Dwyer, February 28, 1950, folder "Housing Projects—Financed by Private Sources #702," box 71, SF, O'Dwyer Papers.

45. Young was also a member of the Long Island Home Builders' Institute, the Jamaica Real Estate Board, and the Long Island Real Estate Board. "Civic Council Leader Named Board Member," *Meadow Lark* (hereafter *ML*), January 12, 1950, 3; "George F. Young Dies; Led Boro Civic Fights," *Long Island Herald* (hereafter *LIH*), January 29, 1953, 1.

46. *LIDP*, April 22, 1948, 1, and *NYT*, April 22, 1948, 2. The Newtown rally was one of the few events of the two-year protest that the *New York Times* reported. Another mass protest was organized by Young: "visits to congressmen and state legislators, distribution of millions of leaflets, mass meetings, and a general program of education." Young even mentioned that "the Civic Council will probably use motion pictures and other visual aids to push the fight" (*LIDP*, January 19, 1950, 20; *LIDP*, January 22, 1950, 1).

47. *Star*, February 25, 1950, 1; *Star*, March 15, 1949, 5; *ML*, March 31, 1949, 1. David H. Brown, one of the organizers of the United Civic Council, the Fresh Meadows Civic Association, and the Hillcrest Jewish Center, was also a "well-known local attorney and realtor" ("Brown Takes Sole Charge at Estates," *LIH*, January 15, 1953, 1).

48. Among the Republicans who lent their support were the moderate state senator Seymour Halpern of Kew Gardens and the conservative councilmen Walter McGahan and Aloysius J. Maickel ("G.O.P. Bloc Drafts Bill to Stop Tax-Free Housing Projects," *Star*, March 29, 1948, 1; Halpern to O'Dwyer, April 6, 1948, folder 2, box 60D7, series 6, NYCHA Papers). Among the Democrats, James A. Roe, leader of the Queens County Democratic Party, condemned the programs, as well as the Parsons and the Jefferson Democratic Clubs. See *Star*, March 20, 1948, 1; *LIDP*, April 1, 1948, 1; "Parson Dem's Oppose Tax-Free Housing Plans," *ML*, April 8, 1948, 1; *LIDP*, April 2, 1948, 1; "Jefferson Dem's Protest Tax-Free Housing Proposal," *ML*, April 22, 1948, 1; "Women Dems Vote against Tax Exemption," *Bayside Times* (hereafter *BT*), March 9, 1950, 15.

49. Details about the formation and the strategies of the real estate lobby can be found in the report of a congressional committee formed in March 1950 to study "the role of lobbying in representative self-government." See *U.S. Congress, Hearings before the House Select Committee on Lobbying Activities*, 81st Cong., 2nd sess., 1950 (hereafter *Housing Lobby*). What became known as "the lobby" is also described in Leonard Freedman, *Public Housing: The Politics of Poverty* (New York: Holt, Rinehart and Winston, 1969), 4–7, and Wright, *Building the Dream*, 220–22. For negative reactions to the lobby's practices, see "Housing: A 1950 Tragedy," by Lee F. Johnson, executive vice president of the National Housing Conference, in *Survey*, December 1950, 551–55, and "What Makes the Real Estate Lobby Tick?" by Leo Goodman, director of the CIO National Housing Committee, in *Journal of Housing*, December 1950, 423–27.

50. See esp. "Some Facts about NAREB's Public Relations Department," *Housing Lobby*, 737–39; for examples of handout material, including "suggested editorial or letter to the editor," 352–57, 700–709, 723–30, 748–80; for Nelson's editorial material sent to the press and radio, 50; on propaganda in schools, 57–58. The NAHB also sent material out to local groups (349–64; 404–11). The grassroots campaigns in various localities were described at length in a series of articles published in the *Journal of Housing*: January 1950, 8–10; May 1950, 158–59; July 1950, 226–27; August 1950, 265–68; January 1951, 9–10, 24–26; February 1951, 49–50; March 1951, 90, 94; May 1951, 153–54. See also Davies, *Housing Reform during the Truman Administration*, 127–28. As described by Elizabeth Fones-Wolf, the business community as a whole and the labor movement to a lesser extent had discovered the value of reaching out to the local communities in this way. See *Selling Free-Enterprise: The Business Attack on the New Deal Order, 1945–1960* (Chicago: University of Chicago Press, 1994).

51. *Housing Lobby*, 714–15, 349, 354.

52. *Housing Lobby*, 37–43, 543–44. The failed attempt by the NAREB to form a nationwide association of home and property owners further supported the allegations that "phony property owners" were unscrupulously used to disguise "selfish private interest." After having dropped for financial reasons the 1945–47 attempt to form a national association of home and property owners, the NAREB encouraged its members "to take part in local civic affairs as actively as possible. This is the best kind of public relations," wrote Nelson (*Housing Lobby*, 568–69, 581–82, 676–77).

53. Samuel O. Dunn, "The Little Man Speaks," *American Builder,* April 1950, 7.

54. Director of public relations, NAREB, to Real Estate Board secretaries, December 21, 1948, *Housing Lobby*, 738; *Star,* March 16, 1948, 1.

55. For a description of white home owners' resistance to residential integration in the 1940s and 1950s, see Arnold R. Hirsch, *Making the Second Ghetto: Race and Housing in Chicago, 1940–1960* (New York: Cambridge University Press, 1983), Thomas J. Sugrue, "Crabgrass-Roots Politics: Race, Rights, and the Reaction against Liberalism in the Urban North, 1940–1964," *Journal of American History* 82 (September 1995): 551–78, and Abrams, *Forbidden Neighbors.*

56. Referred to as an "East Coast Newspaper Advertisement" in the *Journal of Housing*, it likely was emanating from New York, or possibly Connecticut, where Governor Chester Bowles was especially active in promoting moderate-income projects of the type endorsed by Stichman and O'Dwyer (May 1950, 158).

57. *Star*, March 15, 1948, 1.

58. *Star*, March 16, 1948, 4.

59. See Bureau of the Census, *U.S. Census of Population: 1950. Vol. 3, Census Tract Statistics (New York, New York)* (Washington, D.C.: Government Printing Office, 1952).

60. According to its Section 156, amended in 1946 and effective until December 31, 1949, veterans were eligible for public housing if their incomes did not exceed seven or eight times the rental (seven for families of fewer than five persons, eight for larger families; for nonveterans, the corresponding ratios were five and six). Thus, based on a rent of $16, the maximum possible incomes were calculated at $7,900 for a veteran with a large family and $5,900 for a nonveteran. See James England, NYCHA executive director, to four city councilmen, four state senators, a dozen assemblymen, as well as nine civic and home owners' associations, March 30, 1948, folder 2, box 60D7, series 6, NYCHA Papers.

61. Memorandum from Bill Donoghue, May 19, 1948, folder 2, box 60D7, series 6, NYCHA Papers. See memorandum from Farrell to Colonel John J. Bannett, deputy mayor, May 20, 1948, folder "Housing General #668," box 67, SF, O'Dwyer Papers. The City Housing Authority's decision to revise the income ceilings at the level of the state-aided project—$3,984 for a family of seven (for veterans) and $2,988 for nonveterans—was reported in *LIDP*, May 26, 1948, 1, May 27, 1948, 1, 24. For reaction to Farrell's refusal to set a fixed income limit, see "Unbelievable," editorial, *LIDP*, May 21, 1948, 22; about Queens's "victory," see "Queens Is Right, Says O'Dwyer. Insists Only Real Low-Income Families Should Get City's Tax-Free Housing," *LIDP*, May 23, 1948, 1.

62. John M. Dickerman to J. L. Virden, Virden Lumber & Steel Co.,

Greenville, Miss., July 21, 1949, *Housing Lobby*, 405; memorandum to local associations, ibid., 352.

63. *Star*, March 15, 1948, 1.

64. *ML*, March 16, 1950, 1. See also England to elected representatives, March 30, 1948, NYCHA Papers. For two assessments of the overall cost of the tax exemptions thereby granted on municipal finance, see memorandum from Robert Moses to O'Dwyer, February 15, 1950, folder "Housing #702," box 71, SF, O'Dwyer Papers. In 1955, Mayor Wagner sponsored a study of the cost of tax exemptions to the city. Based on an analysis of the case of Electchester, the report concluded that "partial tax exemption . . . can be an excellent thing for the City. It should cost the other taxpayers nothing and result in valuable property eventually going on the tax rolls and then reduce the tax load." See "A Study of the Cost of Tax Exemption for Middle-Income Housing to the City of New York," by Thurman Lee, president of the Dry Dock Savings Bank, June 23, 1955, folder 4, box 68C5, series 6, NYCHA Papers.

65. *Star*, December 7, 1949, 1; December 12, 1949, 1; press release by Moses, December 12, 1949, folder 2, box 68C3, series 6, NYCHA Papers. It was not the first time that Moses reacted negatively to Stichman's public announcement that the city would grant tax exemptions. The same had happened, although privately, during the negotiations for Electchester in May 1949 (folder 10, box 60D6, series 6, NYCHA Papers). In the following months, the local press and many representatives of home owners referred directly to Moses' comments. See "Tax Exempton," *Star*, January 21, 1950, 4. See also Bellerose-Commonwealth Civic Association to Moses, December 22, 1949, folder "Housing Projects—Financed by Private Sources #702," box 71, SF, O'Dwyer Papers.

66. "Extract of the Minutes of the Meeting of the Board of Estimate Held March 18, 1948," folder 2, box 60D7, series 6, NYCHA Papers. See also *Star*, March 18, 1948, 1.

67. "It's 'People versus Pomonok,' Civics Maintain on Eve of Vote," *ML*, May 25, 1950, 3.

68. Bowne Park to Mayor O'Dwyer, April 12, 1948, folder 2, box 60D7, series 6, NYCHA Papers.

69. Henry W. Meissner, president of the Little Neck Community Association, to O'Dwyer, April 1, 1948, folder "Housing General #665," box 67, SF, O'Dwyer Papers.

70. Flushing Manor to O'Dwyer, April 10, 1950, folder "Housing Projects—Financed by Private Sources #702," box 71, SF, O'Dwyer Papers.

71. Lucille Willcutt to John Haugaard, deputy commissioner of housing, November 10, 1949, and Willcutt to Governor Thomas Dewey, June 14, 1950, Minutes of the Oakland Hills-Bayside Hills Civic Association, 1949–51, Bayside Historical Society, Queens, N.Y. (hereafter OHCA Papers).

72. Letter to the editor, *LIDP*, June 13, 1949, 10. Two members of Local 3 of the IBEW, the group that sponsored Electchester, responded to this letter. See *LIDP*, June 19, 1949, Q18, and *LIDP*, July 11, 1949, 8.

73. *LIDP*, August 3, 1946, 22. This is, of course, only one of many requests for zoning restrictions brought forward by home owners' associations. In November 1947, for instance, the Harding Heights Civic Association successfully petitioned the Board of Estimate for a zone change "to protect their own community from the deterioration which might ensue from the development of the adjacent vacant area with unsightly row houses" (see folder "Zoning

#1869," box 174, SF, O'Dwyer Papers). Similarly, the Oakland Hills Civic Association, which protested in 1949 that the construction of apartments would irremediably lead to "the creation of an overcrowded situation and destroy the character of the Borough itself," had been involved in zoning fights for years. See Willcutt to Stichman, with copy to Moses, October 8, 1949; Willcutt to John Haugaard, deputy commissioner of housing, November 10, 1949; and Willcutt to Governor Thomas Dewey, June 15, 1950, OHCA Papers. See also, "Oakland Hills Civics Nominate All-Woman Slate," *BT*, November 11, 1948, 3. The OHCA was organized in 1933.

74. *Star*, January 18, 1950, 1; *Star*, January 26, 1950, 1.

75. *Star*, December 13, 1949, 1. According to another resident, "We fear that the site projected for the eastern Queens high school will be taken from us, and an elementary school substituted if the project is built" (*Star*, January 26, 1950, 1).

76. "Civics Propose Housing Limits," *ML*, December 1, 1949, 1. See copy of proposal, January 27, 1950, folder "Zoning #1872," box 174, SF, O'Dwyer Papers. The Queens Valley Home Owners' Association was formed in 1940 and joined the UCC in 1944 ("Queens Valley Home Owners Group Helps Area's Growth," *Post*, July 21, 1949, folder "Kew Gardens Hills, History," Vertical Files, Long Island Division, Queens Borough Public Library, New York City). In 1960, it claimed 2,000 members, all one- and two-family home owners ("Jewel Ave. Bridge Widening Sought," *Kew Hills News* [hereafter *KHN*], March 1960, 1).

77. See letters to the editor, *ML*, April 15, 1948, 3, and April 7, 1949, 4.

78. See letter from Queens County Board of Business Agents to O'Dwyer, March 21, 1950. Along the same lines, see "A Statement on Tax Exempt Housing by the Queens County Jewish War Veterans, the Queens County Amvets, and the Queens County Disabled American Veterans," February 23, 1950; telegram from New York Building and Construction Trades Council, May 17, 1950; letter to Maurice A. FitzGerald from Stichman, March 23 and 30, 1950, all in folder "Housing Projects—Financed by Private Sources #702," box 71, SF, O'Dwyer Papers.

79. "Bell Park ADA Decries Attacks on Limited Tax," *BT*, February 9, 1950, 19. See also "New ADA Chapter Attacks Critics of State Housing Units," *ML*, February 9, 1950, 1; "Bell Park Directors Hit Co-op Protests," *BT*, February 16, 1950, 1; "Tax Exemption Question Stirs Oakland-Bell Park," *BT*, February 16, 1950, 6; letter to the editor, by Edward Kramer, Joseph Lapal, Joseph Gil, and Sol Schwartz, *ML*, February 16, 1950, 4; "Tax-Free Housing Debate Hits Peak; Battle Lines Form," *ML*, February 23, 1950, 1; "Housing Crossfire Hearing Opens Volley of Arguments," *ML*, March 2, 1950, 1; "Oakland Area, Fresh Meadows ADA Units Unite in Tax Fight," *BT*, March 23, 1950, 7.

80. "Vets in Force for Rally," *BT*, March 2, 1950, 6.

81. Letter to Moses, March 6, 1950, and Moses' response, March 24, 1950, folder 6, box 60D6, series 6, NYCHA Papers.

82. The Wealth and Health Council of New York City, *New York City, 1955–1965: A Report to the Community* (1955), folder 2, box 66B2, series 12, NYCHA Papers.

83. One of the subcommittees formed was mandated to study "middle-income housing, with special emphasis on the proper use of tax concessions and State or City credit for cooperatives and limited dividend projects."

Among its twelve members were Alfred Kazan, one of the sponsors of the Amalgamated Houses; Charles Abrams; Maxwell H. Tretter; and Philip J. Cruise, chairman of the NYCHA. See folder 4, box 68C5, series 6, NYCHA Papers.

84. Mayor's Committee for Better Housing of the City of New York, "Report of Subcommittee on Middle Income Housing with Proper Use of Tax Concessions and State or City Credit," June 1955, folder "Housing (General) July-December 1955," box 143, SF, Mayor Robert F. Wagner Jr. Papers, New York City Municipal Archives. See also memorandum from George D. Brown Jr. to the Subcommittee on Housing & Redevelopment of the Mayor's Advisory Council, folder 4, box 68C5, series 6, NYCHA Papers; speech by Philip J. Cruise, chairman of the NYCHA at Real Estate Board luncheon, April 28, 1954, folder 1, box 60D7, series 6, NYCHA Papers.

85. Again in 1955, both New York State and the city intervened in the moderate-income housing market, the former with the Mitchell-Lama program. These programs and the misuse of public money are discussed in Jack Newfield and Paul DuBrul, *The Abuse of Power* (New York: Viking, 1977), 297–300.

86. "Homes for the Future," 10.

87. See "The Role of the States," in Straus, *Two-thirds of a Nation*, 283–39. He also emphasized the pressure that groups of veterans had applied in 1945 when the Connecticut plan was discussed: "There was no question in their minds, at least, that their state government had the responsibility for providing homes, although such state responsibility was entirely without precedent in Connecticut, as practically everywhere else" (240). The story of Jay Ramsay and his wife, who dragged their four children and furniture to the city hall of Englewood, Colorado, and squatted there until promised a shelter, spoke in favor of Bowles's contention (reported in *Time*, December 24, 1945, 22–23).

Chapter 3. Suburban Radicals

1. See Elaine Tyler May, *Homeward Bound: American Families in the Cold War Era* (New York: Basic Books, 1988). See also her essays "Cold War—Warm Hearth: Politics and the Family in Postwar America," in Steve Fraser and Gary Gerstle, eds., *The Rise and Fall of the New Deal Order: 1930–1980* (Princeton, N.J.: Princeton University Press, 1989), 153–81, and "Explosive Issues: Sex, Women, and the Bomb," in Lary May, ed., *Recasting America: Culture and Politics in the Age of Cold War* (Chicago: University of Chicago Press, 1989), 154–70.

2. Many authors have noted the commitment of Jews to progressive liberalism in the postwar period (namely, on economic, civil rights, and civil liberties issues). In 1952, for instance, the liberal Democrat Adlai Stevenson received 44 percent of the popular vote but 75 percent of the Jewish vote. See Lawrence H. Fuchs, *The Political Behavior of American Jews* (Glencoe, Ill.: Free Press, 1956), esp. chaps. 6 and 7, and Deborah Dash Moore, *To the Golden Cities: Pursuing the American Jewish Dream in Miami and L.A.* (New York: Free Press, 1994), 189–90. See also Nathan Glazer and Daniel Patrick Moynihan, *Beyond the Melting Pot: The Negroes, Puerto Ricans Jews, Italians, and Irish of New York City* (Cambridge: MIT Press and Harvard University Press, 1964), 167–71.

3. Betty Friedan, "The Way We Were—1949," *It Changed My Life: Writings on*

the Women's Movement (New York: Random House, 1976), 16; Daniel Horowitz, *Betty Friedan and the Making of* The Feminine Mystique*: The American Left, the Cold War, and Modern Feminism* (Amherst: University of Massachusetts Press, 1998).

4. In 1936, fourteen out of the twenty-one election districts in the Eighth Assembly District went to Roosevelt ("Bayside Area Joins Sweep," *Bayside Times* [hereafter *BT*], November 5, 1936, 1).

5. "See 8th A.D. as Pivot in Races up to U.S. Senator," *BT*, October 27, 1949, 1.

6. "Electioneering," editorial, *Meadow Lark* (hereafter *ML*), November 2, 1950, 8. See also "Registration Ends Saturday," *ML*, October 12, 1950, 1; "Barrage of Words Awaits Voter as Candidates Seek Ballots in 'Mystery Area,' " *ML*, November 2, 1950, 1.

7. "N.Y. State Will Go as Queens Votes in Nov., Political Pundits Say," *Glen Oaks News* (hereafter *GON*), August 14, 1952.

8. "Boro Registration Shows Record Growth of Queens," *GON*, October 16, 1952, 1. See also "Registration Record Set by 8th A.D.," *Long Island Herald* (hereafter *LIH*), October 16, 1952, 1. For registration figures for Queens County, see *New York Red Book* (Albany: J. B. Lyon, 1953).

9. This is based on an analysis of the results by electoral districts within the Eighth Assembly District as provided in *The City Record*, 1952. For results of the Glen Oaks area, located in the Ninth Assembly District (E.D. 1 to 16), see "Glen Oaks Emerges as Dem. and Liberal Area," *GON*, November 20, 1952, 3, and "Local GOP Trio Does It Again!" *GON*, November 6, 1952, 1.

10. "For Senator Halpern," *ML*, August 31, 1950, 6; "Halpern Campaign Marks Civic OKs," *LIH*, October 30, 1952, 2; "Holtzman and Halpern in Hot Election Battle," *Kew Hills News* (hereafter *KHN*), October 1954, 1; "Political News and Views," *LIH*, October 30, 1958, 8–10; "Cong. Halpern Heads Committee for Lindsay," *LIH*, September 2, 1965, 1.

11. "Rabin Warns Queens against City Taxes," *LIH*, September 25, 1952, 1, and "Meet Your Local Candidates: Samuel Rabin," *Pomonok News* (hereafter *PN*), October 1952, 1.

12. "Meet Your Local Candidates: Edward Sharf," *PN*, October 1952, 1. See bulletin of the Kew Gardens Hills Regular Democratic Club, October 1953, folder "1953 Queens County," box 21, Records of the Liberal Party of New York State, Manuscripts and Archives Division, New York Public Library, Astor, Lenox and Tilden Foundations (hereafter LP Papers).

13. "Latham Scorns ADA, Liberal Party," *GON*, October 9, 1952, 1.

14. "Perrini Stands Anti T-H, Pro Price, Wage Controls," *GON*, October 2, 1952, 1.

15. "Notes for Queens," October 25, 1952, folder 3, box 238, Adlai E. Stevenson Papers, Public Policy Papers, Seeley G. Mudd Manuscript Library, Princeton University.

16. The new district was bounded by Horace Harding Boulevard and Hillside Avenue, 164th Street and the Nassau County Line ("New Democratic Club in Glen Oaks," *GON*, May 6, 1954, 6). On Wallach, see "Democrats Carry 10th; Wallach in Assembly," *GON*, November 4, 1954, 1, and "Louis Wallach," *GON*, November 1, 1956, 1.

17. "Local Politicians Assume New Duties," *BT*, January 6, 1955, 1.

18. "Cong. Halpern Heads Committee for Lindsay," *LIH*, September 2, 1965, 1.

19. "Senator Jack Bronston Presents Legislation," *LIH*, January 29, 1959, 1.

20. In *LIH*, see "Leon Beerman Runs for Senate," August 5, 1954, 1; "Fred Rosenberg Runs for Senate," August 19, 1954, 2; "Supporters Hold Rallies for Demo Fred Rosenberg," September 2, 1954, 5; "Beerman Hits Roe Rule," September 9, 1954, 9. Also on the 1954 primary, see "Thomas Dent for Congress," *LIH*, July 22, 1954, 8; "Julius Feigenbaum Runs for Office," *LIH*, August 26, 1954, 2; "Julius Feigenbaum Conducts Meetings," *LIH*, September 2, 1954, 12; "Jacob Orenstein Runs for Congress," *LIH*, July 29, 1954, 4. On the 1956 primary, see "Jack Bronston Designated State Senator Candidate," *LIH*, April 19, 1956, 1; "Attorney Leonard Finz Enters Primary Fight," *LIH*, May 24, 1956, 1; "Bronston Wins over Finz by 3 to 1 Margin," *BT*, June 7, 1956, 1.

21. In fact, many among these young Democrats supported the renters in their disputes against their lawyers, as they did support the community residents' battles for a variety of services. See "Leonard Finz Demands Justice," *LIH*, May 31, 1956, 1; "Jack Bronston Demo's Choice," *LIH*, November 1, 1956, 1; "Louis Wallach Gets Control Nod," *LIH*, August 30, 1962, 6.

22. Stanley Taxel to Adolph A. Berle Jr., October 3, 1952, folder "Queens County Headquarters," box 18, LP Papers.

23. "Windsor Park Tenants Oppose Rent Increases," *BT*, August 7, 1952, 1; "Windsor Park Tenants Fight Rent Increases," *LIH*, August 7, 1952, 1; "Windsorites Fight Rent Increases," *BT*, August 14, 1952, 1; "Windsorites Raise Funds to Fight Rent Increases," *BT*, August 21, 1952, 1; "Windsor Park Rent Battle Grows as Tenants Organize," *LIH*, August 21, 1952, 1; "Windsor Tenants Meet to Map New Battle Strategy," *LIH*, August 28, 1952, 1; "Seek Court Injunction against Gross-Morton," *BT*, September 4, 1952, 1; "Windsor Park Civic Association Plans Battle Strategy," *LIH*, September 4, 1952, 1.

24. "Tenants Crowd Court to Block Rent Hike" and "Windsor Park Tenants Lose," *Long Island Star-Journal* (hereafter *Star*), September 12, 1952, 4, and September 13, 1952, 6. See also "Please Be Fair," *LIH*, September 11, 1952, 4. Protests against rent increases also touched Campus Hall, where in September 1953 the tenants protested a rent increase of well over 10 percent ("Campus Hall Tenants Protest Rent Hike," *KHN*, September 1953, 1), and Meadowlark Gardens (*LIH*, April 1 and 8, 1954).

25. For the 1952 protest, in which 500 tenants participated, see in *GON*: "Tenants Mass In a Protest against GOV Rent Rise," June 19, 1; "Village Tenants Demand Rent Schedule Lowered," June 26, 1; "Increased Taxes 'n Costs Raise Rents: Management," June 26, 1; "Management and Tenants Agree to Discuss Rents," July 3, 1; "May Settle Rent Dispute Today," July 10, 1; "Tenants Accept Management's Reductions for Lease Renewals," July 17, 1; "Local Tenants' Committee Disbands, Divides Treasury," January 23, 1953, 1. The *GON* reported the 1954 tenants' fight in "Tenants Council Says: 'Withhold All Rents,' " April 29, 1; "Seek Rent Reductions on F.H.A. Disclosures," May 6, 1; "Tenants Council Will Meet Tonight," May 13, 1; "Court Rules against Tenants in Two Cases Brought against G.O.," June 3, 1.

26. Loans totaling $24 million were guaranteed for Glen Oaks Village, while its construction costs were only $20 million (*New York Times* [hereafter *NYT*], April 14, 1954, 1). This was disclosed as part of the Section 608 "windfall" profits scandal, as discussed by Wright, *Building the Dream*, 246–47.

27. Grand Central Apartments was located on Little Neck Parkway between Grand Central Parkway and 73rd Avenue. In *GON*, 1952, see "Many Facilities Not Granted to Grand Central Tenants," January 10, 1; "Grand Central Association to Be Established Monday," January 24, 1; "Grand Central Residents

Vote Permanent Group," January 31, 1; "Tenants Withholding Rent until Conditions Improve," February 14, 1; "The Tenants Speak," letter to the editor, February 14; "Rent Withholding Tenants May Establish Precedent, Legality Still Questioned," February 21, 1. See also "Grand Central Tenants Form Ass'n to Protest Conditions," January 26, 1956, 1.

28. The project was located between 47th and 48th Avenues and 215th and 217th Streets in Bayside. It had been purchased by the Riverside Realty Company in February 1953 and seemed to have been resold twice in the two following years. Already in 1950 the Tenants League had criticized the owner (then Kessler-Hess Corporation) for a lack of maintenance; they did so again in 1956 ("Jeffrey Tenants Form Petition," *BT*, August 3, 1950, 1; "Jeffrey Tenants Ask Assist From Mayor," *BT*, May 13, 1954, 1; "Jeffrey Gardens Apartment Sold," *BT*, July 7, 1955, 1; "Leonard Finz Demands Justice," *LIH*, May 31, 1956, 1).

29. For the developments in the "No Heat" case, see in *BT*: "Oakland Gardens Tenants Organize to Get More Heat," November 26, 1953, 1; "Tenants Take Court Action against Oakland Apt. Owners," December 3, 1953, 6; "Oakland Apt. Owners Promise to Correct All Complaints," December 17, 1953, 6; "Oakland Gardens Tenants Claim Apts. without Heat," January 21, 1954, 1; "Tenant-Owner Dispute Held for Special Sessions," January 28, 1954, 1; "No Heat Trial Starts Today," February 11, 1954, 1; "D.A. to Name Officers in 'No Heat' Case," February 18, 1954, 1; "Oakland Gardens 'No Heat' Case Reopened in Magistrate's Court," April 8, 1954, 1; "Magistrate Orders Complaint against Oakland Apt. Owners," April 22, 1954, 1; " 'No Heat' Case Settled," July 1, 1954, 1; "Oakland 'No Heat' Case Again Being Heard," October 28, 1954, 1; "Oakland Apt. Owners Guilty in 'No Heat' Case," December 16, 1954, 1; "Appeals Court Upholds Sentence in 'No Heat' Case," June 9, 1955, 1.

30. On the Liberal Party's efforts to change the New York State Rent Control Law, see Ben Davidson to Stanley Taxel, October 9, 1952, and "Report on Election Activities—1952," folder "Queens County Headquarters," box 18, LP Papers. Some local Democratic clubs also assisted tenants by providing legal counsel. See, for instance, the relationship between the Hillcrest Democratic Club and the tenants of Meadowlark in 1952 ("Meadowlark Tenants Deny Rent Increase," *LIH*, April 1, 1954, 1; "Meadowlark Tenants Continue Fight," *LIH*, April 8, 1954, 1).

31. The *GON* reported "Wallach's rent crusade" in a series of front-page articles in 1962. See "Wallach Calls for Tenant Aid in Rent Battle," July 12, 1; "Wallach Gains Support of Tenant Group," July 26, 1; "Wallach: Apartment Rent Squeeze Produces the Need for Controls," August 2, 1; "Wallach Reveals Petitions to Aid Rent Control Fight," August 16, 1; "City Speaks Softly on Wallach's Rent Crusade," August 23, 1. Wallach had himself been a tenant at Langdale Apartments in the early 1950s ("Democratic Candidate Unable to Win Liberal Support for Assembly," *GON*, August 21, 1952, 1).

32. Joel Schwartz, "Tenant Power in the Liberal City, 1943–1971," in Ronald Lawson, ed., with the assistance of Mark Naison, *The Tenant Movement in New York City, 1904–1984* (New Brunswick, N.J.: Rutgers University Press, 1986), 150.

33. This controversy is described in newspaper clippings in vertical file "United Nations," Long Island Division, Queens Borough Public Library, New York City. See esp. *NYT*, April 22, 1947, 22; June 5, 1947, 1; June 6,

1947, 5; June 7, 1947, 4; July 15, 1947, 7; July 17 1947, 3; July 18, 1947, 5; July 19, 1947, 4; July 25, 1947, 19; July 31, 1947, 19. Metropolitan Life, also the owner of Stuyvesant Town, was then famous for its successful legal battle to preserve its right to choose "suitable" tenants. On the latter case, see Charles Abrams, *Forbidden Neighbors: A Study of Prejudice in Housing* (New York: Harper & Brothers, 1955), 251–59.

34. "Last Unit Filled at U.N. 'Village,'" *NYT*, August 1, 1948, Section 8, 1; "UN Town," *LIDP*, January 23, 1949, 8; "All-Nation Block Party," *NYT*, June 25, 1949, 14.

35. "U.N. Tenants' Fight Gets New Support," *NYT*, July 11, 1952, 19. The precarious situation of the International School was further discussed in "U.N. Agency Talks of Saving Village," *NYT*, July 24, 1952, 29.

36. "20 to 35% Rent Rise Threatens a 585–Family U.N. Community," *NYT*, June 29, 1952, 1. Parkway Village Inc. argued that the rent increase was necessary to preserve a minimum return on their investment—or, as was reported in the *NYT*, "to put the project on a sound economic basis." See "Report of Parkway Village Inc. Press Conference," June 30, 1952, folder 381, "Parkway Village, working papers, 1952," box 10, Betty Friedan Papers, Schlesinger Library, Radcliffe Institute, Harvard University, Cambridge, Mass. (hereafter Friedan Papers) and "Parkway Village Faces Rent Rises," *NYT*, July 1, 1952, 31.

37. See flyer to announce the June 17 meeting, folder 383, box 10, Friedan Papers.

38. See Sylvia Bader's telegram to Mayor Impellitteri. Bader introduced herself as "Chairman for 208 American Citizens Residing in Parkway Village." She stated, "For the non-American United Nations employees . . . who earn no more than comparable civil service employees, this is a desperate situation. In addition, families from certain Asian and African countries will have to pay a premium to live in this unsegregated community which their salaries will not permit, or face the discriminatory housing practices prevailing elsewhere in New York." The mayor's intervention, she pleaded, was especially urgent considering the "international implications" that the case had. Telegram from Bader to Impellitteri, July 27, 1952, folder "Housing Project—Parkway Village Houses #619," box 53, Subject Files, Mayor Vincent R. Impellitteri Papers, New York City Municipal Archives. See also "Parkway Villagers Appeal on Rent Rise," *NYT*, July 28, 1952, 18.

39. "UN Tenants' Fight Gets New Support," *NYT*, July 11, 1952, 19. Charles Abrams later resigned as counsel to the tenants' association to join this "Citizens' Committee for the Preservation of Parkway Village." See "UN Villagers See Profit on 'Waste,'" *NYT*, July 20, 1952, 13.

40. "UN Personnel Get Offer of Rent Cut," *NYT*, September 23, 1952, 8. For other articles on the negotiations and tenants' response to the proposal, see in *NYT*: "UN Village Compromise on Rent Likely as Banks Agree to Parley," July 25, 1952, 19; "Banks Firm on Rent Rise," July 26, 1952, 21; "UN Tells Tenants: Pay More or Move," September 27, 1952, 19; "UN Tenants to Vote Today on Rent Rises," September 30, 1952, 52; "UN Tenants Reject Rent Offer By Banks," October 1, 1952, 40; "UN Tenants Advised to Drop Rent Battle," December 2, 1952, 50.

41. Folder 381, box 10, Friedan Papers. According to the newsletter's masthead, Friedan was editor of *Parkway Villager* from February 1952 to February 1954. The fact that she systematically kept copies of the *Villager*, from its first issue, dated April 23, 1949, to January 1956 suggested an active involvement,

or at least interest in the affairs of her community, throughout most of her stay in Parkway Village. Folder 382, box 10, Friedan Papers.

42. See "Opening remarks at a membership meeting conveyed to discuss the proposal which the banks have made to the rent committee," typewritten text with handwritten annotation, s.d., folder 381, box 10, Friedan Papers. This was probably the June 17 meeting, for which a flyer was found in folder 383, box 10, Friedan Papers. This theme was reiterated by a resident of Parkway Village who argued, in a letter to the editor, that the community was worth preserving because it was "America's only successful privately owned, unsegregated housing experiment." See "Housing U.N. Employees," *NYT*, September 4, 1952, 26.

43. On Friedan's involvement in Parkway Village and her work as editor of the *Parkway Villager*, see Horowitz, *Betty Friedan*, 155–61; on her involvement in Popular Front labor circles, see chaps. 6 and 7.

44. "They Found Out," folder 384, box 10, Friedan Papers, 7. Or, as she put it in conclusion, "I guess Parkway Village proves that propaganda and prejudice make mighty flimsy curtains when people get to know each other as good neighbors" (9).

45. "This Is Your Community: The Spirit of Brotherhood," *KHN*, March 1955, 1. On Schreier's own move to Kew Gardens Hills, see her "At Home in the Hills," *KHN*, December 1953, 4.

46. See "Desegregation in Washington," *Flushing Guide*, September 1955, 2, Suburban Flushing Civic Association Papers, Marilyn Mossop, Queens, N.Y. For Schreier's articles, see "School News," *KHN*, October 1957, 6, and "Oh, Promised Land!" *KHN*, October 1963.

47. On Staupers, see Darlene Clark Hine, "Mabel K. Staupers and the Integration of Black Nurses into the Armed Forces," in J. H. Franklin and August Meier, eds., *Black Leaders of the Twentieth Century* (Urbana: University of Illinois Press, 1982), 241–58. On Wilkins, see Horowitz, *Betty Friedan*, 158.

48. See "Kew Hills Residents Picket Electchester Woolworth Store," *KHN*, April 1960, 1, and "Chain Store Boycott Termed Effective," *KHN*, May 1960, 2. The picketing took place on Saturday afternoons over the two-month period. A boycott of the store was also called.

49. "Many Kew Hills Residents in Washington Civil Rights March," *KHN*, September 1963, 1, and "Local Committee Organized to Support Pres. Kennedy's Civil Rights Program," *KHN*, October 1963, 1

50. "Osias Residents Urge Liberal Rental Policy," *LIH*, July 3, 1952; "Osias Tenants Further Fight Discrimination," *LIH*, April 10, 1952, 15.

51. See "Neighbors for Brotherhood," *KHN*, September 1954, 2; "New Housing Survey Planned," *KHN*, November 1954, 4. See also "Workshop Is Planned on Integration in Housing," *KHN*, November 1956, 1.

52. "Neighbors for Brotherhood," *KHN*, June 1954, 1. See also "Inter-Cultural Contact," *KHN*, March 1954, 1.

53. It attracted between 700 and 1,000 residents each February. "Brotherhood Week—A History," *ML*, February 15, 1951, 2; "20 KGH Groups Sponsoring a Brotherhood Festival," *KHN*, February 1955, 1; "Brotherhood Festival Set for Next Month," *KHN*, January 1956, 1; "KGH Brotherhood Festival Sponsored by Local Clubs," *KHN*, February 1956, 1; "KGH Meeting Observes U.S. Negro History Week," *KHN*, February 1956, 1; "Overflow Crowd Attends KGH Brotherhood Festival," *KHN*, March 1956, 1; "Annual Brotherhood Festival Attended by Overflow Crowd," KHN, March 1957, 1; "KGH Brother-

hood Festival Sponsored by Local Clubs," *KHN*, January 1958, 1; "Annual Brotherhood Festival Attended by Overflow Crowd," *KHN*, March 1959, 1; "Overflow Crowd Expected at Brotherhood Festival," *KHN*, February 1960, 1; "Annual Brotherhood Festival Planned by Kew Hills Groups," *KHN*, January 1961, 1; "Annual Brotherhood Festival Draws Enthusiastic Crowd," *KHN*, February 1963, 1; "Annual Brotherhood Festival Will Be Here Next Month," *KHN*, January 1964, 1.

54. In addition to the articles cited below, see "Brotherhood Week—A History," *ML*, February 15, 1951, 2; "Brotherhood Week," *BT*, February 26, 1948, 6; "Interfaith Services, Rally Herald Brotherhood Edict," *ML*, February 16, 1950, 1.

55. "Nucleus Formed for Mass Brotherhood Week Program," *ML*, December 7, 1950, 1; "UN Official Sets Theme of Future Brotherhood Week Area Conclaves," *ML*, February 22, 1951, 1.

56. "Be a Brother," *LIH*, February 11, 1954, 7. In 1953, B'nai B'rith and the PTAs had brought the theme to youngsters in public schools, asking them to "design posters illustrating the brotherhood of man" and organizing a pageant of mothers dressed in various national costumes (Indian, Puritan, Scotch, French, Scandinavian, German, Irish, Italian, Czech, and Israeli). The *LIH* proudly reported that " 'Standing Room Only' crowds flocked to the Hillcrest Jewish Center" ("Brotherhood Lives," editorial, *LIH*, January 15, 1953, 4; "Observe Brotherhood Week" and "P.S. 173 Pageant," *LIH*, February 19, 1953, 1).

57. " 'Headlines' Smears Ike in Passing," *GON*, July 3, 1952, 3; "More Mud Means More 'Headlines' " and "Hate," *GON*, July 10, 1952, 2, 3.

58. " 'Third Party' New Hate Cry," *GON*, August 14, 1952, 1, and "Hatists Hide behind Flag," *GON*, August 21, 1952, 1.

59. In the series "Balance Sheet," see the following: "Civil Rights in the United States," July 17; "Study Finds 'Hate Groups' On Wane," July 24; "Fight for Non-Segregated Housing," July 31; and "Modest Assaults Replace Lynching," August 7. See also letter to the editor, *GON*, July 24, 1952, 4. The editors' stand did not bring them only praises. See "Bigotry at Home," *GON*, August 14, 1952, 4.

60. "Windsor Park's Garages May Be A-Bomb Shelters," *BT*, September 28, 1950, 1.

61. "Bomb Shelter for Small Home Owners on Display in Bayside," *BT*, May 3, 1951, 1.

62. For a description of the Civil Defense campaign, see Paul Boyer, *By the Bomb's Early Light: American Thought and Culture at the Dawn of the Atomic Age* (New York: Pantheon Books, 1985), 319, and JoAnne Brown, " 'A Is for Atom, B Is for Bomb': Civil Defense in American Public Education, 1948–1963," *Journal of American History* 75 (June 1988): 68–90.

63. For responses and debate, see in *ML*, 1951: "No Mental Cases in Raid Drills, Educators, State Senator Affirm," February 1, 1; "Civil Defense Fans Out through Area" and letters to the editor, February 8, 1, 7, 12; letter to the editor, February 22, 4; "A Call for Our Self-Defense" and letters to the editor, March 1, 1, 6; "Civil Defense," March 8, 1.

64. "Mrs. Gordon Seeks 200 Housewives for Emergency," *BT*, December 14, 1950, 13; "Organizations Invited to CD Meeting Tonight," *BT*, January 4, 1951, 1; "It's Your Move," editorial, *BT*, January 11, 1951, 12; "Home Defense Lags—Because of Apathy," *BT*, January 11, 1951, 3; "Air Raid Wardens—5,000 Are Needed," *BT*, January 25, 1951; "CD Rally Hears of Plan for Recruitment

Day," *BT*, January 11, 1951, 2; "Basement Phones Tie Local CD," *ML*, May 3, 1951, 1; "Civil Defense Station Ready to Serve," *ML*, June 28, 1951, 1; "Civil Defense to Train Housewives," *ML*, July 19, 1951, 1; Minutes, Meeting of Officers and Directors, 1949–1954, January 22, 1953, 221, Flushing Council of Women's Organizations' Papers, Queens, N.Y. (hereafter FCWO Papers).

65. Minutes, 1945–49, December 12, 1946, 77–79; March 25, 1948, 176; December 9, 1948, 213, FCWO Papers.

66. Robert Griffith, *The Politics of Fear: Joseph R. McCarthy and the Senate*, 2nd ed. (1970; Amherst: University of Massachusetts Press, 1987), 117–22.

67. " 'Stop the Mundt Bill,' Is Citizens' Committee's Cry," *ML*, June 22, 1950, 2, and "Mundt Bill Rally Attracts Throngs," *ML*, July 13, 1950, 2.

68. "McCarthy's Bank Account," *GON*, June 18, 1953, 1. Among the articles published in this series between June 18 and August 6, see "How to Snub the Senate and Succeed," "Anti-Red $ Earn Profit of $17,000," "How to Raise $10,000 Effortlessly," and "Sugar Fight Earns Sweet $20,000." Upon concluding of its series, the *GON* noted, "There are many other things questionable about Senator McCarthy. We even question the sincerity of his fight against communism. If, as the committee discovered, some of the funds sent to the senator for his campaign were diverted to personal investments, then we have some amount of evidence that McCarthy is more money-happy than anti-communist" ("Completed, but Not Completely," editorial, August 6, 1953, 2). For other *GON* editorials attacking McCarthy, see "The Correct Answer," July 16, 1953; "Not Doing Too Well," August 20, 1953, 4.

69. In *GON*, see "A Balloon Is Burst," March 18, 1954, 4; "More Suspicion," April 8, 1954, 4; " 'A Point of Order'," April 28, 1954, 4; "Greater Strength Needed," June 17, 1954, 4. For other Barasch editorials condemning the violation of civil liberties, see "A Frightened America," October 9, 1953, 4; "A Picture of Us," February 18, 1954, 1.

70. In the summer of 1950, the ALP—whose chairman, Vito Marcantonio, had been the only member of the House of Representatives to protest Truman's decision to intervene in Korea—held a rally at Madison Square Garden to protest American intervention in Korea. The text of Marcantonio's intervention from the *Congressional Record* was reproduced in the program of the Peace Festival (see folder "1950," American Labor Party Papers, Tamiment Institute Library, New York University). See also Robert F. Carter, "Pressure from the Left: The American Labor Party, 1936–1954" (Ph.D. diss., Syracuse University, 1965), 410–11.

71. " 'Do Recent Events Spell Peace or War?' Localities Ask Selves," *ML*, June 29, 1950, 2; " 'Peace Councils' Spring Up," *BT*, June 29, 1950, 17; " 'Peace Petitions' Started in Area," *BT*, July 6, 1950, 13.

72. " 'Peace Petitions' Started in Area." See Lawrence S. Wittner, *Rebels against War: The American Peace Movement, 1933–1983* (Philadelphia: Temple University Press, 1984), 203–5.

73. On the ALP and LP, see Carter, *Pressure from the Left*; Kenneth Alan Waltzer, "The American Labor Party: Third Party Politics in New Deal-Cold War New York, 1936–1954" (Ph.D. diss., Harvard University, 1977), and Bernard Rosenberg, "New York Politics and the Liberal Party," *Commentary* 37 (February 1964): 69–75. On the ADA, see Steven M. Gillon, *Politics and Vision: The ADA and American Liberalism, 1947–1985* (New York: Oxford University Press, 1987).

74. Letter to the editor, *ML*, July 13, 1950, 6.

75. "ADA Branch Hits Local Peace Groups," *ML*, July 20, 1950, 3; "An Editorial: There Is No Peace," *BT*, July 20, 1950, 1.
76. Letter to the editor, *BT*, July 20, 1950, 8.
77. "Peace Group Ducks Critics to Hear Nehru Proposals," *BT*, August 10, 1950, 1, and "Anti-Franco Rally to Hear Norman Thomas," *BT*, August 17, 1950, 1.
78. While condemning the peace appeal as "intended to divert world attention from Soviet aggression," the veterans had judged as an infringement of civil liberties a resolution that called upon the post commander to advise each and every member to refrain from participation in the peace appeal, and they refused to endorse it. See "Stormy JWV Meeting Condemns Peace Petitions," *BT*, August 10, 1950, 10.
79. " 'Declaration of Freedom' Campaign Gets under Way," *BT*, October 5, 1950, 1; "Enough of 'Catnip,' " *BT*, October 5, 1950, 18; "Freedom Crusade Winds Up with Signing This Week," *BT*, October 19, 1950, 1.
80. "Renounce 'Peace' Women," letter to the editor, *BT*, November 2, 1950, 28.
81. *ML*, September 21, 1950, 6. Bendiner reiterated his charges in *ML*, October 12, 1950, 5.
82. Letter to the editor, *BT*, October 12, 1950, 18.
83. "Letter to *Lark* Editor Draws Sharp Rebuttal by 26 Executive Body" and "P.S. 26 PTA—Several Opinions," *ML*, September 28, 1950, 1, 4, 5. The editor noted that these opinions were representatives of the letters received in reply to Bendiner. "Leadership Upheld at Stormy PTA Session," *ML*, October 26, 1950, 1.
84. "PTA Queries Stir Ire of Candidates for Group Election," *ML*, May 10, 1951, 1; letters to the editor, *ML*, May 10 and 17, 1951; "Belle Steinglass Named President of 26 PTA," *BT*, May 31, 1951, 9.
85. "Candidate Sets School Plans," *LIH*, January 31 1952, 1.
86. "A Political Fraud," *LIH*, February 7, 1952, 4. The campaign material issued by the "Better Schools Committee" (which listed Bearman's address) and found in the ALP papers did not mention the ALP endorsement. See folder "Queens County," box "1952 Pu-Sta," series I, American Labor Party Papers, Special Collections and Archives, Alexander Library, Rutgers University, New Brunswick, N.J. (hereafter ALP Papers, Rutgers).
87. "Aroused Parents Move to Regain Power at P.S. 26," *LIH*, May 1, 1952; "P.S. 26 Parents Back Leaders; Hit Untruths," *LIH*, May 8, 1952, 1; "Carlin Answers Charges of PTA," *LIH*, May 15, 1952, 3; letters to the editor, *LIH*, May 22, 1952, 4; "P.S. 26 Picks Officers for PTA Season," *LIH*, May 29, 1952, 1; letters to the editor, *LIH*, June 12, 1952, 4.
88. As reported in the former case, "At first the proposal [to withdraw from the Kew Meadows Committee] was turned down by the executive board of the Parent Association. One of the members of the board [Mrs. Evelyn Ranter], however, presented the report to the full membership . . . and the break was officially sanctioned" ("P.S. 164 Parents Quit Kew M'dows School League," *LIH*, April 3, 1952, 1; "PTA Quits Kew Meadows Ass'n," *LIH*, May 1, 1952, 1). The decision of the PTA of P.S. 173 to withdraw from the Kew Meadows Committee was also taken over the opposition of its president, Mary Bancroft. It was initiated by Gertrude Halpern, who had been president of the group from its beginning in September 1949 until June 1951, when she was replaced by Mary Bancroft ("PTA Quits Kew Meadows Ass'n," *LIH*, May 1, 1952, 1). In December 1952, Bancroft's teaching license was suspended when she refused

to respond to a Board of Education's investigation of her Communist sympathies. Her husband, Frank, was also suspended from his position as a document editor for the United Nations ("Mary Bancroft Loses Her City Teaching License" and "Abused Rights!" *LIH*, December 4, 1952, 1 and 4).

89. Letter to the editor, *ML*, October 12, 1950, 3.

90. "The End?" editorial, *ML*, October 26, 1950, 6.

91. "Meadows Assn. Protests Public Opposition Here," *LIH*, May 8, 1952, 1.

92. On the membership of the local ALP, see "New ALP Unit Will Meet in Oakland Gardens," *BT*, December 8, 1949, 9; "Bayside Hills ALP to Elect Chairman," *ML*, February 2, 1950, 8; "ALP Meets Tomorrow," *BT*, March 16, 1950, 1. The total number of ALP members in Queens increased from 321 in January 1949 to 1,318 in February 1950 and 1,380 in August 1952 (Queens ALP Membership Bulletin, January 17, 1949, folder "Queens County," box "1948–49 Q-U," series I; Action Letter, February 7, 1950, folders "Queens County 1949–50" and "Queens County 1951–53," box "1949–1953 Q-Z," series II; all in ALP Papers, Rutgers). On ADA membership, see "Comparison in Branch Membership," April 26, 1951, series III, "Chapter File, 1943–1965," reel 72, Americans for Democratic Action Papers, Wisconsin State Historical Society, Madison. According to enrollment figures compiled by the Liberal Party of New York State, in October 1949 the LP and the ALP were head to head in Queens, each with approximately 11,000 members. This represented a gain of 36 percent for the LP, whose membership had increased from 8,100 since October 1948, and a loss for the ALP, who had 14,502 members a year earlier. In New York City's five boroughs, the membership of the LP was 112,859 and the ALP was 164,229. See "To All Liberal Party Clubs," January 17, 1950, folder "Correspondence—All Clubs, 1950," box 10, LP Papers.

93. "Neighborhood News Capsules," *ML*, September 21, 1950, 9; "P.S. 26 Parents Back Leaders; Hit Untruths," *LIH*, May 8, 1952, 1.

94. "For an End to the Cold War," *Action Letter*, April 21, 1950, folder "Queens County, 1949–50," box "1949–1953 Q-Z," series II, ALP Papers, Rutgers.

95. "Role of Local AVC Chap. Traced at New Unit Meeting," *ML*, March 16, 1950, 4.

96. For the 1950 and 1951 elections, see "Bell Park Forming Council of Residents," *BT*, December 22, 1949, 20; "Bell Park Elects Kramer," *BT*, January 26, 1950, 9; "Vets Elect Gil, Schwartz," *BT*, March 2, 1950, 24; "Bell Park Elects 28 to New Community Council," *BT*, March 30, 1950, 16. See also *BT*, January 11, 1951, 8; January 18, 1951, 1; January 25, 1951, 8.

97. "Minutes, Housing Conference," 2–3, folder "Conference Housing and Rent Control, 1953," box 21, 2–3, LP Papers.

98. See Letter to the Editor, *BT*, August 3, 1950, 8, and *BT*, August 10, 1950, 8; " 'Bell Park Residents for Peace' Change Name," *BT*, September 7, 1950, 13.

Chapter 4. Active Citizenship and Community Needs in Queens

1. "Larger and Stronger," *Bayside Times* (hereafter *BT*), December 28, 1950, 10.

2. Stanley Elkins and Eric McKitrick, "A Meaning for Turner's Frontier," *Political Science Quarterly* 69 (September and December 1954): 321–53, 565–602.

3. William M. Dobriner, *Class in Suburbia* (Englewood Cliffs, N.J.: Prentice-Hall, 1963), 111. Herbert J. Gans also described the multifaceted political in-

volvement of the residents of Levittown, N.J., in *The Levittowners: Ways of Life and Politics in a New Suburban Community* (New York: Pantheon, 1967). So did Harry Henderson with his descriptions of PTA meetings as "jammed and often loud with queries and arguments" ("Rugged American Collectivism: The Mass-Produced Suburbs," *Harper's Magazine*, December 1953, 81).

4. On the meaning of the idea of community in American culture, see Thomas Bender, *Community and Social Change in America* (Baltimore: Johns Hopkins University Press, 1978).

5. Minutes, regular meeting, December 15, 1936, Bayside Hills Civic Association Papers, Bayside Hills Civic Association, Queens, N.Y. (hereafter BHCA Papers). The 1938 edition of the Constitution and Bylaws of the North Shore Civic Alliance, Inc. listed sixteen charter members (Bayside Taxpayers Improvement Association Papers, Bayside Historical Society, Queens, N.Y. [hereafter BTIA Papers]).

6. As noted at a meeting of the BHCA's Board of Directors meeting, June 5, 1950, the associations along Horace Harding Boulevard (now the Long Island Expressway) initiated the formation of the UCC (Minutes, BHCA Papers). Among the early members of the UCC were the Horace Harding, Harding Heights, Utopia Park, Flushing Suburban, and Fresh Meadows Civic Associations, the Queens Valley Home Owners' Association, and the associations near Cunningham Park. Figures on the membership of the UCC were gathered from a variety of sources. See circular letter from Daniel Russo, UCC president, to affiliated civic associations, Oakland Hills Civic Association Papers, Bayside Historical Society, Queens, N.Y. (hereafter OHCA Papers); "Russo Resigns from Presidency of UCC," *Long Island Herald* (hereafter *LIH*), December 31, 1952, 1; "Join United Civic" and "Daniel Russo Returned as United Civic Proxy," *Meadow Lark* (hereafter *ML*), September 16, 1948, 4, and December 21, 1950, 8; "Julia E. Jerry Named to Board," *LIH*, June 9, 1960, 1; and "Recommendations of the Queens Federation of Civic Councils, New York City Program," January 1967, manuscript, Julia Jerry Papers, Queens, N.Y. (hereafter Jerry Papers). For a description of the UCC's major functions in its first ten years of existence, see Daniel Russo to Lucille G. Willcutt, August 7, 1950, OHCA Papers.

7. Besides the UCC the other councils were the North Shore Council of Home Owners, which in 1967 had twenty-three affiliated associations (previously the North Shore Civic Alliance), the Central Queens Allied Civic Council (founded in 1927), the United Civic Council of Southern Queens, the Eastern Queens Civic Council, and the Queens County Civic Council. The formation of the Federation is described in "Meet Edward Costello—Organizer of Civic Federation of All Queens," *Home Town News* (hereafter *HTN*), March 12, 1957, 1.

8. "Queens Is Growing, and So Are Its Troubles," *New York Times* [hereafter *NYT*], November 29, 1963, 39.

9. Federation's stationery, Jerry Papers.

10. For the text of the declaration of purposes of the FCWO, see Certificate of Incorporation of the Flushing Council of Woman's Organizations, Inc., 1949, in Scrapbook "Flushing's Freedom Mile." The same statement of purposes was included in the foreword to the Revised Constitution and Bylaws, 1987 edition. Information about the formation of the FCWO is available in a scrapbook of newspaper clippings (mostly from the *Flushing Journal*) compiled by Suzanne R. Knowles, founder of the FCWO, in March 1973. Information

about the membership was found in the FCWO minutes (1945–49, 20; 1954–59, October 18, 1954) and in "Flushing's Freedom Mile." For Streator's notes, see President's Book, 1941–51, March 22, 1945. All in FCWO Papers, FCWO, Queens, N.Y.

11. "Say It with Civics," *ML*, September 21, 1950, 6.

12. "Something to Think About," *HTN*, December 31, 1957, 1.

13. *Beacon*, June 1956, BHCA Papers.

14. "Burke Lauds Home Show as Model House Opens," *Long Island Daily Press*, March 27, 1949, 5. In a letter to Commissioner Tayler, Home Relief Bureau, dated May 13, 1933, the Bayside Taxpayers and Improvement Association also boldly stated that its members "look upon home owners as much more better [*sic*] citizens" than renters (folder "correspondence, 1932–1936," BTIA Papers). For a good overview of the ideological connections between home ownership and good citizenship, especially after World War I, see Margaret Marsh, *Suburban Lives* (New Brunswick, N.J.: Rutgers University Press, 1990), 130–34.

15. Constitution and Bylaws of the Bayside Hills Civic Association, Inc., September 1953. The emphasis has been added. Its official purpose, as stated in 1936, was "to bring together . . . those who are interested in civic betterment of any nature, with the purpose of promoting the cause of good citizenship ("Preamble to the Constitution," bylaws, circa 1936, BHCA Papers).

16. October 1940, 4, BHCA Papers.

17. Typescript, s.d., Jerry Papers.

18. "Salute Oakland Gardens" and "The Toughest Year," editorial, *BT*, February 2, 1950, 1, 8.

19. The OGCA cooperated with the Greater Bayside Citizens' Association to improve bus service in the area ("Citizens' Meeting at Legion Hall Probes Bus Problem Tonight," *BT*, March 10, 1949, 1, and "OGCA to Hear Bus, Community House Talks," *BT*, November 3, 1949, 1). See also "Form Oakland Garden Civic-Social Group," *BT*, February 10, 1949, 1. In a similar fashion, 350 tenants of Windsor Park formed a civic association in the summer of 1952 to obtain public services such as traffic lights (letter to the editor, *BT*, January 24, 1952, 16).

20. See the program souvenir, *Bell Park Gardens: Independence Celebration, 1950–1991*, May 5, 1991, Bell Park Gardens Community Council Papers, Sidney and Beatrice Ifshin, Bayside, N.Y. See also "Bell Park Forming Council of Residents," *BT*, December 22, 1949, 20.

21. "Kew Hills News Marks Its Tenth Birthday," *Kew Hills News* (hereafter *KHN*), September 1963, 1.

22. See "Mid-Queens Community Council, A Seven-Year Story," *KHN*, September 1962, 10; "Coordinating Council Holds First Meeting," *KHN*, October 1955, 5.

23. "Mid-Queens Community Council, A Seven-Year Story."

24. *The Community Press in an Urban Setting: The Social Elements of Urbanism* (1952; Chicago: University of Chicago Press, 1967), x–xii. In 1963, sixty community papers catered to New York City neighbourhoods, and their concentration was apparently even greater in Brooklyn and Queens (Janowitz, xiii; see also "Weeklies' Voice Is Strong in City," *NYT*, November 26, 1963, 3). For a description of the Queens weeklies, see "Queens Community Newspapers," appendix I.

25. See Wallace S. Sayre and Herbert Kaufman, *Governing New York City* (1960; New York: Russell Sage Foundation, 1965), 84.

26. "Love Thy Neighbor," *LIH*, February 4, 1954, 4. For examples of the *ML*'s support of local merchants, see "Cooperation Necessary," editorial, April 22, 1948, 4, and "In the Works!" editorial, April 8, 1948, 4. The *BT* similarly relied on advertising and supported local merchants (see December 26, 1946, 6; May 15, 1947, 10). For relationships between the weekly press and local businesses and merchants associations, see also Janowitz, *The Community Press*, 23, 35–36.

27. "Growing . . . Growing . . . Growing . . .," editorial, *Pomonok News* (hereafter *PN*), September 10, 1952, 2.

28. *PN*, October 1952, 2; November 1952, 2.

29. Important Announcement," *KHN*, February 1958.

30. "Tenants Honor First President," *KHN*, December 1955, 12.

31. "Fourth Anniversary," editorial, *Glen Oaks News* (hereafter *GON*), June 5, 1952, 1; "Paper Began as 8–Page Weekly in '48, Still 8–Page Weekly," *GON*, June 4, 1953, 1; "A Statement," editorial, *ML*, October 5, 1950, 6. As we saw in Chapter 3, the *Bayside Times* took position during the debate stirred by the pacifists. During the debate over moderate-income public housing discussed in Chapter 2, the weeklies remained impartial, while the Long Island dailies conducted a systematic campaign of distortion. A good example of the dailies' sensationalism is their treatment of women's public role, especially in the case of baby carriage parades (see Chapter 6).

32. "Good Luck!" *LIH*, January 22, 1953, 4.

33. "Will You Be There?" *LIH*, October 29, 1953, 4; See also "Did You Register?" October 7, 1954, 4; "Will You Be There?" November 3, 1955, 4.

34. In *LIH*, see the following: "Let Freedom Ring," June 28, 1956, 4; "Your Vote Counts," August 23, 1956, 4; "Look, Listen and Vote," October 4, 1956, 4; "New Political Column to Appear in *Herald*," October 11, 1956, 3; "Voting Is Privilege," November 1, 1956, 4. One finds the same litany in 1957 and in the following years: see "Let Freedom Ring!" July 4, 1957, 4; "Have You Registered?" July 11, 1957, 4; "Voting Is Your Privilege," October 31, 1957, 4; "Vote Tuesday," October 30, 1958, 4; "Vote Tuesday," October 29, 1959, 4; "Our Final Word," November 4, 1960, 4; "Vote Vote Vote," November 2, 1961, 4; "Be Sure You Vote!" October 31, 1963; "Every Vote Counts, So Vote and Be Counted," October 29, 1964, 4; "Voting Is Up to You," September 2, 1965, 8.

35. "Privilege of Voting," *GON*, September 18, 1952, 4.

36. "Pomonok Tenants' Council to Hold First '52–'53 Meeting," *PN*, September 10, 1952, 1.

37. "Which One Are You?" *HTN*, July 15, 1958, 1.

38. "Protecting Your Interests," editorial, *GON*, August 21, 1952, 1.

39. The Fresh Meadows branch was organized in June 1948 ("Women Voters Organized in Area," *ML*, June 10, 1948, 1; "Gals Pick New Officers," *ML*, October 6, 1949, 8). The North Shore branch was formed in early 1949 to regroup women living in the Bayside and Little Neck area ("League of Women Voters to Meet," *BT*, February 17, 1949, 13). The third branch was located in Glen Oaks. In 1959, an internal report noted that "Fresh Meadows continues to be the strongest branch in Queens." See folder "Analysis of Branch Annual Reports, 1958–1963," box 7, Papers of the League of Women Voters of New York City, Rare Book and Manuscript Library, Butler Memorial Library, Columbia University.

On the importance that the League attributed to "promoting political responsibility" in the postwar period, see minutes of the New York City Convention,

1947, p. 8, box 27. See also their publication *The Art of Citizenship* (New York: League of Women Voters, 1948), folder "Membership," box 42. Finally, see Susan Ware, "American Women in the 1950s: Nonpartisan Politics and Women's Politicization," in Louise A. Tilly and Patricia Gurin, eds., *Women, Politics, and Change* (New York: Russell Sage Foundation, 1990), 281–99.

On the LWV's activities in Queens, see "Only 2 Days Left to Register for Elections," *ML*, October 13, 1949, 1; "Register or Lose Vote, Public Told," *ML*, October 5, 1950, 1; "Primary Day Aug. 21 Queens to Vote for 9; 'Run, Don't Walk to Polls' Urges Women's League," *ML*, August 16, 1951, 1; "Women Voters Visit Meadows," *LIH*, May 31, 1956, 5; "Primary Day and Before," *GON*, June 7, 1956, 1; "LWV Opens Voters Info Booth at Dan's," *GON*, October 12, 1961, 1. Rubin's quote is from *GON*, January 31, 1952, 4.

40. "Zionists Plan 'Town Meeting,' " *ML*, February 10, 1949, 2; " 'Town Hall' Zoning Conclaves Sketched," *ML*, September 14, 1950, 1; "Vets Hold Town Meeting on Community Center," *BT*, August 24, 1950, 16; "Vets Have a Problem," *BT*, August 31, 1950, 16, 1; "Vets Weigh BP Surplus," *ML*, November 2, 1950, 1; "Merits of Town Meetings," *BT*, October 16, 1952, 14.

41. *Beacon*, April 1940, 6.

42. Minutes of the Regular Meeting, November 25, 1952 and October 13, 1953, BHCA Papers. Again, in 1950, Daniel Russo described the UCC meeting as reminiscent of "the old form of 'Town Hall' meetings . . . truly an expression of democratic principle and action" (Russo to Willcutt, October 20, 1950).

43. "Wallach Organizes Town Get-Together," *GON*, October 23, 1958, 4; "Lou Wallach Calls Civic Town Meeting," *LIH*, October 30, 1958, 1. The editor of the *Home Town News* expressed the same idea when he wrote, "Civic associations are instituted for one purpose. To hold check reins on government. To make the word of the people heard within government chambers" (editorial, *HTN*, April 20, 1955, 2).

44. "Meet Your Local Candidates: Edward Sharf," *PN*, October 1952, 1.

45. "Burke Installs Kuhn," *BT*, September 30, 1948, 6.

46. "An Exclusive to the *Home Town News*," *HTN*, June 3, 1958, 7. Crisona's plans, deferred at the end of 1958 as his tenure ended, were to create "direct contact with every community through the community planning councils" in order to assist the borough president. Composed of civic leaders and of a myriad of professionals (engineers, architects, lawyers, businessmen, and bankers) from the various communities, the councils were planned to assist the Queens Advisory Planning Board, an official body authorized by the city charter whose members were appointed by the borough president. They were designed to bring to the attention of the borough president problems and suggested solutions regarding zoning, traffic, parking, transit, and other improvements. The areas covered by the planning councils corresponded to the territories within the sphere of the six civic councils comprising the Federated Civic Councils of Queens ("Crisona Delays Planning Councils So Successor Can Review Planning," *HTN*, December 9, 1958, 5; see also *LIH*, December 11, 1958, 1).

47. "Boro President Notes Civic Importance," *LIH*, February 13, 1964, 1. In June, it was reported that Cariello "again praised 350 civic organizations for their cooperation with the borough president's office and help in the proper development of the borough" (*LIH*, June 11, 1964, 1; see also "Cariello Calls Civic Meeting," *LIH*, July 2, 1964, 1 and "Top Civic Leaders Back Boro Presi-

dent's Requests," *LIH*, July 9, 1964, 1). For discussion of the new Community Planning Boards, see "Borough Hall Seeks Community Planners," *LIH*, January 3, 1963, 1. See also "Boro Prexy Announces Local Planning Boards," *LIH*, January 23, 1964 and *By Laws of Community Boards: Borough of Queens*, typescript, Jerry Papers, s.d.

48. "Support Your Civic Groups," editorial, *BT*, September 4, 1952, 20. See also "It's Your Job, Too!" *LIH*, September 11, 1952, 4, and "Join Now!" *ML*, August 4, 1949, 1.

49. "Civic Workers," editorial, *BT*, September 17, 1936, 6.

50. "Heart Fells Osterman," *LIH*, February 21, 1952, 2.

51. "Our Civic Groups," *BT*, January 22, 1942, 6.

52. Ibid.

53. The constitution of the North Shore Civic Alliance (1938) explicitly excluded "political organizations" from membership (BTIA Papers). The preamble to the 1936 constitution of the Bayside Hills Civic Association specified that "we shall have no affiliation with any political organization"; its revised 1953 version read, "we shall have no affiliation with any Commercial, Political, or Religious organizations" (BHCA Papers).

54. "Civics in Political Swim" and "Unleased," *ML*, June 15, 1950, 1, 6. See also "Civics to Draw Campaign Maps," *ML*, June 22, 1950, 1; "Civics Set Political Timetable," *ML*, July 20, 1950, 1; "Parties Eye UCC Endorsements as Races Tighten," *ML*, October 19, 1950, 1. In a letter to an affiliated association dated October 1950, UCC president Daniel Russo explained the Council's decision as such. "The consensus of opinion at that June 12th meeting, without a single voice expressing its disapproval, was that while we perhaps should not be politicians, we should be interested in the background and cooperative action of those who seek political and public office." Russo to Lucille Willcutt, Oakland Hills Community Association, October 20, 1950, OHCA Papers.

55. Letter to the editor, by John J. O'Connor, *ML*, October 12, 1950, 3; letter to the editor, by Joseph A. Corello, *ML*, November 2, 1950, 8.

56. For classic negative assessments of the independent voter, see Angus Campbell et al., *The American Voter* (New York: John Wiley, 1960), 143; Norman H. Nie, Sidney Verba, and John R. Petrocik, *The Changing American Voter* (1976; Cambridge: Harvard University Press, 1979), esp. chap. 2, "The American Public in the 1950s," 14–42; Fuchs, *The Political Behavior of American Jews* (Glencoe, Ill.: Free Press, 1956), 132–33. In *Revolt of the Moderates* (New York: Harper & Brothers, 1956), Samuel Lubell also characterized 1950s middle-class voters as being in "restless revolt against both parties" (6). He noted that ticket splitting was seen as a way to "get more honest men" (111), which is also in line with the approach taken in Queens.

57. Bulletin of the Kew Gardens Hills Regular Democratic Club, October 1953, folder "1953 Queens County," box 21, Records of the Liberal Party of New York State, Manuscripts and Archives Division, New York Public Library, Astor, Lenox and Tilden Foundations.

58. "Queens Independent Demos Support Halley," *LIH*, August 13, 1953, 1. See also "Queens Civic Committee to Back Impy's Reelection," *BT*, July 23, 1953, 1, and "Queens Ind. Party Formed," *LIH*, August 27, 1953, 2. The "Independent, Unbossed, Unbossable" is from "Halley Fights On," a campaign pamphlet published for Halley's 1951 bid for City Council (folder "1951 campaign," box 16, LP Papers). See also "Halley Pledges! Clean Up City!" (*LIH*,

July 30, 1953, 1), which highlighted Halley's investigation for the Kefauver Commission as illustration of his commitment to uphold the rights of "upstanding citizens" against corrupt government. Halley polled 81,381 votes in Queens, behind Robert Wagner Jr. (207,958) and Republican candidate Harold Riegelman (206,782). See "Queens Re-elects Lundy; Barnes Wins Council Seat," *BT*, November 5, 1953, 1.

59. See "Julius Feigenbaum Conducts Meetings," *LIH*, September 2, 1954, 12; "Julius Feigenbaum Runs for Office," *LIH*, August 26, 1954, 2; "Civic Leader. Julius Feigenbaum," *HTN*, April 23, 1957, 1.

60. " 'Petticoat Brigade' Backs Nat H. Hentel," *LIH*, August 30, 1956, 1; "Hentel's Petticoat Brigade Begins Campaign Tactics," *BT*, August 30, 1956, 1; "Independent Party Opens Offices Drive to Elect Nat H. Hentel," *HTN*, October 2, 1956, 2; "Headquarters Opened to Elect Nat Hentel," *LIH*, October 4, 1956, 1; "IFV for Hentel Urges Election Reform," *LIH*, October 11, 1956, 10; "Report Dems Swing to Hentel," *GON*, November 1, 1956.

Chapter 5. The School Crisis and Citizens' View of Metropolitan Development

1. Steve Fraser and Gary Gerstle, eds., *The Rise and Fall of the New Deal Order, 1930–1980* (Princeton, N.J.: Princeton University Press, 1989), and Alan Brinkley, *The End of Reform: New Deal Liberalism in Recession and War* (New York: Vintage Books, 1995).

2. In *The Great School Wars: A History of the New York City Public Schools* (1974; New York: Basic Books, 1988), Diane Ravitch argued that by 1940 the New York City school system had solved its chronic overcrowding problem (239). Her analysis does not take into account the postwar baby boom or the tremendous migration that brought families from Manhattan and the older sections of Brooklyn and the Bronx to undeveloped areas in the Bronx and Queens. Racial integration is the only "great school war" of the postwar period that she analyzed during this period.

3. Rose Shapiro to Mayor O'Dwyer, December 31, 1945, folder "PTA #300," box 992 #37, General Correspondence (hereafter GC), Mayor William O'Dwyer Papers, New York City Municipal Archives (hereafter O'Dwyer Papers).

4. Shapiro to O'Dwyer, April 18, 1946, folder "PTA #302," box 992 #37, GC, O'Dwyer Papers; Streator to O'Dwyer, May 5, 1946, folder "Education, Board of, April–June 1946," box 4, Departmental Correspondence (hereafter DC), O'Dwyer Papers.

5. Lateiner to Impellitteri, March 1, 1951, folder "Schools—Queens, 1950–1951 #1274," box 115, Subject Files (hereafter SF), Mayor Vincent R. Impellitteri Papers, New York City Municipal Archives (hereafter Impellitteri Papers).

6. See "Confidential Memorandum on School Building Program," September 10, 1946, folder "Education, Board of, Jan.–March 1947," box 21, DC, O'Dwyer Papers.

7. Shapiro to O'Dwyer, September 14, 1947, folder "PTA, Part 2," box 1018 #97, GC, O'Dwyer Papers.

8. "Mayor O'Dwyer's Report on the Financing, Activities, and Progress of New

York City's Public School System since January 1st, 1946," 1949, folder "Mayor's Departmental Reports, Education #998," box 95, SF, O'Dwyer Papers.

9. Before the opening of P.S. 46, most of Oakland Gardens and Bell Park Gardens children attended P.S. 31, in Bayside Hills, P.S. 41, at 35th Avenue and 214th Street in Bayside (three miles from Oakland Gardens), and P.S. 109, in Queens Village. The home owners of the area had long been fighting for the addition of a wing to P.S. 31. See "The Case for Public School 31, Queens," Presented by William V. Kuhn on behalf of Bayside Hills Civic Association, Inc., Parent-Teachers Association of Public School 31, Oakland Hills Community Association, Rocky Hill Terrace Residents Association, Bellside Civic Association, October 26, 1949, Collection "Oakland Hills–Bayside Hills Civic Associations," Bayside Historical Society, Queens, N.Y. For the participation of the parents of Oakland Gardens and Bell Park Gardens to the struggle to secure an addition to P.S. 31, see "P.S. 46 in Mind, OGCA Supports P.S. 31 Wing Drive," *Bayside Times* (hereafter BT), January 12, 1950, 12, and "Bell Park Backs Hills Wing Drive," *BT*, February 2, 1950, 6. For the construction of P.S. 46, see "Oakland Garden School Expected," *BT*, February 10, 1949, 15; "Break Ground for School Today," *BT*, August 11, 1949, 1; "200 Oakland Gardens Kids Transferred," *BT*, October 13, 1949, 5; "Parents Study School Problems in Oakland Area," *BT*, September 28, 1950, 1; "1,150 Schooled Closer to Home as PS 46 Opens," *Meadow Lark* (hereafter ML), April 12, 1951, 1.

10. See the letters sent to Mayor Impellitteri by Mrs. Arthur Zwickel, chairman, School Committee, Bell Park Gardens Community Council, and C. Nardiello, corresponding secretary, Oakland Area School Committee, November 19 and December 4, 1951, and "File Note" by Austin J. Collins, educational aide to the mayor, December 17, 1951, all in folder "Schools—Queens, 1951–1953 #1275," box 115, SF, Impellitteri Papers. See also "Parents Seek Quick Action on 2 Schools," *Long Island Herald* (hereafter LIH), October 23, 1952, 1; "Parents Win Battle," *LIH*, November 26, 1952, 1; "Bd. of Estimate OK's Site for New P.S. 213," *BT*, November 27, 1952, 1.

11. "500 More Seats Asked for Proposed P.S. 26," *Long Island Daily Press* (hereafter LIDP), March 26, 1946, 9.

12. "Separate School Urged for Fresh Meadows," *LIDP*, May 22, 1946, 11, and "Too Big!" editorial, *LIDP*, May 23, 1946, 22.

13. "School Drive Launched by United Civic Council," LIDP, October 30, 1946, 11. See also Russo to William Ellard, September 25, 1946, Russo to James A. Burke, December 10, 1946, and Russo to O'Dwyer, July 31, 1947, all in folder "Education, Board of—April–December 1947," box 21, DC, O'Dwyer Papers. First planned to be built at 73rd Avenue and 190th Street, P.S. 26 was finally built to accommodate 1,508 pupils, and relocated at 73rd avenue and 196th street, on a site donated to the city by the New York Life Insurance Company. On Moses' comments regarding P.S. 165, see Moses to O'Dwyer, April 14, 1947, folder "Education, Board of—April–December 1947," box 21, DC, O'Dwyer Papers.

14. "Last Five Schools for Oakland Area," *BT*, June 29, 1950, 15, and " 'Battle of the Budget' Forces Start of Bayside School Council," *BT*, August 24, 1950, 1. See also letter from Edith Hack, president of the Bayside Joint School for Schools, to Mayor Impellitteri, April 23, 1953, folder "Educational Aide—Queens Schools, 1950–53 #362," box 35, SF, Impellitteri Papers.

15. "Independent Groups Organize to Fight for High School," *LIH*, March 27,

1952, 2. See letter from Naomi Garstein, secretary, to Mayor Wagner, November 15, 1954, folder "School, Construction of, Capital Budget Requests (Queens) 1954," box 291, Mayor Robert F. Wagner Jr. Papers, New York City Municipal Archives (hereafter Wagner Papers). The parents of the Kew Hills area had similar organizations: In 1951, a Joint School Committee represented eleven community associations; the Kew Meadows School Committee represented parents' associations of six public schools (letter from Evelyn Ratner to Mayor Impellitterri, June 18, 1951, and memorandum, November 21, 1951, both in folder "Schools—Queens, 1950–1951 #1274," box 115, SF, Impellitteri Paper.)

16. Diana Glotzer to Impellitteri, May 11, 1953, folder "Educational Aide—Queens Schools, 1950–1953, #362," box 35, SF, Impellitteri Papers.

17. About the rally, see "Irate Parents Call Mass Protest Rally," *LIH*, September 25, 1952, 1; "Protest Rally Sets Plans for Campaign," *LIH*, October 2, 1952, 2; "Parents' Rally Hears Halpern on Schools," *LIH*, October 9, 1952, 1; "March to School Site," *BT*, October 9, 1952, 1; "School Parents Parade," editorial, BT, October 9, 1952, 30. See also telegram from Wang to Impellitteri, September 30, 1952, folder "Schools—Queens, 1951–1953 #1275," box 115, Subject Files, Impellitteri Papers.

18. In addition to the documents cited below, see a six-page report from the PTA of P.S. 184, Flushing Manor, Whitestone, sent to Mayor Wagner on March 8, 1954 ("P.S. 184 Queens School Surveys and Estimates of School Age Children in the District, 1953–1957," in folder "School, Construction of, Capital Budget Requests [Queens], 1955–57," box 291, Wagner Papers). See also the memorandum reporting child population surveys and estimates of future school-age population sent by the Kew Meadows Committee, P.S. 201, November 21, 1951, and a seven-page brief prepared by the "overcrowding committee" of the Parents' Association of P.S. 154, November 8, 1952 (folders "Schools—Queens, 1950–1951 #1274" and "Schools—Queens, 1951–1953 #1275," box 115, SF, Impellitteri Papers); a brief from Esther Seider, PTA of P.S. 187, Little Neck, June 4, 1954 (folder "School, Construction of, Capital Budget Requests [Queens], 1954," box 291, Wagner Papers); one from Adeline Rubin and Adelaide Arons, PTA of P.S. 115, Floral Park, November 16, 1951 (folder "Schools—Queens, 1950–1951 #1274," box 115, SF, Impellitteri Papers).

19. In *BT*, see "Survey Area School Kids," May 4, 1950, 18; "Official Bell Park School Committee Starts Survey," May 11, 1950, 23.

20. Emphasis in the original. Memorandum, "Kew Meadows School Committee, P.S. 201, Queens," folder "Schools—Queens, 1950–1951 #1274," box 115, SF, Impellitteri Papers.

21. In *BT*, see "Survey Area School Kids," May 4, 1950, 18; "Official Bell Park School Committee Starts Survey," May 11, 1950, 23; "P.S. 46 Faces Delayed Flood," May 18, 1950, 1; "Not So Bad?" May 18, 1950, 8; "Letters to the Editor," June 1, 1950, 24; "School Group Reports on Parley with Dr. Chinook," June 1, 1950, 22; "Sen. Halpern Sees School Committee," June 15, 1950, 16; "Last Five Schools for Oakland Area," June 29, 1950, 15.

22. "School Committee Extracts Promise," *ML*, June 28, 1951.

23. Letter to the editor, *BT*, June 14, 1951, 20

24. See "The Case of P.S. 24, Queens," folder "School, Construction of, Capital Budget Requests (Queens), 1955–57," box 291, SF, Wagner Papers. The letter was signed by Mrs. Everett Young and Mrs. Elias Gruber.

25. James F. Gaffney to Nelson Seital, October 11, 1954, in folder "School, Construction of, Capital Budget Requests [Queens], 1955–57," box 291, Wagner Papers.

26. "Independent Groups Organize to Fight for High School," *LIH*, March 27, 1952, 2.

27. P.S. 41, which was supposed to absorb the school-age population until the construction of a new school, already had an average of thirty-four pupils per class and was running split sessions for its first and second graders. "Many Visit Sales Office of Bay Terrace Apt. Project," *BT*, April 16, 1953, 3. See also *New York Times*, April 12, 1953, section 8, 1, *BT*, April 23, 1953, 16, and "P.S. 41 Mothers Fear Overcrowding," *BT*, April 23, 1953, 1.

28. "1,100 Persons Attend 'School Crisis' Rally," *BT*, May 7, 1953, and Don Sieverman to Impellitteri, May 6, 1953, folder "Schools—Queens 1953 #1276," box 115, SF, Impellitteri Papers. The Bayside Club of the American Labor Party condemned the Board of Education's "false economy policy." The ALP even considered suing "both the Federal Housing Administration for granting permission for such a project in violation of their property requirements [which stated that "essential community facilities and services such as employment centers, shopping centers, schools, . . . shall be readily accessible to the property"] and . . . the Board of Education for not adequately providing for the health and welfare of the children of the community." (For documents pertaining to the Bay Terrace case, see "The Crisis in Our Schools!" *Baysider*, May 1953 and "Proposal of the Bayside ALP for Publicity Campaign and Legal Suit on Overcrowded Schools and New Housing in Connection with the Bay Terrace Housing Project in Bayside," s.d., folder "Queens County," box "1953 P-R," series I, American Labor Party Papers, Special Collections and Archives, Alexander Library, Rutgers University, New Brunswick, N.J.).

29. "PTA Census Shows New School Need," *BT*, November 1, 1962, 1.

30. The mayor's papers are filled with letters from ordinary citizens demanding better services. Robert A. Caro described many residents' struggles against highway construction and urban redevelopment in *The Power Broker: Robert Moses and the Fall of New York* (New York: Vintage, 1975). Jack Newfield and Paul DuBrul characterized New York City politics as dominated by the banking and real-estate interests in *The Abuse of Power: The Permanent Government and the Fall of New York* (New York: Viking Press, 1977). For a recent analysis that also insists on the power of this group and its neglect of quality-of-life services, especially in the outer boroughs, see Roger Sanjek, *The Future of Us All: Race and Neighborhood Politics in New York City* (Ithaca, N.Y.: Cornell University Press, 1998).

Chapter 6. As Mothers or as Parents?

1. "Why Not 8 P.M.?" editorial, *Long Island Daily Press* (hereafter *LIDP*), April 15, 1949, 16.

2. As more accurately noted by E. N. Lindheimer, zoning chairman of the Oakland Hills Civic Association, following the City Planning Commission's failure to respond to their letter requesting an audience: "A group of housewives were prepared to attend the meeting." "Oakland Hills Loses New Bid for Rezoning," *Long Island Star-Journal* (hereafter *Star*), August 20, 1948, folder

"Clippings and Correspondence Late 1940s–Early 1950s," Oakland Hills Civic Association Papers, Bayside Historical Society, Queens, N.Y. (hereafter OHCA Papers).

3. "Ross Retires as Fresh Meadows Civic President," *Meadow Lark* (hereafter *ML*), May 27, 1948, 1. Margaret Rose has noted the same dynamics in the Mexican American community organizations that she studied. See her "Gender and Civic Activism in Mexican American Barrios in California: The Community Service Organization, 1947–1962," in Joanne Meyerowitz, ed., *Not June Cleaver: Women and Gender in Postwar America, 1945–1960* (Philadelphia: Temple University Press, 1994), 189.

4. "It's Wonderful" and "2,000 Sign Petitions for Lowering of Gas Rates," *ML*, February 17, 1949, 1, 4. The emphasis is mine.

5. See, e.g., "Meadow Civic Organizes Rate Reduction Campaign, Reports Safety Measures," *ML*, March 3, 1949, 1.

6. "Women Chart Future of Oakland Hills Area," *Star*, January 6, 1948, Clippings and Correspondence, OHCA Papers. See also "Oakland Hills Civics Nominate All-Woman Slate," *Bayside Times* (hereafter *BT*), November 11, 1948, 3.

7. The sentiment expressed here was common to women in the twentieth century. As Nancy F. Cott has noted in her study of modern feminism, after the winning of the suffrage, women's struggle to achieve equality with men and to claim their individuality was characterized by a denial of gender differences. See her *Grounding of Modern Feminism* (New Haven, Conn.: Yale University Press, 1987). Cott also reviews the various forms of consciousness that women have embraced historically (feminist, feminine, and communal) in "What's in a Name? The Limits of 'Social Feminism'; or, Expanding the Vocabulary of Women's History," *Journal of American History* 76 (December 1989): 826–28.

8. Amy Swerdlow and Dee Garrison have documented the struggle of white middle-class women against nuclear and civil defense policies. As Garrison makes especially clear, these activists were similar in profile to the female activists that I analyzed here. In fact, some Queens community activists, such as Shirley Margolin of Fresh Meadows, were active in Women Strike for Peace as well ("Parents Report on Survey," *Long Island Herald* [hereafter *LIH*], October 16, 1952, 1, and " 'Strike for Peace' Ladies Visit Washington Lawmakers," *LIH*, February 1, 1962, 1). See Swerdlow, *Women Strike for Peace: Traditional Motherhood and Radical Politics in the 1960s* (Chicago: University of Chicago Press, 1993), and Dee Garrison, " 'Our Skirts Gave Them Courage': The Civil Defense Protest Movement in New York City, 1955–1961," in Meyerowitz, ed., *Not June Cleaver*, 201–26.

9. For a good analysis of the transformation of American political culture and its growing "desexualization" at the turn of the century, see Paula Baker, "The Domestication of Politics: Women and American Political Society, 1780–1920," *American Historical Review* 89 (June 1984): 620–47. See also her *Moral Frameworks of Public Life: Gender, Politics, and the State in Rural New York, 1870–1930* (New York: Oxford University Press, 1991).

10. "Control Signals," *ML*, April 29, 1948, 4.

11. "Fresh Meadows Area to Receive Traffic Lights Says Local Precinct," *ML*, June 24, 1948, 1.

12. Before the creation of a centralized municipal agency to handle traffic problems, the police department through its neighborhood precincts handled

requests for traffic control. The problem of traffic congestion and motor vehicle accidents had been building up ever since the construction of modern highways and parkways. But it was especially acute after the removal of the wartime ban on purchase of gasoline. According to New York governor Thomas E. Dewey, who called a statewide conference on highway and traffic safety in February 1946, "traffic accidents have increased at an alarming rate" (Dewey to Mayor O'Dwyer, February 13, 1946, folder "Safety #1569," box 149, Subject Files [hereafter SF], Mayor William O'Dwyer Papers, New York City Municipal Archives [hereafter O'Dwyer Papers]).

13. The department's expense budget for 1949–50, its first year of operation, was $180,967. It was headed by a licensed professional engineer and staffed with "traffic engineering experts." The Traffic Commission was also formed then. See *City Traffic Control*, report of Citizens Budget Commission to William O'Dwyer, October 1, 1948; "A Local Law to Establish a Traffic Commission," November 20, 1948; "Department of Traffic Engineering," Mayor's Message, second draft, March 30, 1949; all in folders "Parking, #1305–1307," box 124, SF, O'Dwyer Papers. See also "Mayor O'Dwyer's Report on the Traffic Commission and the Department of Traffic Engineering," folder "Mayor's Departmental Reports #1006," box 95, SF, O'Dwyer Papers.

14. "Outlook Is Bleak in Traffic Agency," *New York Times* (hereafter *NYT*), April 28, 1952, 21; "Reid Quits City Job as Chief of Traffic," *NYT*, June 16, 1951, 32; "Wiley Named Traffic Chief," *NYT*, August 20, 1952, 1; "City Traffic Staff Lacking Engineers," *NYT*, August 21, 1952, 21.

15. "Traffic Control Too Centralized," *Star*, May 18, 1953, 14. In 1956, the Emergency Safety Committee in the Bellerose area called for the establishment of a separate Department of Traffic for Queens County ("Far-reaching Implications," *Glen Oaks News* [hereafter *GON*], August 2, 1954).

16. See, e.g., the coordinated efforts of thirteen local civic groups in the Fresh Meadows area reported in *ML*, August 5, 1948, 1 ("United Civics Meets Tonight to Outline Traffic Safety Plan") and August 12, 1948, 1 ("Council Maps Safety Plans for Community").

17. "Road Signals Weighed," *NYT*, September 17, 1957, 71.

18. As a case in point, consider state senator Jack Bronston's own efforts to obtain a traffic light in Bay Terrace, which included thirty-five phone calls, three personal visits to the Traffic Department, and nine letters ("Parley Friday on Bay Terrace Traffic Signal," *BT*, April 30, 1959, 1; " 'Professional Snobs' Veto Bay Terrace Traffic Light after City Hall Conference," *BT*, November 19, 1959, 1; "Bay Terrace Gets Traffic Controls at Intersection," *BT*, December 27, 1959, 1).

19. See "Tyholland to Erect Own Safety Signs," *BT*, February 26, 1953, 1; "Traffic Signs," editorial, *LIDP*, April 7, 1953, 14; "To Save a Life," *BT*, April 9, 1953, 1; "Tyholland Civic Assn. Backs School Committee," *BT*, May 21, 1953, 1.

20. "Community Improvement thru Grassroots Action," editorial, *BT*, September 8, 1960, 6.

21. Wiley to Hon. Thomas J. Mirabile, July 14, 1952, and Wiley to Mrs. Clarice Kirchman, January 13, 1953 (in this letter to a member of a Brooklyn PTA, he explained, "Traffic signals reduce some accident hazards, have no effect on others, and actually increase some traffic hazards"), both in folder "Parking, #1051 and 1053," box 96, SF, Mayor Vincent Impellitteri Papers, New York City Municipal Archives (hereafter Impellitteri Papers). The same argument was presented to Bayside residents ("Partial Victory in Traffic Light

Fight," *Star*, February 27, 1953, 7) and at a monthly luncheon of the Queens Borough Chamber of Commerce ("Road Signals Weighed," *NYT*, September 17, 1957, 71).

22. "An Urgent and Disturbing Situation in Traffic Control," *BT*, August 13, 1959, 6.

23. "Mothers String Along with Traffic Problems," *ML*, June 15, 1950, 1.

24. "Mothers in Kew Hills to Block Off Traffic," *Star*, June 12, 1950, 1; "They Want a Light! Kew Hills Mothers Block Road with Baby Buggies," *Star*, June 13, 1950, 1; "Kew Hills Mothers Win Civic Battle: Patrolman Guards Crossing," *Star*, June 14, 1950, 1.

25. "Traffic Light Installed for 154's Pupils," *ML*, October 7, 1948, 1; "Marching Mothers Win School Crossing Fight," *LIDP*, September 30, 1948, 1.

26. The *New York Times* reported a few baby carriage blockades every year, occurring throughout New York City. In 1953, for instance, mothers in Manhattan's Lower East Side blocked traffic for three days to request a traffic light at Avenue D and Eighth Street after a five-year-old girl was injured at the intersection. See "Blockade Women Called," *NYT*, April 18, 1953, 29; "Blockade Mothers Get Traffic Lights," *NYT*, April 29, 1953, 30. Coverage of such events was traced through the *New York Times Index*, under "Traffic and Parking—NYC," "Pedestrian" or "School Crossings." Robert Caro describes the action of mothers who put themselves and their children in front of bulldozers to stop the construction of a parking lot for the restaurant Tavern-on-the-Green in Central Park in *The Power Broker: Robert Moses and the Fall of New York* (New York: Vintage, 1975), 984–96.

27. "Tenants League Is Organized in Langdale Apts.," *GON*, April 30, 1953, 1. According to the *Long Island Herald*, it was only after ten months of silence since they had petitioned the Traffic Department for traffic lights or stop signs that 50 "militant mothers" and children, with baby carriages and bicycles, blocked the intersection of 174th Street and 75th Avenue in South Flushing. "Mothers Demonstrate in Plea for Stop Sign," *LIH*, June 11, 1953, 1; "Direct Action," *Star*, June 9, 1953, 7; "Pull Out the stops!" *LIH*, July 2, 1953, 4.

28. "Petition to Traffic Dept. Gets stop Sign," *GON*, May 12, 1955, 1; "Threat of Buggy Blockade Gets Promise from Traffic Departm't," *GON*, May 19, 1955, 1.

29. "Civic Groups Hits Traffic Lite Lack," *LIH*, February 12, 1913, 2. The *Star* referred to a "30–day truce" in "Baby Carriage Blockade of Expressway Delayed," February 6, 1953, 12.

30. "Civic Group Attacks Baby Carriage Blockades," *Star*, September 10, 1952, 6.

31. Already in December 1951, when the PTA of P.S. 46 was organized, more than 1,000 families were members ("Expect 1,000 at Formation of P.S. 446 Parents Group," *BT*, December 13, 1951, 13). About the rally, see "Irate Parents Call Mass Protest Rally," *LIH*, September 25, 1952, 1; "Protest Rally Sets Plans for Campaign," *LIH*, October 2, 1952, 2; "Parents' Rally Hears Halpern on Schools," *LIH*, October 9, 1952, 1; "March to School Site," *BT*, October 9, 1952, 1; "School Parents Parade," editorial, *BT*, October 9, 1952, 30. See also telegram from Wang to Impellitteri, September 30, 1952, folder "Schools—Queens, 1951–1953 #1275," box 115, SF, Impellitteri Papers.

32. See Hack to Impellitteri, April 23, 1953, and Winterbottom to Impellitteri, April 29, 1953, folder "Educational Aide—Queens Schools, 1950–1953 #362," box 35, SF, Impellitteri Papers. See also "P.S. 41 Mothers Fear Over-

crowding," *BT*, April 23, 1943, 1, and "Attend the Rally," editorial, *BT*, April 30, 1953, 20.

33. Mr. and Mrs. Winterbottom to Impellitteri, April 29, 1953, folder "Educational Aide—Queens Schools, 1950–1953 #362," box 35, SF, Impellitteri Papers.

34. Don Sieverman to Impellitteri, May 6, 1953, folder "Schools—Queens 1953 #1276," box 115, SF, Impellitteri Papers.

35. *LIDP*, October 17, 1950. See, in comparison, *BT*, October 19, 1950, 2.

36. "Hundreds of Parents Set for School 'Zero Hour,' " *ML*, November 16, 1950, 1. For other examples of mass delegations to public hearings covered in the weeklies and emphasizing the participation of "parents," see "Parents Seek Quick Action on 2 Schools," *LIH*, October 23, 1952, 1; "A Report on Public School 165," *Pomonok News*, December 1952, 3; "Proposed P.S. 230 Scuttle by Planning Commission," *Kew Hills News* (hereafter *KHN*), October 1955; and "Commission Reverses Self: Favors Addition to P.S. 165," *KHN*, November 1955.

37. *LIH*, November 8, 1951, 1.

38. "Mothers to Protest at Bd. of Ed.," *LIH*, February 21, 1952, 3.

39. "1,100 Persons Attend 'School Crisis' Rally," *BT*, May 7, 1953.

40. "Kew Hills School News," *KHN*, November 1953, 1.

41. Letter from C. Nardiello, corresponding secretary, Oakland Area School Committee, to Mayor Vincent Impellitteri, December 4, 1951, folder "Schools—Queens, 1951–1953 #1275," box # 115, SF, Impellitteri Papers.

42. Paula Baker has also made this argument in her analysis of politics in rural New York in the early twentieth century: "Politics was no longer a public space where the ideals of manhood and womanhood could be acted out." See *The Moral Frameworks*, xvii.

Chapter 7. Betty Friedan, the Volunteers for Stevenson, and 1950s Housewives

1. *The Feminine Mystique* (1963; New York: Laurel, 1983).

2. "Personalities at Fresh Meadows" was written by Annette Winn, one of the two staff members of the newspaper ("The *Meadow Lark* Announces the Addition of Two New Members of Its Editorial Staff," *Meadow Lark* [hereafter *ML*], February 12, 1948, 1).

3. Joanne Meyerowitz, "Beyond the Feminine Mystique: A Reassessment of Postwar Mass Culture, 1946–1958," *Journal of American History* 79 (March 1993): 1455–82, reprinted in Meyerowitz, ed., *Not June Cleaver: Women and Gender in Postwar America, 1945–1960* (Philadelphia: Temple University Press, 1994), 229–62.

4. See "Growing . . . Growing . . . Growing," editorial, *Pomonok News* (hereafter *PM*), September 10, 1952, 2; "Sidewalk Chatter," *PM*, October and December 1952, 2.

5. "Perserverance [*sic*] Usually Gets Results in Community Group Relations with City Officials," *Long Island Herald* (hereafter *LIH*), July 7, 1955, 7.

6. "Adeline Rubin's Many Projects All Lead to a Better Community," by Vivian Potemkin, *Glen Oaks News* (hereafter *GON*), December 22, 1960, 2. Along similar lines, see also "Sue Noreika, Veteran Campaigner," *GON*, March 2, 1961, 1.

7. "Attention: Men," *GON*, December 6, 1956, 4. Again, in 1959, the editor reasserted his belief that men should get involved in the community, more specifically in the Little League ("The Silent 400," editorial, *GON*, July 11, 1959, 4). On many occasions in the following years, the *Glen Oaks News* continued to encourage men's participation in parents' associations by publicizing PTAs' "Fathers' Nights" (in *GON*, see "Program Set for Dads by PTA 186," November 8, 1956, 6; "PTA 115 Slates Fathers' Night," January 9, 1958, 1; "Mike Lee Reports to P-TA 115 Fathers," December 10, 1959, 9).

8. "Whitestone Boosters Civics to Name Queen August 26th," *Home Town News* (hereafter *HTN*), August 26, 1958, 4.

9. See "North Shore Civic Seeks Beauty Queen," *Bayside Times* (hereafter *BT*), April 10, 1958, 1; "Calling All Girls! Enter Miss Civics Beauty Pageant," *GON*, September 17, 1959, 1; "Van Buren Coeds First to Enter 'Miss Civic Queen' Beauty Pageant," *GON*, September 24, 1959, 1; "Queens Civic Week to Be Held Oct. 22nd-29th," *HTN*, June 29, 1960, 8.

10. Studies of women's participation in national party politics have overlooked these organizations, focusing on the two major parties' Women's Divisions and National Committees and on figures such as Eleanor Roosevelt, India Edwards, and Margaret Chase Smith. See, e.g., Cynthia Harrison, *On Account of Sex: The Politics of Women's Issues, 1945–1968* (Berkeley: University of California Press, 1988).

11. See Dick to David Bailey, Woodstock, Vt., October 9, 1952, folder 9, box 234. Unless otherwise indicated, the references in this section are from the Adlai Stevenson Papers, Public Policy Papers, Seeley G. Mudd Manuscript Library, Princeton University. An active participant in many associations of "amateurs," from Wendell Willkie's in 1940 to Stevenson's in 1952 and 1956, Jane Dick has published the only study of these movements. See *Volunteers and the Making of Presidents* (New York: Dodd, Mead, 1980).

12. "Eisenhower Gets Optimistic Report on Economic Path," *New York Times* (hereafter *NYT*), November 16, 1952, 1; "Martin Supports Gesture to South " *NYT*, November 17, 1952, 16.

13. John B. Martin, *Adlai Stevenson of Illinois: The Life of Adlai E. Stevenson* (Garden City, N.Y.: Doubleday, 1976), 620–21. See also Porter McKeever, *Adlai Stevenson: His Life and Legacy* (New York: William Morrow, 1989), 209–10.

14. See memorandum from Barry Bingham to Dick, June 22, 1956, folder 1, box 288.

15. See "Women's Votes Will Decide Election," October 2, 1956, 8, folder 2, box 295; "The Women—and the Results?" *Newsweek*, November 5, 1956, 29–30; and Angus Campbell et al., *The American Voter* (New York: John Wiley, 1960), 483–93.

16. "Suggestions for State and Local Volunteers-for-Stevenson Groups," prepared and distributed by Volunteers for Stevenson, Chicago, 1952, folder 4, box 229. Other information regarding the efforts to recruit women can be found in "Notes for Hubert Will, New Jersey," [1952], folder 9, box 234; and memorandum from Kathleen Whitehead to Ralph Martin and Martha Ragland, October 6, 1956, folder 2, box 302.

17. See folders 4–6, box 235.

18. According to Sara Evans, Stevenson's speech illustrated that "There was no strong sense of public or civic life where women could put into practice the values of domesticity, nor were those values easily expressed in communal terms." See *Born for Liberty: A History of Women in America* (New York: Free

Press, 1989), 255. For the *New York Times* coverage of the speech, see the issue of June 7, 1955, 36.

19. "No Women's Issues?" *New York Post*, September 25, 1956, 34. Both Porter's article and notes for the pamphlet discussed below are in folder 4, box 295.

20. Ibid. The emphasis is in the original.

21. See, e.g., Campbell, *The American Voter*, 143, and Norman H. Nie, Sidney Verba, and John R. Petrocik, *The Changing American Voter* (1976; Cambridge: Harvard University Press, 1979), esp. chap. 2, "The American Public in the 1950s," 14–42.

22. In "A Study of the New York State Voters in 1956" sponsored by the Volunteers for Stevenson, Herbert Hyman, professor of sociology at Columbia University, argued that Stevenson needed to capture only 2.5 percent more of New York's votes to win (see folder 6, box 299 and folder 9, box 227). In the last month of the 1956 campaign, when polls emphasized the importance of the undecided voter, a state-by-state survey conducted by the *New York Times* revealed that the balance of power lay with the Eisenhower Democrats and Independents of 1952. See memorandum from Stanley Karson to Barry Bingham, October 8, 1956, and memorandum by Lemoine Skinner Jr., public relation adviser for the Volunteers to state and local public relations chairmen, October 15, 1956, both in folder 7, box 301.

23. *The Bandwagon* was intended primarily for distribution among independent voters by Volunteer groups around the country. Half of the 100,000 copies initially printed were requested by the New York group (folder 2, box 295).

24. Folder 7, box 301.

25. "Five Minute Radio Broadcast: 'Paper Prosperity,' " folder 4, box 295.

26. Folder 7, box 301.

27. The first five-minute national television special, on which voters who were switching their support from Eisenhower to Stevenson gave their reasons for doing so, was broadcast at 3:00 P.M. on ABC. Daytime radio broadcasts addressed to women voters had also been organized in the last two weeks of the 1952 campaign. See "Broadcasting to Women," *NYT*, October 27, 1952, 15, and letter from Dick to Mrs. Max Stern, October 18, 1952, folder 9, box 234.

28. Memorandum from Bingham, Dick, Archibald to chairmen of all state and local volunteer committees, October 20, 1956, folder 2, box 302, and "Let's Talk Sense for Victory," folder 4, box 295.

29. "Invite as many friends and neighbors as possible to your home for a discussion of the issues," suggested a memorandum sent to state and local groups. "Time your meeting to allow at least an hour for discussion, not including the time taken for Stevenson's speech." See "Are You a Host or Hostess for Stevenson?" memorandum from Jean Massel to Dick, October 13, 1952, folder 9, box 234.

30. Folder 2, box 302.

31. Memorandum from Finnegan to Arthur Schlesinger, October 12, 1956, and letter from Joan Smith, October 20, 1956, both in folder 6, box 269.

32. William H. Chafe, *The Unfinished Journey: America since World War II* (1986; New York: Oxford University Press, 1991), 126.

33. For Taylor's letter, Barry Bingham's response, March 16, 1956, and related correspondence, see folders 4–5, box 287.

34. Dick, *Volunteers*, 246. A college-educated woman, mother of three, and

wife of a prominent Chicago industrialist and philanthropist, Dick had begun her political career as a campaign worker for Wendell Willkie in 1940 (she remained a registered Republican until 1954). During the 1948 Illinois gubernatorial race, she had cochaired the Stevenson for Governor Committee along with Herman Smith, also a Republican and close friend of Stevenson. For Barry Bingham's comments, see his memorandum to Dick, June 22, 1956, folder 1, box 288. According to Dick, Stevenson himself, as well as Stephen A. Mitchell, chairman of the Democratic National Committee, and Wilson Wyatt, campaign manager, "understood and encouraged the Volunteers for Stevenson" (*Volunteers*, 193–94, 197, 200). On the tensions between the Citizens for Eisenhower and the Republican National Committee, see Dick, *Volunteers*, 137, "G.O.P. Denies Deal with Dixiecrats," *NYT*, August 3, 1952, 50, and "Eisenhower Amateurs Win Separate Role in Campaign," *NYT*, August 4, 1952, 1.

35. For the first solid treatment of Friedan's background, see Daniel Horowitz, *Betty Friedan and the Making of* The Feminine Mystique*: The American Left, the Cold War, and Modern Feminism* (Amherst: University of Massachusetts Press, 1998).

36. "'They Found Out 'Americans Aren't So Awful, After All!' " folders 381–85, box 10, Betty Friedan Papers, Schlesinger Library, Radcliffe Institute, Harvard University, Cambridge, Mass. (hereafter Friedan Papers).

37. Folders 378–79, box 10, Friedan Papers. Another version of this story, "They Made the City into 'Country' for Their Kids," can be found in folder 478, box 13. For the published version, see *Parents' Magazine*, May 1957, 36–37, 131–34.

38. "More than a Nosewiper," 1. It is significant to note that the specific information indicating the socioeconomic status of the residents—"they'd paid $1,200 down" and "salesmen and postal clerks and $100–a-week accountants"—was omitted from the version published in *Parents' Magazine*. The published version referred simply to "ex-GI couples." The result of these editorial changes was to turn lower-middle-class families into generic, classless families. In "They Made the City into 'Country' for Their Kids," the author was even more specific about the residents' socioeconomic status, including information about which neighborhood of Manhattan they had moved from: "Most of them had grown up playing on the streets themselves, city kids from New York's lower east side and Hell's kitchen, Brooklyn and the Bronx. It's not a rags to riches story, because most of them are still young, still not rich, still living in the city. But their kids aren't playing in the streets."

39. "More than a Nosewiper," 1–2.

40. Not included in the final printed version were the passages where Friedan described Alice Barski's feelings of being "absolutely liberated" and the triumphant reference to "this new breed of Jill" (see below).

41. "More than a Nosewiper," 3.

42. Ibid., 4–7.

43. Ibid., 10–11

44. Ibid., 11–12.

45. Ibid., 20–21.

46. Ibid., 2.

47. *The Feminine Mystique*, xi, 342, 344, 346, 355, 369, 370.

48. Whyte, *The Organization Man*, 317–18; Harry Henderson, "Rugged American Collectivism: The Mass-Produced Suburbs, Part II," *Harper's Magazine,* December 1953, 81. See also "The Mass-Produced Suburbs: How People

Live in America's Newest Towns," *Harper's Magazine*, November 1953, 25–32. Friedan was directly influenced by this literature.

49. On African American women's demand for education, see Paula Giddings, *When and Where I Enter: The Impact of Black Women on Race and Sex in America* (New York: Bantam Books, 1984), 101; on white upper-class women, see Nancy F. Cott, *The Grounding of Modern Feminism* (New Haven, Conn.: Yale University Press, 1987). See also Barbara Miller Solomon, *In the Company of Educated Women: A History of Women and Higher Education in America* (New Haven, Conn.: Yale University Press, 1985).

50. For a review of the abundant literature on women's participation in voluntary associations, see Karen J. Blair, *The History of American Women's Voluntary Organizations, 1810–1960: A Guide to Sources* (Boston: G. K. Hall, 1989). For examples of its importance in the 1920s, see Cott, *The Grounding of Modern Feminism*.

51. For an example of 1970s feminists' criticism of volunteerism, see Doris B. Gold, "Women and Voluntarism," in Vivian Gornick and Barbara K. Moran, eds., *Woman in Sexist Society: Studies in Power and Powerlessness* (New York: Basic Books, 1971), 533–54.

52. Stanley Elkins and Eric McKitrick, "A Meaning for Turner's Frontier," *Political Science Quarterly* 69 (September and December 1954): 325–26.

53. *The Feminine Mystique*, 244–45.

54. Meyerowitz, *Not June Cleaver*, 248.

55. *The Feminine Mystique*, 345, 346.

56. On the pool, see Horowitz, *Betty Friedan*, 171–79; the quotes are, respectively, from 176 and 179. Horowitz described as such the valuable experience that she gained during her leadership of the group from 1958 to 1964: "Through her efforts she gained experience building and leading a complex and far-flung organization, writing grant proposals, chairing meetings, administering a budget, establishing support groups, generating press releases, and overcoming political resistance" (172). On Friedan's hostility to volunteerism, see 203 and 211–12. For some handwritten notes on the issue of "fulfillment in community," see folders 496 and 497, box 13, Friedan Papers.

Chapter 8. Middle-Class Antiliberalism Revisited

1. The popular and academic representation of the white backlash in the 1970s is well described by Barbara Ehrenreich in *Fear of Falling: The Inner Life of the Middle Class* (New York: HarperCollins, 1989), chap. 3. Richard Rogin's *New York Times* article is a good example of the journalistic portrayal of "Middle America." See "Joe Kelly Has Reached His Boiling Point," reprinted in Murray Freedman, *Overcoming Middle-Class Rage* (Philadelphia: Westminster, 1971).

2. See David Halle, *America's Working Man: Work, Home, and Politics among Blue-Collar Property Owners* (Chicago: University of Chicago Press, 1984); Jonathan Rieder, *Canarsie: The Jews and Italians of Brooklyn against Liberalism* (Cambridge: Harvard University Press, 1985); Ronald P. Formisano, *Boston against Busing: Race, Class, and Ethnicity in the 1960s and 1970s* (Chapel Hill: University of North Carolina Press, 1991); Thomas J. Sugrue, "Crabgrass-Roots Politics: Race, Rights, and the Reaction against Liberalism in the Urban North, 1940–1964," *Journal of American History* 82 (September 1995): 551–78,

and *The Origins of the Urban Crisis: Race and Inequality in Postwar Detroit* (Princeton, N.J.: Princeton University Press, 1996); Arnold Hirsch, *Making the Second Ghetto: Race and Housing in Chicago, 1940–1960* (New York: Cambridge University Press, 1983) and "Massive Resistance in the Urban North: Trumbull Park, Chicago, 1953–1966," *Journal of American History* 82 (September 1995): 522–50; Michael Kazin, *The Populist Persuasion: An American History* (New York: Basic Books, 1995). For an older study of the same topic, see Charles Abrams, *Forbidden Neighbors: A Study of Prejudice in Housing* (New York: Harper & Brothers, 1955).

Robert Johnston has questioned the automatic association of populism with reactionary, antiliberal views in "American Populism and American Language of Class," a paper presented at the 1997 meeting of the Organization of American Historians (see esp. 15–16). Andrew Hurley's analysis of environmentalist activism in Gary, Indiana, presents a refreshing exception to this association of postwar middle-class politics with antiliberalism. See *Environmental Inequalities: Class, Race, and Industrial Pollution in Gary, Indiana, 1945–1980* (Chapel Hill: University of North Carolina Press, 1995).

3. Diane Ravitch, *The Great School Wars: A History of the New York City Public Schools* (1974; New York: Basic Books, 1988), 252–55.

4. The Board's recommendations on integration and the local PTA's position were presented favorably in the *Glen Oaks News* (hereafter *GON*): see "Integration in the Schools," March 7, 1957, 1; "PTA 186 Supports Integration," March 21, 1957, 1; "PTA 186 Urges More Money for Teachers," April 18, 1957, 1; "Integration Commission Accepts Report," May 23, 1957, 1. The Chamber of Commerce's opposition was reported in community newspapers. See "Queens Chamber Blasts Integration Program," *Long Island Herald* (hereafter *LIH*), March 14, 1957, 4; "Chamber Rejects 2 State Plans to End Segregation," *GON*, March 28, 1957, 3; "Chamber of Commerce Urges Civic Opposition," *LIH*, April 11, 1957, 1.

5. The resistance in Glendale and Ridgewood is described briefly in Ravitch, *The Great School Wars*, 258–60, and in Adena Back, "Up South in New York: The 1950s School Desegregation Struggles" (Ph.D. diss., New York University, 1997), chap. 5. Back also analyzes a failed attempt at initiating desegregation of a Bedford-Stuyvesant public school in 1955 in "Blacks, Jews and the Struggle to Integrate Brooklyn's Junior High School 258: A Cold War Story," *Journal of Ethnic History* (Winter 2001): 38–69. On the PAT, see *Our Community, Its History and People* (Ridgewood, N.Y.: Greater Ridgewood Historical Society, 1976), 49. This local history is available at the Long Island Division, Queens Borough Public Library.

6. The Board of Education's Commission on Integration described as such its use of rezoning for the purpose of integration: "Zoning lines are constantly being redrawn as new housing and population changes occur. The rezoning now envisioned simply means that, wherever possible, zoning lines will be drawn in such a way as to encourage integrated instead of segregated schools. This would apply particularly to so-called 'fringe' areas—neighborhoods made up of several racial groups." Document reprinted in "Integration in the Schools," *GON*, March 7, 1957, 1.

7. The debates over the pairing of these two junior high schools can be traced in the minutes of Local School Board, Districts 51 and 52, available in the New York City Board of Education Papers, Special Collections, Milbank Memorial Library, Teachers College Library, Columbia University. See "Min-

utes of the Open Meeting of September 24, 1963" and "Minutes of the Meeting on October 22, 1963," folder "LSB #51–52, 1963–64," box 23. Unless otherwise indicated, the references in this chapter are from this collection.

8. "Minutes of Open Meeting Held on November 26, 1963," December 10, 1963, folder "LSB #51–52, 1963–64," box 23. At the December meeting, one member of the Bell Park Manor Terrace Community Council also openly supported the plan and "cited the advantages to all children in integrated schools," only to be refuted by two other residents of the same garden apartment.

9. Helfat to Hon. James B. Donovan, Board of Education, February 4, 1964, folder "LSB #51–52, 1964," box 27.

10. Helfat and the Local School Board's position was clear from the beginning of the controversy. It was expressed at the October meeting, as cited above, and reiterated later. In January, for instance, Helfat told opponents of integration at the Local School Board's monthly meeting that "in June of 1963 the LSB had stated in its report that it would do what it could to further the Board's plan of integration and that we do support the principle of integration" ("Minutes of Meeting, January 28, 1964," folder "LSB #51–52, 1963–64," box 23). For information about Helfat's background, including his active involvement in Douglaston and his connection with the Democratic Party, see "Kennedy Names Bernard Helfat," *LIH*, October 27, 1960, 1.

11. The Local School Board for District 51 and 52, which covered a territory extending west from the city line to Jamaica and south from Little Neck Bay to the vicinity of Jamaica Avenue, was created in 1962 as part of the Board of Education's major reorganization. The Board had been at the center of a major scandal the previous year, when it was revealed that the city's school-construction funds had been misappropriated with the complicity of Board officials. The committee investigating these irregularities also revealed a level of administrative chaos that impaired the Board's ability to appropriately enforce safety level in the city's schools. As a result of these revelations, New York State ordered the formation of a new nine-member Board of Education along with a revival of Local School Boards. The number of Local Boards was reduced from fifty-four to twenty-five, and their members were appointed by the Board from nominations made by local communities. On the 1961 scandal and following reorganization of the Board and Local Boards, see Ravitch, *The Great School Wars*, 263–64.

12. "School Board Schedules Its First Public Meeting," *GON*, October 18, 1962, 1.

13. Helfat to Hon. James B. Donovan, Board of Education, February 4, 1964, folder "LSB #51–52, 1964," box 27.

14. Helfat to the Board of Education, March 25, 1965, 3, folder "Blueprint, District 51–52," box 25.

15. "A P.A.T. [*sic*] Branch Is Formed Here," *Bayside Times* (hereafter *BT*), March 19, 1964, 4; "School Groups in Opposition to PAT Opening Day Boycott," *BT*, September 3, 1964, 1; "Northeast Queens Council Supports Bd of Ed Plan," *LIH*, September 3, 1964, 1; and "School Boycott Shows Little Effect in Area," *LIH*, September 17, 1964, 1. As reported in "School Absenteeism Is Low in District despite Boycott" (*BT*, September 17, 1964, 1), "In School Districts 51 and 52, . . . 22.3% failed to attend on the first day of school. This was reduced to 16.7% the second day. The Board of Education says 10% absence is normal."

16. Ravitch, *The Great School Wars*, presents a good explanation and criticism of the plan on 280–86. The figures are from 284 and 286.

17. Helfat to the Board of Education, March 25, 1965, 3, folder "Blueprint, District 51–52," box 25.

18. For a brief discussion of the protest against the 1964 pairing plan, see Roger Sanjek, *The Future of Us All: Race and Neighborhood Politics in New York City* (Ithaca, N.Y.: Cornell University Press, 1998), 42; on the LSB 47/48 support for the initiative, see its newsletter, *Local School Board News, Districts 47–48*, February 1964, 1, and "Minutes of Meeting, District 47–48," February 13, 1964, 3, both in box 23, folder "District 47–48, 1963–64."

19. "Special News Letter from Local School Board 47/48"; report of the Local School Board to the Board of Education on "Blueprint for Further Action toward Quality Integrated Education," folder "Blueprint, District 47–48," box 25.

20. "Minutes of Meeting, Dist. 47–48," February 13, 1964, 3, folder "District 47–48, 1963–64," box 23. Observers of the New York integration controversy have noted the lack of adequate communication between the Board of Education and citizens as creating, in Bert E. Swanson's words, an "extreme sense of resentment against the system." David Rogers also identified the Board's bureaucratic and administrative flaws as a major problem with the mid-1960s integration plans (his use of the term bureaucratic pathologies clearly reflects his perspective). See Bert E. Swanson, *The Struggle for Equality: School Integration Controversy in New York City* (New York: Hobbs, Dorman, 1966), esp. 91, and David Rogers, *110 Livingston Street: Politics and Bureaucracy in the New York City Schools* (New York: Random House, 1968), esp. 30–35, 85, chap. 7, and appendix A, 499–500.

21. "Special News Letter from Local School Board 47/48"; report of the Local School Board to the Board of Education on "Blueprint," 3, folder "Blueprint, District 47–48," box 25.

22. Jewel Bellush, "Housing: The Scattered-Site Controversy," in J. Bellush and Stephen M. David, eds., *Race and Politics in New York City: Five Studies in Policy Making* (New York: Praeger, 1971), 114.

23. In addition to Bellush, see Mario Cuomo, *Forest Hills Diary: The Crisis of Low-Income Housing* (New York: Vintage, 1974), and Sanjek, *The Future of Us All*, 44–46.

24. "Protest Delays Plans for Low Cost Housing Project," *Kew Hills News*, May 1966, 1. Flushing Suburban was truly integrated: Moore also stated that blacks constituted about 40 percent of the neighborhood and about 50 percent of the Civic Association's membership. As also reported by borough president Mario Cariello in his presentation to the City Planning Commission on this issue, "As of May 9, 1966 [the area contained] predominantly one- and two-family homes, occupied by 361 white families and 285 non-white families. Practically every block in the area contains white and non-white families." (Document made available to the author by Julia Jerry, Queens, N.Y., from her personal papers.) This is consistent with the information provided by Marilyn Mossop, a black resident of the area, whom I have interviewed.

25. Home owners from the Fresh Meadows area, west of Kew Gardens Hills, also opposed the selection of a site in their middle-class neighborhood, at Fresh Meadows Lane and 59th Avenue (a site which was also opposed by Cariello in that presentation to the City Planning Commission). The residents resented the two thirteen-story and one nine-story buildings planned in this area of one- and two-family houses, and they feared the imposition on already taxed public services. They cited specifically: "High schools already . . . on

triple session. Fire house is too small to handle such large population." See "Residents Plan New March to Protest Housing Project," newspaper clipping (source and date unavailable, probably September 1967), and manuscript notes on the back of typescript document titled "Recommendations of the Queens Federation of Civic Councils, New York City Program, Submitted January 1967," both in Jerry Papers.

26. Text of Mario Cariello's statement to the City Planning Commission's public hearings, September 11, 1967, Jerry Papers.

27. "Many of Lindsay's own people saw this as a questionable selection," including Roger Starr, executive director of the Citizens Housing and Planning Council, and several staff members of the Planning Department (Bellush, "Housing," 119).

28. Bellush, "Housing," 110–12.

29. As Bellush again noted perceptively, "Part of the problem lay in the reformers' objective. The creation of racially balanced communities within the city was a concept built on abstract notions about democracy and social justice. Acceptable as a normative position, these notions were unsupported by the perceptive reasoning and empirical data so necessary to effective implementation. The reformers entered a field in which they had little background or experience, and their lack of understanding or appreciation of the delicacy and complexity of achieving their goal was unfortunate" ("Housing," 116).

Conclusion

1. This lack of agency is especially clear in Mills's work, as in most studies of mass society informed by the Frankfurt School. The problem of agency in Friedan's *Feminine Mystique* is more complex. As Rachel Bowlby noted, her analysis alternated between female victimization and agency. See " 'The Problem with No Name': Rereading Friedan's *The Feminine Mystique*," *Feminist Review* 27 (September 1987): 61–75.

2. See, e.g., Richard Wightman Fox and T. J. Jackson Lears, eds., *The Culture of Consumption: Critical Essays in American History, 1880–1980* (New York: Pantheon, 1983), and Stuart Ewen, *Captains of Consciousness: Advertising and the Social Roots of the Consumer Culture* (New York: McGraw-Hill, 1976). For a critical review of this literature, see Jean-Christophe Agnew, "Coming Up for Air," in John Brewer and Roy Porter, eds., *Consumption and the World of Goods* (New York: Routledge, 1993), 19–39. For studies of popular culture, see Warren Susman, with the assistance of Edward Griffin, "Did Success Spoil the United States? Dual Representations in Postwar America," in Lary May, ed., *Recasting America: Culture and Politics in the Age of the Cold War* (Chicago: University of Chicago Press, 1989), 19–37, and William S. Graebner, *The Age of Doubt: American Thought and Culture in the 1940s* (Boston: Twayne, 1991).

3. See Elaine Tyler May, *Homeward Bound: American Families in the Cold War Era* (New York: Basic Books, 1988). See also her essays "Cold War—Warm Hearth: Politics and the Family in Postwar America," in Steve Fraser and Gary Gerstle, eds., *The Rise and Fall of the New Deal Order: 1930–1980* (Princeton, N.J.: Princeton University Press, 1989), 153–81, and "Explosive Issues: Sex, Women, and the Bomb," in May, ed., *Recasting America*, 154–70. See also Sara Evans, *Born for Liberty: A History of Women in America* (New York: Free Press, 1989), 246–47, 255; Rochelle Gatlin, *American Women since 1945* (Jackson:

University Press of Mississippi, 1987), 7, 53; and more recently, Rosalind Rosenberg's *Divided Lives: American Women in the Twentieth Century* (New York: Hill and Wang, 1992), chap. 5. For a more balanced interpretation of the period, see Eugenia Kaledin, *Mothers and More: American Women in the 1950s* (Boston: Twayne, 1984), and William H. Chafe, *The Unfinished Journey: America since World War II* (1986; New York: Oxford University Press, 1991), 125. For a good review of the traditional historiography on women in the 1950s, see Joanne Meyerowitz's introduction to *Not June Cleaver: Women and Gender in Postwar America* (Philadelphia: Temple University Press, 1994), 1–10.

4. Harry C. Boyte, *Commonwealth: A Return to Citizen Politics* (New York: Free Press, 1989), 10. Brian Balogh offers a good review of the scholarship on the twentieth-century managerial state and an incisive critique of the false dichotomy established between claims to technical expertise and mass-based political movements. See his *Chain Reaction: Expert Debate and Public Participation in American Commercial Nuclear Power, 1945–1975* (New York: Cambridge University Press, 1991), 1–18. Ellen Herman provides another analysis of the rise of expertise in postwar society, but she also notes that the popular school of humanist psychology posited an active and empowered subject. See *The Romance of American Psychology: Political Culture in the Age of Experts* (Berkeley: University of California Press, 1995). Most recently, Robert D. Johnston provided a compelling example of ordinary citizens' challenge to medical and public health expertise in his analysis of the anti-vaccination movement. See his *Radical Middle Class: Populist Democracy and the Question of Capitalism in Progressive Era Portland, Oregon* (Princeton, N.J.: Princeton University Press, 2003).

5. See my introduction and bibliography for specific references to these authors' works.

6. See Stanley Elkins and Eric McKitrick, "A Meaning for Turner's Frontier," *Political Science Quarterly* 69 (September and December 1954): 321–53, 565–602.

7. Robert A. Caro documented the emphasis put on large infrastructural projects in *The Power Broker: Robert Moses and the Fall of New York* (New York: Vintage Books, 1975). He provides many examples of the disregard of neighborhood needs and their representatives, including housewives, that this emphasis on parks and transportation entailed (470, 478–80, 521–25, 614, 752–53, chaps. 37 and 38, 986–87). For the particular case of schools, and the failure to implement an effective master plan to coordinate the city's various needs in the early 1950s, see 780–82. David Rogers also noted the absence of planning to ensure a balance between residential construction and school facilities. See his *110 Livingston Street: Politics and Bureaucracy in the New York City Schools* (New York: Random House, 1968), 431–32.

8. Roger Sanjek, *The Future of Us All: Race and Neighborhood Politics in New York City* (Ithaca, N.Y.: Cornell University Press, 1998), esp. 28 and note 3, 398. Sanjek's analysis is partly based on journalists Jack Newfield and Paul DuBrul's identification of a relatively small network of political, financial, and real estate interests that dominates New York City politics for private gain ("the permanent government"). See *The Abuse of Power: The Permanent Government and the Fall of New York* (New York: Viking, 1977). For the lack of power that ordinary citizens have against this power structure, see esp. 83.

9. Caro, *Power Broker*, 645, 657; Amy Swerdlow, *Women Strike for Peace: Traditional Motherhood and Radical Politics in the 1960s* (Chicago: University of Chicago Press, 1993); Dee Garrison, " 'Our Skirts Gave Them Courage': The

Civil Defense Protest Movement in New York City, 1955–1961," in *Not June Cleaver*, 201–28.

10. See, e.g., Caro, *Power Broker*, on the relationship between the borough president and the city construction coordinator, Robert Moses (743–53). A classic analysis of the formal power of the borough presidents in the city's administrative structure is provided by William S. Sayre and Herbert Kaufman, *Governing New York City* (New York: Russell Sage Foundation, 1960). Bert Swanson has described the "vetoing and negating" role that citizens played in the school integration controversy. See his *Struggle for Equality: School Integration Controversy in New York City* (New York: Hobbs, Dorman, 1966), 57, 79.

11. See Robert Wood, *Suburbia: Its People and Their Politics* (Boston: Houghton Mifflin, 1958). The quote is from 107.

12. The figures for Levittown are taken from Harold Wattel, "Levittown: A Suburban Community," in William M. Dobriner, ed., *The Suburban Community* (New York: Putnam, 1958), 292, and Rosalyn Baxandall and Elizabeth Ewen, *Picture Windows: How the Suburbs Happened* (New York: Basic Books, 2000), 131.

13. David Halle, *America's Working Man: Work, Home, and Politics among Blue-Collar Property Owners* (Chicago: University of Chicago Press, 1984), 16–22.

14. See Charles Abrams, *Forbidden Neighbors* (New York: Harper & Brothers, 1955); Mike Davis, *City of Quartz* (New York: Vintage, 1990); Thomas J. Sugrue, "Crabgrass-Roots Politics: Race, Rights, and the Reaction against Liberalism in the Urban North, 1940–1964," *Journal of American History* 82 (September 1995): 551–78, and *The Origins of the Urban Crisis* (Princeton, N.J.: Princeton University Press, 1996); Arnold Hirsch, *Making the Second Ghetto* (New York: Cambridge University Press, 1983), and "Massive Resistance in the Urban North: Trumbull Park, Chicago, 1953–1966," *Journal of American History* 82 (September 1995): 522–50; Jonathan Rieder, *Canarsie* (Cambridge: Harvard University Press, 1985); Ronald P. Formisano, *Boston against Busing* (Chapel Hill: University of North Carolina Press, 1991); Theresa Mah, "The Limits of Democracy in the Suburbs: Constructing the Middle Class through Residential Exclusion," in Burton J. Bledstein and Robert D. Johnston, eds., *The Middling Sorts: Explorations in the History of the American Middle Class* (New York: Routledge, 2001), 256–66.

15. Sugrue, "Crabgrass-Roots Politics," 557–58.

16. Halle, *America's Working Man*, 192–93, 201, 235.

17. "In the late 1940s, populism began a migration from Left to Right. The rhetoric once spoken primarily by reformers and radicals . . . was creatively altered by conservative groups and politicians (zealous anti-Communists, George Wallace, the Christian Right, and the campaigns and presidential administrations of Richard Nixon and Ronald Reagan)" (Michael Kazin, *The Populist Persuasion* [New York: Basic Books, 1995], 4). Theresa Mah also examined the rhetoric of civic associations in San Francisco and found that a democratic language focusing on majority rights was prevalent.

Appendix

1. On community newspaper chains, see Morris Janowitz, *The Community Press in an Urban Setting: The Social Elements of Urbanism* (1952; Chicago: University of Chicago Press, 1967), 57; "*Times* Newspapers Keep Pace with

Growth of Area," *Bayside Times,* October 22, 1936, 1, and "To Our Reader," *Bayside Times,* December 5, 1946, 1.

2. In *Meadow Lark,* see "Weekly Charge of Five Cents to Be Made for *Meadow Lark* Starting July," June 24, 1948, 1; "Worthwhile Greeting," editorial, September 15, 1949, 4; "Thank You," June 29, 1950, 2; "Fourth Year," February 1, 1951, 1; "*Lark* Renamed," October 18, 1951, 1. See the masthead for circulation figures.

3. In *Glen Oaks News,* see "A New Policy," January 3, 1952, 4; "Let's Call It 'Corliss Field,' " July 31, 1952, 4; "For This Community," July 22, 1954, 4; "Paper Began as 8–Page Weekly in '48," June 4, 1953, 1. Information about the editor, publisher, cost, and areas of distribution was printed on the masthead.

4. In *Home Town News,* see "Editorial," January 11, 1956, 2, and "Open Letter to Our Readers on Sale of *Home Town News,*" November 25, 1958, 8.

5. This information can be found on the masthead. See also "*Kew Hills News* Marks Its Tenth Birthday," *Kew Hills News,* September 1963, 1.

Bibliography

Manuscript Collections

American Labor Party. Special Collections and Archives, Alexander Library, Rutgers University, New Brunswick, N.J.

American Labor Party. Tamiment Institute Library, Bobst Library, New York University, New York City.

Americans for Democratic Action. Wisconsin State Historical Society, Madison, Wis.

Bayside Hills Civic Association. Bayside Hills Civic Association, Queens, N.Y.

Bayside Taxpayers and Improvement Association. Bayside Historical Society, Queens, N.Y.

Bell Park Gardens Community Council. Sidney and Beatrice Ifshin, Bayside, N.Y.

Flushing Council of Woman's Organizations. Flushing Council of Woman's Organizations, Queens, N.Y.

Friedan, Betty. Schlesinger Library, Radcliffe Institute, Harvard University, Cambridge, Mass.

Impellitteri, Mayor Vincent R. New York City Municipal Archives, New York City.

Jerry, Julia (papers of various civic organizations, including the Harding Heights Civic Association, the United Civic Council, and the Federation of Civic Councils). Julia Jerry, Queens, N.Y.

League of Women Voters of New York City. Rare Book and Manuscript Library, Butler Memorial Library, Columbia University, New York City.

Liberal Party of New York State. Manuscripts and Archives Division, New York Public Library, Astor, Lenox and Tilden Foundations, New York City.

Long Island Division, Vertical Files. Queens Borough Public Library, New York City.

Municipal Reference and Research Center, Vertical Files. New York City.

New York City Board of Education. Special Collections, Milbank Memorial Library, Teachers College Library, Columbia University, New York City.

New York City Housing Authority. LaGuardia and Wagner Archives, LaGuardia Community College, New York City.

Oakland Hills–Bayside Hills Civic Association. Bayside Historical Society, Queens, N.Y.

Oakland Hills Civic Association. Bayside Historical Society, Queens, N.Y.

O'Dwyer, Mayor William. New York City Municipal Archives, New York City.

Stevenson, Adlai E. Public Policy Papers, Seeley G. Mudd Manuscript Library, Princeton University, Princeton, N.J.
Suburban Flushing Civic Association. Marilyn Mossop, Queens, N.Y.
Wagner, Mayor Robert F., Jr. New York City Municipal Archives, New York City.

Queens Local History and Community Newspapers

(The works in this section are held at the Long Island Division, Queens Borough Public Library, Queens, N.Y.)

Bayside Historical Society. *Bayside Was a Wilderness Then . . . Voices from Bayside's Black Community*. Bayside, N.Y.: Bayside Historical Society, 1988.
Bayside—Its Yesterdays and Tomorrows. With original illustrations by James Flux. Bayside, N.Y.: Bayside Times Publishing Corporation, 1957.
Bayside Times
Bell Park Gardens. *Independence Celebration, 1950–1991*. New York: Bell Park Gardens Community Council, May 1991.
Glen Oaks News
Home Town News
Kew Hills News
Long Island Herald
Lovely, Thomas J. *The History of Jamaica Estates, 1929–1969*. Jamaica, N.Y.: Jamaica Estates Association, 1969.
Meadow Lark
Our Community, Its History and People. Ridgewood, Glendale, Maspeth, Middle Village, Greater Ridgewood Historical Society, 1976.
Pomonok News

Other Sources

Abrams, Charles. *Forbidden Neighbors: A Study of Prejudice in Housing*. New York: Harper & Brothers, 1955.
———. "The Ghetto Makers." *Nation*, October 7, 1961, 222–25. Reprinted in Jon Pynoos, Robert Schafer, and Chester W. Hartman, eds., *Housing Urban America*, 274–78. Chicago: Aldine, 1973.
Agnew, Jean-Christophe. "Coming Up for Air." In John Brewer and Roy Porter, eds., *Consumption and the World of Goods*, 19–39. New York: Routledge, 1993.
American Builder (National Association of Home Builders)
American Federationist (American Federation of Labor)
Aronowitz, Stanley. *False Promises: The Shaping of American Working-Class Consciousness*. 1973. Durham, N.C.: Duke University Press, 1992.
Back, Adena. "Blacks, Jews and the Struggle to Integrate Brooklyn's Junior High School 258: A Cold War Story." *Journal of Ethnic History* (Winter 2001): 38–69.
———. "Up South in New York: The 1950s School Desegregation Struggles." Ph.D. diss., New York University, 1997.
Baker, Paula. "The Domestication of Politics: Women and American Political Society, 1780–1920." *American Historical Review* 89 (June 1984): 620–47.

———. *The Moral Frameworks of Public Life: Gender, Politics, and the State in Rural New York, 1870–1930*. New York: Oxford University Press, 1991.

Balogh, Brian. *Chain Reaction: Expert Debate and Public Participation in American Commercial Nuclear Power, 1945–1975*. New York: Cambridge University Press, 1991.

Baritz, Loren. *The Good Life: The Meaning of Success for the American Middle Class*. New York: Alfred A. Knopf, 1989.

Bauer, Catherine. "The Middle Class Needs Houses, Too." *New Republic*, August 29, 1949, 17–20.

Baxandall, Rosalyn, and Elizabeth Ewen. *Picture Windows: How the Suburbs Happened*. New York: Basic Books, 2000.

Bellush, Jewel. "Housing: The Scattered-Site Controversy." In J. Bellush and Stephen M. David, eds., *Race and Politics in New York City: Five Studies in Policy Making*, 98–133. New York: Praeger, 1971.

Bender, Thomas. *Community and Social Change in America*. Baltimore: Johns Hopkins University Press, 1978.

Berger, Benneth M. *Working-Class Suburb: A Study of Auto Workers in Suburbia*. Berkeley: University of California Press, 1960.

Binford, Henry C. *The First Suburbs: Residential Communities on the Boston Periphery, 1815–1860*. Chicago: University of Chicago Press, 1985.

Blackmar, Elizabeth. *Manhattan for Rent, 1785–1850*. Ithaca, N.Y.: Cornell University Press, 1989.

Blair, Karen J. *The History of American Women's Voluntary Organizations, 1810–1960: A Guide to Sources*. Boston: G. K. Hall, 1989.

Bledstein, Burton J., and Robert D. Johnston, eds. *The Middling Sorts: Explorations in the History of the American Middle Class*. New York: Routledge, 2001.

Blumin, Stuart M. *The Emergence of the Middle Class: Social Experience in the American City, 1760–1900*. Cambridge: Cambridge University Press, 1989.

———. "The Hypothesis of Middle-Class Formation in Nineteenth-Century America: A Critique and Some Proposals." *American Historical Review* 90 (1985): 299–338.

Bowlby, Rachel. " 'The Problem with No Name': Rereading Friedan's *The Feminine Mystique*." *Feminist Review* 27 (September 1987): 61–75.

Boyer, Paul. *By the Bomb's Early Light: American Thought and Culture at the Dawn of the Atomic Age*. New York: Pantheon Books, 1985.

Boyte, Harry C. *Commonwealth: A Return to Citizen Politics*. New York: Free Press, 1989.

Brinkley, Alan. *The End of Reform: New Deal Liberalism in Recession and War*. New York: Vintage Books, 1995.

———. "The New Deal and the Idea of the State." In Steve Fraser and Gary Gerstle, eds., *The Rise and Fall of the New Deal Order, 1930–1980*, 85–121. Princeton, N.J.: Princeton University Press, 1989.

———. "The Problem of American Conservatism." *American Historical Review* 99 (April 1993): 409–29.

Brown, JoAnne. " 'A Is for Atom, B Is for Bomb': Civil Defense in American Public Education, 1948–1963." *Journal of American History* 75 (1988): 68–90.

Buder, Stanley. *Visionaries and Planners: The Garden City Movement and the Modern Community*. New York: Oxford University Press, 1990.

Calhoun, Craig, ed. *Habermas and the Public Sphere*. Cambridge: MIT Press, 1992.

Campbell, Angus, et al. *The American Voter*. New York: John Wiley, 1960.

Caro, Robert A. *The Power Broker: Robert Moses and the Fall of New York*. New York: Vintage, 1975.

Carter, Robert F. "Pressure from the Left: The American Labor Party, 1936–1954." Ph.D. diss., Syracuse University, 1965.

Chafe, William H. *The Unfinished Journey: America since World War II*. 1986. New York: Oxford University Press, 1991.

Chase, Stuart. "The Case against Home Ownership." *Survey Graphic*, May 1938, 260–67.

Chinoy, Ely. *Automobile Workers and the American Dream*. Boston: Beacon Press, 1985.

Clark, Clifford E., Jr. *The American Family Home, 1800–1960*. Chapel Hill: University of North Carolina Press, 1986.

———. "Ranch-House Suburbia: Ideals and Realities." In Lary May, ed., *Recasting America: Culture and Politics in the Age of Cold War*, 171–91. Chicago: University of Chicago Press, 1989.

Cohen, Lisabeth A. "Citizens and Consumers in the Century of Mass Consumption." In Harvard Sitkoff, ed., *Perspectives on Modern America: Making Sense of the Twentieth Century*, 145–61. New York: Oxford University Press, 2001.

———. "The Class Experience of Mass Consumption: Workers as Consumers in Interwar America." In Richard Wightman Fox and T. J. Jackson Lears, eds., *The Power of Culture: Critical Essays in American History*, 135–60. Chicago: University of Chicago Press, 1993.

———. "Embellishing a Life of Labor: An Interpretation of the Material Culture of American Working-Class Homes, 1885–1915." *Journal of American Culture* 3 (winter 1980): 752–75.

———. *Making a New Deal: Industrial Workers in Chicago, 1919–1939*. New York: Cambridge University Press, 1990.

Commission on Intergroup Relations. *Trends in the Racial Distribution in New York City between 1950 and 1957: An Ecological Analysis*. Prepared by Harold Goldblatt. February 1961.

Community Council of Greater New York. *Queens Communities: Population Characteristics and Neighborhood Social Resources*. New York: Bureau of Community Statistical Services, Research Department, 1958.

Congress and the Nation, 1945–1964. Washington, D.C.: Congressional Quarterly Service, 1965.

Cott, Nancy F. *The Bonds of Womanhood: "Woman's Sphere" in New England, 1780–1835*. New Haven, Conn.: Yale University Press, 1977.

———. *The Grounding of Modern Feminism*. New Haven, Conn.: Yale University Press, 1987.

———. "What's in a Name? The Limits of 'Social Feminism'; or, Expanding the Vocabulary of Women's History." *Journal of American History* 76 (December 1989): 809–29.

Cuomo, Mario. *Forest Hills Diary: The Crisis of Low-Income Housing*. New York: Vintage, 1974.

Danielson, Michael N. *The Politics of Exclusion*. New York: Columbia University Press, 1976.

Davies, Richard O. *Housing Reform during the Truman Administration*. Columbia: University of Missouri Press, 1966.

———. " 'Mr. Republican' Turns 'Socialist': Robert A. Taft and Public Housing." *Ohio History* 73 (summer 1964): 136–43.

Davis, Mike. *City of Quartz: Excavating the Future in Los Angeles.* New York: Vintage, 1990.

Dean, John P. "The Ghosts of Home Ownership." *Journal of Social Issues* 7, nos. 1 & 2 (1951): 59–68.

———. *Home Ownership: Is It Sound?* With a foreword by Robert S. Lynd. New York: Harper & Brothers, 1945.

Dick, Jane. *Volunteers and the Making of Presidents.* New York: Dodd, Mead, 1980.

Dobriner, William M. *Class in Suburbia.* Englewood Cliffs, N.J.: Prentice-Hall, 1963.

———, ed. *The Suburban Community.* New York: Putnam, 1958.

Ehrenreich, Barbara. *Fear of Falling: The Inner Life of the Middle Class.* New York: Harper Perennial, 1989.

Elkins, Stanley, and Eric McKitrick. "A Meaning for Turner's Frontier." *Political Science Quarterly* 69 (September and December 1954): 321–53, 565–602.

Ethington, Philip. "Hypotheses from Habermas: Notes on Reconstructing American Political and Social History, 1890–1920." *Intellectual History Newsletter* 14 (1992): 21–40.

Evans, Sara M. *Born for Liberty: A History of Women in America.* New York: Free Press, 1989.

Ewen, Stuart. *Captains of Consciousness: Advertising and the Social Roots of the Consumer Culture.* New York: McGraw-Hill, 1976.

Fones-Wolf, Elizabeth A. *Selling Free Enterprise: The Business Attack on the New Deal Order, 1945–1960.* Urbana: University of Illinois Press, 1994.

Formisano, Ronald P. *Boston against Busing: Race, Class, and Ethnicity in the 1960s and 1970s.* Chapel Hill: University of North Carolina Press, 1991.

Fox, Kenneth. *Metropolitan America: Urban Life and Urban Policy in the United States, 1940–1980.* Jackson: University of Mississippi Press, 1986.

Fox, Richard Wightman, and T. J. Jackson Lears, eds. *The Culture of Consumption: Critical Essays in American History, 1880–1980.* New York: Pantheon, 1983.

Frank, Dana. *Purchasing Power: Consumer Organizing, Gender, and the Seattle Labor Movement, 1919–1929.* New York: Cambridge University Press, 1994.

Fraser, Steve, and Gary Gerstle, eds. *The Rise and Fall of the New Deal Order, 1930–1980.* Princeton, N.J.: Princeton University Press, 1989.

Freedman, Leonard. *Public Housing: The Politics of Poverty.* New York: Holt, Rinehart and Winston, 1969.

Freedman, Murray. *Overcoming Middle-Class Rage.* Philadelphia: Westminster, 1971.

Friedan, Betty. "Day Camp in the Driveways." *Parents' Magazine,* May 1957, 36–37, 131–34.

———. *The Feminine Mystique.* Twentieth anniversary edition. 1963. New York: Laurel, 1983.

———. *It Changed My Life: Writings on the Women's Movement.* New York: Random House, 1976.

Friedman, Lawrence M. *Government and Slum Housing: A Century of Frustration.* Chicago: Rand McNally, 1968.

Fuchs, Lawrence H. *The Political Behavior of American Jews.* Glencoe, Ill.: Free Press, 1956.

Gans, Herbert J. "The Failure of Urban Renewal: A Critique and Some Proposals." *Commentary* 39 (April 1965): 29–37

————. *The Levittowners: Ways of Life and Politics in a New Suburban Community.* New York: Pantheon, 1967.

Garrison, Dee. " 'Our Skirts Gave Them Courage': The Civil Defense Protest Movement in New York City, 1955–1961." In Joanne Meyerowitz, ed., *Not June Cleaver: Women and Gender in Postwar America, 1945–1960,* 201–26. Philadelphia: Temple University Press, 1994.

Gatlin, Rochelle. *American Women since 1945.* Jackson: University Press of Mississippi, 1987.

Gelfand, Mark I. *A Nation of Cities: The Federal Government and Urban America, 1933–1945.* New York: Oxford University Press, 1975.

Genevro, Rosalie. "Site Selection and the New York City Housing Authority, 1934–1939." *Journal of Urban History* 12 (August 1986): 334–52.

Giddings, Paula. *When and Where I Enter: The Impact of Black Women on Race and Sex in America.* New York: Bantam Books, 1984.

Gillon, Steven M. *Politics and Vision: The ADA and American Liberalism, 1947–1985.* New York: Oxford University Press, 1987.

Glazer, Nathan, and Daniel P. Moynihan. *Beyond the Melting Pot: The Negroes, Puerto Ricans, Jews, Italians, and Irish of New York City.* Cambridge: MIT Press and Harvard University Press, 1964.

Gold, Doris. "Women and Voluntarism." In Vivian Gornick and Barbara Moran, eds., *Women in a Sexist Society: Studies in Power and Powerlessness,* 539–42. New York: Basic Books, 1971.

Goldstein, Sidney. "American Jewry, 1970: A Demographic Profile." In Marshall Sklare, ed., *The Jew in American Society,* 97–162. New York: Behrman House, 1974.

Goodman, Leo. "What Makes the Real Estate Lobby Tick?" *Journal of Housing,* December 1950, 423–27.

Graebner, William S. *The Age of Doubt: American Thought and Culture in the 1940s.* Boston: Twayne, 1991.

————. "The Unstable World of Benjamin Spock: Social Engineering in a Democratic Culture, 1917–1950." *Journal of American History* 67 (December 1980): 612–29.

Griffith, Robert. "Forging America's Postwar Order: Domestic Politics and Political Economy in the Age of Truman." In Michael J. Lacey, ed., *The Truman Presidency,* 57–88. Cambridge: Cambridge University Press, 1989.

————. *The Politics of Fear: Joseph R. McCarthy and the Senate.* 1970. Amherst: University of Massachusetts Press, 1987.

Habermas, Jürgen. *The Structural Transformation of the Public Sphere: An Inquiry into a Category of Bourgeois Society.* 1962. Cambridge: MIT Press, 1989.

Halle, David. *America's Working Man: Work, Home, and Politics among Blue-Collar Property Owners.* Chicago: University of Chicago Press, 1984.

Hamilton, Richard. *Working-Class Suburb: A Study of Auto Workers in Suburbia.* New York: John Wiley, 1972.

Harris, Richard. "Working-Class Home Ownership in the American Metropolis." *Journal of Urban History* 17 (November 1990): 46–69.

Harrison, Cynthia. *On Account of Sex: The Politics of Women's Issues, 1945–1968.* Berkeley: University of California Press, 1988.

Hartman, Chester W. *Housing and Social Policy.* Englewood Cliffs, N.J.: Prentice-Hall, 1975.

Henderson, Harry. "The Mass-Produced Suburbs: How People Live in America's Newest Towns." *Harper's Magazine,* November 1953, 25–32.

————. "Rugged American Collectivism: The Mass-Produced Suburbs, Part II." *Harper's Magazine*, December 1953, 80–86.

Herman, Ellen. *The Romance of American Psychology: Political Culture in the Age of Experts*. Berkeley: University of California Press, 1995.

Hine, Darlene Clark. "Mabel K. Staupers and the Integration of Black Nurses into the Armed Forces." In J. H. Franklin and A. Meier, eds., *Black Leaders of the Twentieth Century*, 241–58. Urbana: University of Illinois Press, 1982.

Hirsch, Arnold R. *Making the Second Ghetto: Race and Housing in Chicago, 1940–1960*. New York: Cambridge University Press, 1983.

————. "Massive Resistance in the Urban North: Trumbull Park, Chicago, 1953–1966." *Journal of American History* 82 (September 1995): 522–50.

Hodgins, Eric. *Mr. Blandings Builds His Dream House*. New York: Simon and Schuster, 1946.

Horowitz, C. Morris, and Lawrence J. Kaplan. *The Jewish Population of the New York Area, 1900–1975*. New York: Federation of Jewish Philanthropies of New York, 1959.

Horowitz, Daniel. *Betty Friedan and the Making of* The Feminine Mystique: *The American Left, the Cold War, and Modern Feminism*. Amherst: University of Massachusetts Press, 1998.

————. "Rethinking Betty Friedan and *The Feminine Mystique*: Labor Union Radicalism and Feminism in Cold War America." *American Quarterly* 48 (March 1996): 1–42.

————. *Vance Packard and American Social Criticism*. Chapel Hill: University of North Carolina Press, 1994.

Hurley, Andrew. *Environmental Inequalities: Class, Race, and Industrial Pollution in Gary, Indiana, 1945–1980*. Chapel Hill: University of North Carolina Press, 1995.

"Ideas from Sweden for an American Co-operative Housing Program." *American City*, March–May 1949, 84–86, 110–42

Ifshin, Sidney and Beatrice. Interview by author. Bayside, N.Y. May 1992.

Jackson, Kenneth T. *Crabgrass Frontier: The Suburbanization of the United States*. New York: Oxford University Press, 1985.

————. "Race, Ethnicity, and Real Estate Appraisal: The Home Owners Loan Corporation and the Federal Housing Administration." *Journal of Urban History* 6 (August 1980): 419–52.

Jackson, Walter A. *Gunnar Myrdal and America's Conscience: Social Engineering and Racial Liberalism, 1938–1987*. Chapel Hill: University of North Carolina Press, 1990.

Janowitz, Morris. *The Community Press in an Urban Setting: The Social Elements of Urbanism*. 1952. Chicago: University of Chicago Press, 1967.

Jay, Martin. *Permanent Exiles: Essays on the Intellectual Migration from Germany to America*. New York: Columbia University Press, 1985.

Johnson, Lee F. "Housing: A 1950 Tragedy." *Survey*, December 1950, 551–55.

Johnston, Robert D. "American Populism and American Language of Class." Paper presented at the annual meeting of the Organization of American Historians, 1997.

————. *The Radical Middle Class: Populist Democracy and the Question of Capitalism in Progressive Era Portland, Oregon*. Princeton, N.J.: Princeton University Press, 2003.

Journal of Housing (National Association of Housing Officials)

Kaledin, Eugenia. *Mothers and More: American Women in the 1950s*. Boston: Twayne, 1984.

Katz, Donald. *Home Fires: An Intimate Portrait of One Middle-Class Family in Post-war America*. New York: HarperCollins, 1992.

Katznelson, Ira. *City Trenches: Urban Politics and the Patterning of Class in the United States*. Chicago: University of Chicago Press, 1981.

Kazin, Michael. "The Grass-Roots Right: New Histories of U.S. Conservatism in the Twentieth Century." *American Historical Review* 97 (February 1992): 136–55.

———. "A People Not a Class: Rethinking the Political Language of the Modern U.S. Labor Movement." In Mike Davis and Michael Sprinkler, eds., *Reshaping the American Left: Popular Struggles in the 1980s*, 257–86. New York: Verso, 1988.

———. *The Populist Persuasion: An American History*. New York: Basic Books, 1995.

Keats, John. *The Crack in the Picture Window*. Boston: Houghton Mifflin, 1956.

Keeley, John B. *Moses on the Green*. The Inter-University Case Program, no. 45. Tuscaloosa: University of Alabama Press, 1959.

Keith, Nathaniel S. *Politics and the Housing Crisis Since 1930*. New York: Universe Books, 1973.

Kelly, Barbara Mae. "The Politics of House and Home: Implications in the Built Environment of Levittown, Long Island." Ph.D. diss., State University of New York–Stony Brook, 1988.

Kerber, Linda. *Women of the Republic: Intellect and Ideology in Revolutionary America*. New York: Norton, 1980.

Komarovsky, Mirra. *Blue-Collar Marriage*. New Haven, Conn.: Yale University Press, 1962.

Kornbluh, Mark Lawrence. "Men, Women, and Politics in the Nineteenth and Twentieth Centuries." *Reviews in American History* 20 (1992): 72–77.

Kramer, John, ed. *North American Suburbs: Politics, Diversity, and Change*. Berkeley: Glendessary Press, 1972.

Kroessler, Jeffrey A. "Building Queens: The Urbanization of New York's Largest Borough." Ph.D. diss., City University of New York, 1991.

———. "Suburban Growth, Urban Style. Patterns of Growth in the Borough of Queens." In Barbara Mae Kelly, ed. *Long Island: The Suburban Experience*, 25–35. Interlaken, N.Y.: Heart of the Lakes, 1990.

Lichtenstein, Nelson. "The Making of the Postwar Working Class: Cultural Pluralism and Social Structure in World War II." *Historian*, November 1988, 42–63.

Loeser, Herta. *Women, Work, and Volunteering*. Boston: Beacon Press, 1974.

Long Island Daily Press

Long Island Star-Journal

Lubell, Samuel. *The Future of American Politics*. New York: Harper, 1951.

———. *Revolt of the Moderates*. New York: Harper, 1956.

Lynn, Susan. *Progressive Women in Conservative Times: Racial Justice, Peace, and Feminism, 1945 to the 1960s*. New Brunswick, N.J.: Rutgers University Press, 1992.

Mah, Theresa. "The Limits of Democracy in the Suburbs: Constructing the Middle Class through Residential Exclusion." In Burton J. Bledstein and Robert D. Johnston, eds., *The Middling Sorts: Explorations in the History of the American Middle Class*, 256–66. New York: Routledge, 2001.

Marchand, Roland. "Visions of Classlessness, Quests for Dominion: American

Popular Culture, 1945–1960." In Robert H. Bremner and Gary W. Reichard, eds., *Reshaping America: Society and Institutions, 1945–1960*, 163–90. Columbus: Ohio State University Press, 1982.

Marsh, Margaret. "From Separation to Togetherness: The Social Construction of Domestic Space in American Suburbs, 1840–1915." *Journal of American History* 76 (September 1989): 506–27.

———. *Suburban Lives*. New Brunswick, N.J.: Rutgers University Press, 1990.

Marshall, T. H., and Tom Bottomore. *Citizenship and Social Class*. 1950. London: Pluto Press, 1992.

Martin, John B. *Adlai Stevenson of Illinois: The Life of Adlai E. Stevenson*. Garden City, N.Y.: Doubleday, 1976.

May, Elaine Tyler. "Cold War—Warm Hearth: Politics and the Family in Postwar America." In Steve Fraser and Gary Gerstle, eds., *The Rise and Fall of the New Deal Order: 1930–1980*, 153–81. Princeton, N.J.: Princeton University Press, 1989.

———. "Explosive Issues: Sex, Women, and the Bomb." In Lary May, ed., *Recasting America: Culture and Politics in the Age of Cold War*, 154–70. Chicago: University of Chicago Press, 1989.

———. *Homeward Bound: American Families in the Cold War Era*. New York: Basic Books, 1988.

May, Lary, ed. *Recasting America: Culture and Politics in the Age of Cold War*. Chicago: University of Chicago Press, 1989.

McDonnell, Timothy. *The Wagner Housing Act: A Case Study of the Legislative Process*. Chicago: Loyola University Press, 1957.

McKeever, Porter. *Adlai Stevenson: His Life and Legacy*. New York: William Morrow, 1989.

Merton, Robert. "Patterns of Influence: Local and Cosmopolitan Influentials." In *Social Theory and Social Structure*, 441–74. 1949. New York: Free Press, 1968.

Message from the Governor Transmitting Report of the Commission of Housing and Regional Planning for Permanent Housing Relief. New York State Legislative Document No. 66, 1926.

Meyer, Donald. "Betty Friedan." In G. J. Barker-Benfield and Catherine Clinton, eds., *Portraits of American Women: From Settlement to the Present*, 599–615. New York: St. Martin's Press, 1991.

Meyer, Gerald. *Vito Marcantonio, 1902–1954: Radical Politician*. Albany: State University of New York Press, 1989.

Meyerowitz, Joanne. "Beyond the Feminine Mystique: A Reassessment of Postwar Mass Culture, 1946–1958." *Journal of American History* 79 (March 1993): 1455–82.

———, ed. *Not June Cleaver: Women and Gender in Postwar America, 1945–1960*. Philadelphia: Temple University Press, 1994.

Miller, Herman P. *Income of the American People*. New York: John Wiley, 1955.

Mills, C. Wright. "Mass Media and Public Opinion." In *Power, Politics and People*, 577–98. New York: Oxford University Press, 1963.

———. "The Middle Classes in Middle-Sized Cities." In *Power, Politics and People*, 274–91. New York: Oxford University Press, 1963.

———. *The Power Elite*. New York: Oxford University Press, 1956.

———. *The Sociological Imagination*. New York: Oxford University Press, 1959.

———. *White Collar: The American Middle Classes*. New York: Oxford University Press, 1951.

Moore, Deborah Dash. *To the Golden Cities: Pursuing the American Jewish Dream in Miami and L.A.* New York: Free Press, 1994.

Mossop, Marilyn. Interview by author. Flushing, N.Y. March 1992.

Mouffe, Chantal, ed. *Dimensions of Radical Democracy: Pluralism, Citizenship, Community.* London: Verso, 1992.

Mumford, Lewis. "The Sky Line." *New Yorker,* October 22, 1949, 102–6.

Murray, Sylvie. "Suburban Citizens: Domesticity and Community Politics in Queens, New York, 1945–1960." Ph.D. diss., Yale University, 1994.

Newfield, Jack, and Paul DuBrul. *The Abuse of Power: The Permanent Government and the Fall of New York.* New York: Viking, 1977.

New York City, Board of Election. *Election Map. 1952. Borough of Queens. Eighth Assembly District.* 1952.

New York City. *City Record,* 1952.

New York City Housing Authority. *Community Facilities and Activities in New York City Public Housing Projects.* 1946.

New York City Planning Commission. *Plan for New York City. A Proposal. 5: Queens.* New York, 1969.

New York Red Book. Albany: J. B. Lyon, 1953.

New York Times

Nie, Norman H., Sidney Verba, and John R. Petrocik. *The Changing American Voter.* Enlarged ed. Cambridge: Harvard University Press, 1979.

Orleck, Annelise. " 'We Are That Mythical Thing Called the Public': Militant Housewives during the Depression." *Feminist Studies* 19 (spring 1993): 147–72.

Palen, J. John. *The Suburbs.* New York: McGraw-Hill, 1995.

Pells, Richard H. *The Liberal Mind in a Conservative Age: American Intellectuals in the 1940s and 1950s.* New York: Harper & Row, 1985.

Radford, Gail. *Modern Housing for America: Policy Struggles in the New Deal Era.* Chicago: University of Chicago Press, 1996.

———. "Reconsidering New Deal Housing Policy Alternatives: A Step toward 'Getting Housing In' to Mainstream U.S. History." Paper presented at the annual meeting of the Organization of American Historians, Anaheim, Calif., 1993.

Ravitch, Diane. *The Great School Wars: A History of the New York City Public Schools.* 1974. New York: Basic Books, 1988.

Rieder, Jonathan. *Canarsie: The Jews and Italians of Brooklyn against Liberalism.* Cambridge: Harvard University Press, 1985.

Riesman, David, with Nathan Glazer and Reuel Denney. *The Lonely Crowd: A Study of the Changing American Character.* 1950. New Haven, Conn.: Yale University Press, 1969.

Robbins, Ira S., and Marian Sameth, eds. *Directory of Large-Scale Rental and Co-operative Housing: With a Summary of Legislation Relating to Housing and Urban Renewal in New York City.* New York: Citizens' Housing and Planning Council of New York, 1957.

Rogers, David. *110 Livingston Street: Politics and Bureaucracy in the New York City Schools.* New York: Random House, 1968.

Rose, Margaret. "Gender and Civic Activism in Mexican American Barrios in California: The Community Service Organization, 1947–1962." In Joanne Meyerowitz, ed., *Not June Cleaver: Women and Gender in Postwar America, 1945–1960,* 177–200. Philadephia: Temple University Press, 1994.

Rose, Mark H. *Interstate: Express Highway Politics, 1939–1989.* Rev. ed. Knoxville: University of Tennessee Press, 1990.

Rosenberg, Bernard. "New York Politics and the Liberal Party." *Commentary* 37 (February 1964): 69–75.

Rosenberg, Rosalind. *Divided Lives: American Women in the Twentieth Century.* New York: Hill and Wang, 1992.

Rosenman, Dorothy. *A Million Homes a Year.* New York: Harcourt, Brace, 1945.

Rupp, Leila J., and Verta Taylor. *Survival in the Doldrums: The American Women's Rights Movement, 1945 to 1960s.* New York: Oxford University Press, 1987.

Sanjek, Roger. *The Future of Us All: Race and Neighborhood Politics in New York City.* Ithaca, N.Y.: Cornell University Press, 1998.

Sayre, Wallace S., and Herbert Kaufman. *Governing New York City.* 1960. New York: Russell Sage Foundation, 1965.

Scammon, Richard M. *America at the Polls: A Handbook of American Presidential Election Statistics, 1920–1964.* Pittsburgh: University of Pittsburgh Press, 1965.

Schwartz, Joel. "Tenant Power in the Liberal City, 1943–1971." In Ronald Lawson, ed., with the assistance of Mark Naison, *The Tenant Movement in New York City, 1904–1984*, 134–208. New Brunswick, N.J.: Rutgers University Press, 1986.

Seeley, Evelyn. "The House: A Success Story." *Survey Graphic*, February 1948, 70–74, 85.

Shishkin, Boris. "Homes for the Brave." *American Federationist*, March 1946, 8–11.

Shklar, Judith N. *American Citizenship: The Quest for Inclusion.* Cambridge: Harvard University Press, 1991.

Smith, Governor Alfred. "Annual Message," January 6, 1926. New York Senate. *Journal, 1926*, vol. 2, "Executive Journal."

———. "Special Message," April 1, 1926. New York Senate. *Journal, 1926*, vol. 2, "Executive Journal."

Solomon, Barbara Miller. *In the Company of Educated Women: A History of Women and Higher Education in America.* New Haven, Conn.: Yale University Press, 1985.

Spigel, Lynn. *Making Room for TV: Television and the Family Ideal in Postwar America.* Chicago: University of Chicago Press, 1992.

State of New York, Division of Housing. *Building Homes for Those with Lower Middle Incomes.* New York, 1949.

Stock, Catherine McNicol. *Main Street in Crisis: The Great Depression and the Old Middle Class on the Northern Plains.* Chapel Hill: University of North Carolina Press, 1992.

Straus, Nathan. *Two-thirds of a Nation: A Housing Program.* New York: Alfred A. Knopf, 1951.

Sugrue, Thomas J. "Crabgrass-Roots Politics: Race, Rights, and the Reaction against Liberalism in the Urban North, 1940–1964." *Journal of American History* 82 (September 1995): 551–78.

———. *The Origins of the Urban Crisis: Race and Inequality in Postwar Detroit.* Princeton, N.J.: Princeton University Press, 1996.

———. "Reassessing the History of Postwar America." *Prospects* 20 (1995): 493–509.

Susman, Warren, with the assistance of Edward Griffin. "Did Success Spoil the United States? Dual Representations in Postwar America." In Lary May, ed., *Recasting America: Culture and Politics in the Age of Cold War,* 19–37. Chicago: University of Chicago Press, 1989.

Swados, Harvey. "The Myth of the Happy Worker." *Nation*, August 17, 1957, 65–68.

Swanson, Bert E. *The Struggle for Equality: School Integration Controversy in New York City*. New York: Hobbs, Dorman, 1966.

Swerdlow, Amy. *Women Strike for Peace: Traditional Motherhood and Radical Politics in the 1960s*. Chicago: University of Chicago Press, 1993.

Tilly, Louise A., and Patricia Gurin, eds. *Women, Politics, and Change*. New York: Russell Sage Foundation, 1990.

Tobey, Ronald, Charles Wetherell, and Jay Brigham. "Moving Out and Settling In: Residential Mobility, Home Owning, and the Public Enframing of Citizenship, 1921–1950." *American Historical Review* 95 (December 1990): 1395–1422.

Tracy, James. "Forging Dissent in an Age of Consensus: Radical Pacifism in America, 1940 to 1970." Ph.D. diss., Stanford University, 1992.

Tretter, Maxwell H. "Cooperative Project Is Planned as Example, Guide." *Journal of Housing*, April 1949, 121–22.

United States Bureau of the Census. *U.S. Census of Housing, 1950*. Washington, D.C.: Government Printing Office, 1951.

———. *U.S. Census of Housing, 1960*. Washington, D.C.: Government Printing Office, 1961.

———. *U.S. Census of Population, 1950*. Washington, D.C.: Government Printing Office, 1952.

———. *U.S. Census of Population, 1960*. Washington, D.C.: Government Printing Office, 1952.

United States Congress. *Congressional Record*, 81st Cong., 2nd sess. Washington, D.C.: Government Printing Office, 1950.

———. *Hearings before the House Select Committee on Lobbying Activities*, 81st Cong., 2nd sess. Washington, D.C.: Government Printing Office, 1950.

Vose, Clement E. *Caucasians Only: The Supreme Court, the NAACP, and the Restrictive Covenant Cases*. 1959. Berkeley and Los Angeles: University of California Press, 1967.

Wallock, Leonard. "The Myth of the Master Builder: Robert Moses, New York, and the Dynamics of Metropolitan Development since World War II." *Journal of Urban History* 17 (August 1991): 339–62.

Waltzer, Kenneth Alan. "The American Labor Party: Third Party Politics in New Deal–Cold War New York, 1936–1954." Ph.D. diss., Harvard University, 1977.

Ware, Susan. "American Women in the 1950s: Nonpartisan Politics and Women's Politicization." In Louise A. Tilly and Patricia Gurin, eds., *Women, Politics, and Change*, 281–99. New York: Russell Sage Foundation, 1990.

Weiner, Lynn Y. *From Working Girl to Working Mother: The Female Labor Force in the United States, 1820–1980*. Chapel Hill: University of North Carolina Press, 1985.

Weiss, Nancy Pottishman. "Mother, the Invention of Necessity: Dr. Benjamin Spock's *Baby and Child Care*." *American Quarterly* 29 (winter 1977): 519–46.

Wendt, Paul F. *Housing Policy: the Search for Solutions*. Berkeley: University of California Press, 1962.

Westbrook, Robert B. "Fighting for the American Family: Private Interests and Political Obligation in World War II." In Richard W. Fox and T. J. Jackson Lears, eds., *The Power of Culture: Critical Essays in American History*, 195–221. Chicago: University of Chicago Press, 1993.

———. " 'I Want a Girl, Just like the Girl That Married Harry James': American Women and the Problem of Political Obligation in World War II." *American Quarterly* 42 (December 1990): 587–614.

Whyte, William H., Jr. *The Organization Man*. New York: Simon and Schuster, 1956.

Wiebe, Robert H. *The Search for Order, 1877–1920*. New York: Hill and Wang, 1967.

Wilson, Leslie. "Dark Spaces: An Account of Afro-American Suburbanization, 1890–1950." Ph.D. diss., City University of New York, 1992.

Wilson, Sloan. *The Man in the Gray Flannel Suit*. New York: Simon and Schuster, 1955.

Wittner, Lawrence S. *Rebels against War: The American Peace Movement, 1933–1983*. Philadelphia: Temple University Press, 1984.

Wolfe, Alan. *America's Impasse: The Rise and Fall of the Politics of Growth*. New York: Pantheon, 1981.

————. "Middle-Class Moralities." *Wilson Quarterly*, summer 1993, 49–72.

Wood, Robert C. *Suburbia: Its People and Their Politics*. Boston: Houghton Mifflin, 1959.

Wright, Gwendolyn. *Building the Dream: A Social History of Housing in America*. New York: Pantheon Books, 1981.

Index

(CIO): and electoral politics, 64; and housing, 43, 45
Consumer culture, 5, 166
Corello, Joseph A., 104
Corona, 161, 163
Costello, Edward, 93, 106
Crisona, James (borough president), 100
Cunningham Park, 22, 29

Davis, Mike, *City of Quartz*, 172
"Day Camp in the Driveways" (Friedan), 144–45
Dean, John, 40–41, 43
Declaration of Freedom, 82
Democratic Party: and electoral politics, 62–65; and housing controversy, 49; and liberal Democrats, 66–67, 104–5; and rent protest, 70
Dent, Thomas, 67
Dick, Jane, 135, 142, 152; *Volunteers and the Making of Presidents*, 143
DiLeonardo, John, 67
Disabled American Veterans, and housing, 47, 57
Douglaston, 31, 66–67, 93, 120, 157

East Queens Civic Organization, 105
Economic liberalism. *See* New Deal liberalism
Education, of Queens residents, 31–32. *See also* Schools, overcrowding of; Schools, public
Electchester (garden apartment): construction of, 30, 47, 53–54, 57; and electoral politics, 64; and progressive politics, 75–76; Women's Committee of, 96
Elkins, Stanley, and Eric McKitrick, "A Meaning for Turner's Frontier," 92, 150, 168
Elmhurst, 161
The Emergence of the Middle Class (Blumin), 39
England, James, 51
Environmental Inequalities (Hurley), 167, 173
Expertise, 10, 166–67. *See also* Political strategy, and expertise

Family, housing congenial to, 22, 25–26, 28–30, 36, 41, 144, 171

Farrell, Thomas, 48, 51
Federal Housing Administration (FHA): and mortgage insurance, 40–41, 45; Section 608, 22, 27–28, 30, 69
Federation of Civic Councils, 93, 134
Feigenbaum, Julius, 67, 106
Feldman, Harold, 84
The Feminine Mystique (Friedan), 6, 11–12, 133, 149–52, 166
Finnegan, James A., 141
Finz, Leon, 67
Flushing, 18, 65–66, 93
Flushing Council of Woman's Organizations (FCWO), 78–79, 93
Flushing Guide (Flushing Suburban Civic Association), 75
Flushing Hillcrest Civic Association, 106
Flushing Manor Civic Association, 125; and housing controversy, 54–55
Flushing Society of Friends, 79
Flushing Suburban, black population in, 35, 75, 163, 165
Flushing Suburban Civic Association, 75, 77, 96, 163, 203n. 6
Fones-Wolf, Elizabeth, *Selling Free Enterprise*, 58
Foreign-born population, 36
Forest Hills, 161, 163
"Forging America's Postwar Order" (Griffith), 58
Formisano, Ronald, *Boston against Busing*, 154, 172
Fresh Meadows, 77, 112–13
Fresh Meadows (garden apartment), 22, 25–26, 120; Jews in, 36, 77; and progressive politics, 55, 77, 82–83; and racial segregation, 72; residents as upper-middle class, 31; and school construction, 112–13; suburban qualities of, 22, 25–26, 68
Fresh Meadows Civic Association, 118, 189n. 47, 203n. 6
Fresh Meadows Community Association, 77
Friedan, Betty, 1–2; and community politics, 62; "Day Camp in the Driveways," 144–45; *The Feminine Mystique*, 6, 11–12, 133, 149–52, 166; "More than a Nosewiper," 144–49; at Parkway Village, 26, 61–62, 143, 152; pre-*Feminine Mystique* writings,

Acknowledgments

Writing this book was a long process, during which I accumulated many debts. I am grateful to Nancy F. Cott and David Montgomery for their support and advice during my years at Yale University. I am indebted to my editor, Peter Agree, who took on this project ten years ago and showed patience and understanding as my revisions were delayed by teaching and family obligations. His professional intuition and experience and his personal knowledge of northeastern Queens (he attended Alice Barsky's day camp, after all!) confirmed me in the knowledge that I was on the right track. The encouragement and constructive criticism of three historians in particular—Daniel Horowitz, Thomas Sugrue, and Robert Johnston, who read and commented on the manuscript at key points in the production of the book—were invaluable. They helped me sharpen my arguments and see the forest for the trees. They have made the writing of this book a challenging and most rewarding endeavor.

Before historians set their eyes on this material, the people of Queens shared with me their memories and knowledge of their communities' life and politics. Some even dug dusty papers and documents out of their closets and basements and invited me into their offices and homes to consult them. I am especially grateful to William Caulfield and the Bayside Hills Civic Association, Steven Blank and *The Bayside Times*, the Bell Park Gardens Community Council, the Flushing Council of Woman's Organizations, Marguerite D'Emidio, Marjorie Ferrigno, Beatrice and Sidney Ifshin, Julia Jerry, Marilyn Mossop, John Sims, and Della Stametz. The volunteers and staff of the Bayside Historical Society and the Queens Historical Society also provided invaluable assistance. Finally, I thank Dora Galacatos and Joel Forman for opening their home in Astoria and sharing their love of New York City with me. Roger Sanjek also offered friendship (and restaurant tips) during my stay in New York.

Librarians and archivists in Queens and beyond helped make my archival work pleasant and fruitful. I thank the staff of the Long Island

Division of the Queens Borough Public Library, the New York City Municipal Archives, the Municipal Research and Reference Center, the LaGuardia and Wagner Archives at LaGuardia Community College, the Rare Book and Manuscript Library and the Teachers College Library at Columbia University, the Manuscripts and Archives Division of the New York Public Library, the Tamiment Institute Library at New York University, the Alexander Library at Rutgers University, the Seeley G. Mudd Library at Princeton University, and the Schlesinger Library at Radcliffe Institute, Harvard University.

Many friends and colleagues have commented on conference papers and excerpts over the years. I thank especially Burton Bledstein, Ceil Bucki, Lizabeth Cohen, Eric Davis, Sarah Deutsch, Jack Gaston, Yvette Huginnie, Andrew Hurley, Jeff Kroessler, Kenneth Kusmer, Joanne Meyerowitz, Jeffrey Morgan, Bruce Nelson, Roger Sanjek, Bob Smith, David Waldstreicher, Karolle Wall, Susan Ware, and Leslie Wilson.

The financial assistance of the following institutions eased the completion of this project: the Social Sciences and Humanities Research Council of Canada, through its Aid to Small Universities Grant; and the University College of the Fraser Valley, through its Professional Development, Scholarly Activity, and Research Leave funds. I am also grateful to Kathy Gowdridge, faculty assistant at the University College of the Fraser Valley, who helped me reformat the whole manuscript, to Patti Sawatsky, who produced the maps, and to Jan Jaap ter Haar, who assisted in the production of the index and in the proofreading. The staff of the University College of the Fraser Valley library, especially its interlibrary loan division, also provided much appreciated assistance. Thanks go as well to Erica Ginsburg and her staff at the University of Pennsylvania Press for their meticulous work.

Finally, my families, the Murrays and the Schlitts, provided encouragement and support throughout the writing of this book, though they wondered why it took so long! Above all, I thank my husband, Greg Schlitt, who not only did more than his share of parenting in critical periods but read and reread multiple revised versions of the introduction and various parts of the book. He and our children, Michelle, Alexa, and Christopher, have my deepest gratitude for the joy that they bring into my life. Historians and other readers might criticize this book for all kinds of reasons. But no criticism will be more to the point than Michelle's complaint that her mother's book is "broken," because it has no pictures.